THE ITCA GUIDE
TO COACHING WINNING TENNIS

THE ITCA GUIDE
TO COACHING WINNING TENNIS

David A Benjamin, Editor

Prepared by the Intercollegiate Tennis Coaches Association

With a Foreword by Arthur R. Ashe, Jr.

PRENTICE HALL
Englewood Cliffs, New Jersey 07632

Prentice-Hall International (UK) Limited, *London*
Prentice-Hall of Australia Pty. Limited, *Sydney*
Prentice-Hall Canada, Inc., *Toronto*
Prentice-Hall Hispanoamericana, S.A., *Mexico*
Prentice-Hall of India Private Limited, *New Delhi*
Prentice-Hall of Japan, Inc., *Tokyo*
Simon & Schuster Asia Pte. Ltd., *Singapore*
Editora Prentice-Hall do Brasil, Ltda., *Rio de Janeiro*

© 1989 *by*

PRENTICE-HALL, Inc.
Englewood Cliffs, NJ

10 9 8 7 6 5 4 3 2 1

Library of Congress Cataloging-in-Publication Data

The ITCA guide to coaching winning tennis.

Includes index.
1. Tennis—Coaching. I. Benjamin, David A.,
1945— . II. Intercollegiate Tennis Coaches
Association.
GV955.18 1989   796.342'07'7   88-31796
ISBN 0-13-507955-1

ISBN 0-13-507955-1

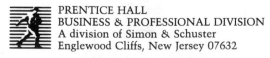
PRENTICE HALL
BUSINESS & PROFESSIONAL DIVISION
A division of Simon & Schuster
Englewood Cliffs, New Jersey 07632

Printed in the United States of America

ACKNOWLEDGMENT

I would like to express my deepest appreciation to the Board of Directors of the Intercollegiate Tennis Coaches Association for their support of this important project, as well as to our ITCA coaches who have contributed their unique expertise in working on this book.

I would also like to pay tribute to Tracy Kenny, who devoted so much valuable time and incandescent energy in helping me edit this manuscript.

And finally, I would like to thank Princeton University for providing such a special home for myself and the ITCA over these many past years.

David A Benjamin
Executive Director, ITCA
Men's Tennis Coach
Princeton University

for Alex and Nicky

FOREWORD

By Arthur R. Ashe, Jr.

This collection of thoughts, strategies, records, and recollections by America's best college tennis coaches provides the reader with a detailed and interesting tour of the world of college tennis.

I feel I am a fairly good judge of the college tennis scene, since I spent four years at UCLA before graduating in 1966. Though Open tennis—amateurs and professionals in the same events—in 1968 changed the attraction of the collegiate game, the preparation, dedication, team unity, and sacrifice are still as relevant today as in the pre-1968 era.

This book is timely for several reasons; first because there presently exists no other compendium of information like it anywhere. It should have been done earlier, but it was not. Second, there exists today large gaps of knowledge concerning the collegiate game among parents, junior players, and coaches. Though we may assume that successive generations of parents are more aware than those in the past, this is not so. Each set of parents with college-bound sons and daughters is, in general, just as lacking in information as their counterparts twenty years ago.

Third, collegiate tennis is a more important segment of the total tennis picture than it was in the past simply because it is the last level of amateur tennis before the professional game. The majority of American male players who turn professional try college tennis first. It is less so for women, but no less important. As such, the college game is now more competitive, with more and better coaching. Any NCAA champion is taken seriously as a rookie professional, and a past list of NCAA winners reads like a *Who's Who* of American tennis.

Finally, this book gives a variety of opinions and approaches that should prove once and for all that there is no one way to produce outstanding teams. There are no magic formulas, and some of the revelations are brutally honest and forthright. Dr. Allen Fox, in particular, speaks of his methods of communicating with players who were not brought up in a team environment as junior stars. In truth, this is one of the major contributions herein: that tennis players, by and large, grow as centers of influence unto themselves. In nearly every other sport, athletes are parts of teams. Not so, tennis players.

I only wish I could have read something like this book in 1960 in my high school senior year. In hindsight, I believe I would have done the same thing, but I, my parents, and my coach would have been much more informed.

A.R.A.
1987

PREFACE

Welcome to the special world of college tennis—special not only in terms of the quality and excitement of competition, but also in structure. Unlike most collegiate sports, the format and many theories of college tennis are strikingly different from the way the sport is played on the junior, and high school level, and on the professional tour.

In the case of football, basketball or baseball, the manner in which a high school athlete participates in a sport is very similar to the college experience and often similar to the professional games. However, a high school tennis player arriving as a freshman on a college tennis team will discover that our Intercollegiate Tennis Coaches Association rules mandate a scoring system radically different from regular tennis scoring, that coaching is allowed continuously throughout the match as long as it does not interfere with play (on the junior and professional tennis scene, coaching is strictly prohibited), and collegiate match competition centers around dual meet team matches consisting of six singles and three doubles matches, often with the same players playing both singles and doubles. This format is unique to college tennis, and creates a sense of team camaraderie vastly different from the individual tournament experience common for most junior players on the professional tour.

Our primary purpose in writing this book is to better educate our college and high school coaches in the complex and wide-ranging array of opportunities and responsibilities involved in their role.

The Intercollegiate Tennis Coaches Association (ITCA) was founded in 1956 by the late J. D. Morgan, who started out as an innovative tennis coach at UCLA and went on to become the dynamic Director of Intercollegiate Athletics at the same institution.

Initially, the ITCA represented a small number of men's coaches from Division I tennis teams. But over the past decade the ITCA has evolved into an active service organization with close to a thousand member coaches representing men's and women's college tennis teams from all three NCAA divisions, as well as the NAIA and junior and community college tennis. Despite our greater size and the myriad new programs and opportunities which have become the essence of the

ITCA, our primary goals have remained the same over the past three decades:

> To foster and encourage the playing of intercollegiate tennis in accordance with the highest traditions of sportsmanship and consistent with the general objective of higher education . . .

> To develop among the intercollegiate coaches a deeper sense of responsibility in teaching, promoting, maintaining and conducting the game of tennis . . .

> To educate and serve those individuals and groups who are involved in collegiate tennis: junior and college players, their coaches and parents, and the at large tennis public . . .

We hope that in publishing this book we shall provide a much needed educational service for both high school and college coaches, as well as young players and their parents interested in participating in collegiate tennis. In doing so we shall have fulfilled one of the charter goals envisioned by J. D. Morgan.

David A Benjamin
Executive Director, ITCA
Princteon, New Jersey
December 1988

CONTENTS

Dick Gould

Dick Gould
Men's Tennis Coach
Stanford University

Under the tutelage of Dick Gould, Men's Tennis Coach at Stanford University, some of the world's finest tennis players have developed their games during collegiate play. A list of former players reads like a Who's Who of U.S. Tennis—Wimbledon quarterfinalist Tim Mayotte, Roscoe Tanner, John McEnroe, and Gene and Sandy Mayer. All in all, ten different Stanford players have reached at least the finals of the NCAA singles tournament while playing for Gould. Five have reached at least the semifinals of Wimbledon. Twenty-six of his players have earned ITCA All-America honors during his twenty-year tenure. The Cardinal men's team has finished in the NCAA top five in sixteen out of the last seventeen years, and in NCAA team competition Stanford has won thirty-one of thirty-four matches during the nine years in which they were invited to participate.

Gould is renowned not only for his coaching and recruiting skills, but also as a pioneer in the collegiate tennis world. The forty-nine-year-old coach initiated major college indoor matches back in 1974, opening the doors of Stanford's spacious Maples Pavilion so that up to 8,000 fans could view major collegiate competition in the comfort of an indoor arena.

"Courtside With the Stars" was another brainchild of Gould's. The endowed scholarship fundraising exhibition took place two years in a row and raised $75,000 in the collective name of "Stanford Tennis Professionals." John McEnroe, Roscoe Tanner, Sandy Mayer, Nick Saviano, Pat Dupre, Tim Mayotte, Peter Rennert, Gene Mayer and Scott Davis are among the tennis alumni who have returned to aid Gould in his fundraising effort through the Courtside With the Stars exhibition match.

In 1971, Gould founded the Stanford Tennis School, a two week summer camp attracting an enrollment capacity of 432. Proceeds from the all level instructional camp are used as supplemental funding for the Stanford tennis program. He is the author of *Tennis Anyone?*, one of the most popular instructional guides ever.

Gould did his undergraduate and graduate work at Stanford where he was a Dean's list scholar and a master's degree recipient. After graduation from Stanford, Gould coached at Mountain View High School and in 1962 moved to Foothill College to become head tennis coach, winning state championships in 1964 and 1965. From 1960 through 1966, he was the tennis professional at the Fremont Hill Country Club in Los Altos Hills.

In 1966 the Lifetime Sports Foundation honored Gould as one of the twenty-five original Master Clinicians for his teacher training seminars. In 1974 he received the ITCA Wilson Coach of the Year Award and in 1983 he was presented with the Educational Merit Award by the United States Tennis Association.

Gould has hosted four U.S. Junior Davis Cup training camps at Stanford University. He also directed the USTA National Junior training camp in 1985, 1986, and 1987 at Stanford.

He has conducted tennis clinics in Mexico, the Caribbean, China, Japan and Central America. In 1981, he was named an honorary member of the United States Professional Tennis Association and has served as president of the NorCal Tennis Professionals Association in past years.

Gould and his wife, Anne, the former Stanford University women's coach from 1976 to 1979, reside in Menlo Park with their daughter, Kimberly Anne. Gould has three older daughters and a son who currently attends Stanford.

CHAPTER · 1

RECRUITING

―――――

Dick Gould, Men's Tennis Coach, Stanford University

When I began coaching at Stanford University in 1967, we had never been out of the top ten and yet our average finish was around seventh. We finished second one year only because either USC or UCLA was ineligible because of a football violation and the school was on probation. There was a tremendous gap between the Number 1 and Number 2 teams in the country and everyone else. We considered a 7–2 or 8–1 defeat or the loss of some three-set matches to UCLA or USC moral victories. That was, realistically, the closest we could come to either UCLA or USC back in the sixties.

I kept thinking though—we had great facilities and a great area, and enough good players could get into Stanford, yet they were going elsewhere. That was a situation we should be able to change. I became almost obsessed with proving that we could create a great team. I was hired in May and the recruiting season was all but over. I made a few calls to players, but they were committed to other schools. So I had to wait until the next year to begin recruiting.

No coach was visiting recruits in those days, but I really worked hard to get Zan Guerry and Stanley Pasarell. They were the two guys who were admitted to Stanford who were really top players. I was told Zan was all sewed up for Rice. I made one of my few recruiting trips to St. Louis to see Bobby McKinley, I went down to Miami and saw Bill Colson and Matt Kaplan, to Chattanooga, came back via Texas and saw Mike Estep and Stanley Pasarell, both at St. Mark's School, and said hello to Woody Blocker, who was younger. It was a tremendous experience for me.

The main reason for my trip was to try to get Zan Guerry. Mr. Guerry simply said, "There's no reason to visit. He's going to Rice." But I was persistent, and I said, "Alex, I'm going to be in Chattanooga on this date, will you be in town?" He finally just capitulated and said, "Come on up for lunch." So look out, Zan, here I come! His Dad was really hard on me, asked me every question in the book; but we established a rapport. I talked him into letting Zan come out for a visit and Zan really liked the school. Mr. Guerry had me answering questions like: "What's the wind velocity in the Spring? What's the average temperature? What's the average rainfall? How tall are the mountains?" Questions you can't believe! It really prepared me, because I had to do my homework. I was very thorough. I wrote back ten page, single spaced typed letters answering these amazing questions.

I grew as a recruiter because of Alex Guerry. Then all of a sudden Zan decided he wanted to go to Stanford, but he didn't want to go by himself. Charlie Pasarell, Stan's brother, had gone to UCLA, and that was the place Stanley was considering first. Zan called Stanley and said, "Let's go to Stanford." In the meantime, I went back and visited Mike and Stanley at St. Mark's. Stanley got excited and said, "Hey, now I'm going to come to Stanford." He called back Zan and said, "Okay, let's go to Stanford." In the meantime, Zan had made a final commitment to Rice; still, Stanley Pasarell finally did come to Stanford.

Anyway, in my first recruiting year I almost landed two top players, and that was a very good experience: I learned how to talk to players; how to prepare for parents' questions—the kind of information I should be expected to know. If I have any talent as a recruiter at all, it's because of Alex Guerry who was, ironically, a losing cause at that time.

THE REAL SECRET OF SUCCESSFUL RECRUITERS

There really is no secret to recruiting. The best advice I can give to a coach is to be yourself. Don't try to be somebody you are not. You must be honest in answering questions. If you don't have a strong academic program, you have to say that. If there is something about a course of study that is very difficult, you had better tell them it is difficult. If there is a problem with the dormitory situation, you have to tell them straight. If the question is about guys on the team, again you have to answer honestly.

We often hear horror stories of recruiting violations in college athletics! But the word *recruit* is not necessarily a dirty word and certainly does not have to have negative connotations, nor does it mean that it is universally a negative experience. However, because of past experiences the governing body of college athletics, the National Collegiate Athletic Association, has established many rules to help ensure that the recruiting process is fair and honorable both to the student and to the recruiter. Strict regulations exist in terms of amateurism, transferring from one school to another, the number and timing of recruiting visits, the number of personal contacts, and athletic tryouts. If you have any questions about recruiting rules, you should always check with your athletic director or contact the NCAA enforcement office for clarification. The address is P.O. Box 1903, Mission, KS 66201, and the phone number is (913) 384-3220.

I hope the recruiting process will be one that will enable the students to make a more valid choice as to which school should be selected to continue their education and tennis development. Essentially recruitment is selling. It may represent the school or coach trying to sell a product to a prospective athlete, or it might instead be the prospective athlete trying to sell himself or herself to the school. Recruiting is a very common practice in almost all phases of life. Industries and businesses compete with each other for the recruitment of specially trained personnel just as graduate schools compete with each other for the most outstanding students and universities compete for the most renowned professors. At the undergraduate level, schools recruit aggressively for students who can add something special to that university, whether in purely academic terms or some extremely well-developed and highly successful avocation or hobby or a very strong talent in a special field, such as the arts, music, or in our case, athletics.

ACCENT THE POSITIVE

As a coach, you should always emphasize the positive when recruiting. You are a salesman for your school or tennis program. You have to project your enthusiasm, your belief in what you are selling. Never talk down another player or coach or another program; instead, emphasize what is good about your program.

Recruiting is extremely competitive in all forms of athletics, including tennis. It is aggressively undertaken, both for male and female athletes, at Division II and III schools as well as Division I schools, and also at the NAIA and junior college level.

When I started coaching at Stanford, the USTA was looking for a place to hold its Junior Davis Cup try-out camp. Stanford was available, and the Northern California Tennis Association came to me asking if we would host the Junior Davis Cup Try-out Camp, because it would help get the players into the National Hardcourts in Burlingame and ensure their coming to that tournament. I jumped at the chance and said I would be happy to be the host, but only if we could put on a first class event. And we did. The players still talk about that camp. That gave me, a rookie coach with no tour or playing experience, a chance to get to know the kids. This was in 1967, 1968, 1969—three straight years. Frankly, this was a great opportunity for the kids to get to see Stanford. I was the host, not the coach, which was a very positive situation for me personally vis á vis the players.

I went to Kalamazoo only once my first year; it was such a meat market that I never went back. Running the camp and raising all the money for it was hard work, and I couldn't do it more than three years, but it helped me get to know players and them to know Stanford.

A few years later, the Northern California Tennis Association came back to me in an emergency situation and asked me to do the camp, but at that point you had to get NCAA permission. They said, "Yes, but you can't have any contact with the players, whatsoever." So what this meant was that they would be using Stanford facilities, but I could not contact or even be nice to players, not even say Hello to them! This would have created a negative effect because the kids wouldn't have known why I couldn't talk to them and would have wondered what's going on with me; why didn't I care about them? So I never did it again because of the new NCAA rules. Ironically, college coaches now are permitted to travel with the Junior Davis Cuppers, so apparently the NCAA rules are not as strict as they once were.

THREE STEPS TO EFFECTIVE RECRUITING

Step 1. The first thing to find out before recruiting players is whether they have a chance for admission. Generally speaking, at Stanford this means someone in the 1100 range of the SATs, and about 3.5 GPA in solid courses. If one is a little higher than the other, that might help. But someone who is 1100 and a 3.5 better be one of my top two or three prospects or he's still not going to get in. Naturally, these standards vary tremendously at the different colleges throughout the country.

Step 2. Try to identify those players who are possible admission candidates—usually by correspondence during their Sophomore or Junior year. For me, it then becomes a matter of continuous contact, especially in a player's senior year, through mail or the phone about every week or ten days. I have a list of about fifteen kids which as the SAT scores come in gets whittled down to about eight kids. Then when you start talking about money and scholarships, it gets down to about two or three kids. I usually write these players myself, by hand, though sometimes I'll dictate. I like to let them know what is happening out here. There is always enough going on to tell them about.

Step 3. Once you establish the potential of the candidate, try to begin and sustain some kind of dialogue. I don't use the phone so much. I try to hold off on visits to Stanford until nearer the time of a decision because I don't want to spend money on someone who might not be admitted. If someone wants to come in the Fall, fine, but I prefer that he come out a little later. I know for sure who will be admitted to Stanford by April 1, sometimes the week before, and I've been around long enough to have a pretty good idea even earlier. I rank kids in order of playing ability for Admissions, which is the usual procedure for coaches at most colleges.

The most difficult thing for us to overcome is the fact that Stanford is so highly regarded academically. Many players wonder if they can cope academically and still keep up with varsity tennis. That is a very fair question from parents, but when I point out our current players' GPAs, that usually takes care of that question. It is natural when kids hear of valedictorians with 1400 boards who are turned down to wonder how they themselves can make it. In order to offset this, I show our recruits a list of guys on the team and what their GPAs were when they applied and what they have now, and how well they are doing in tennis with the same kinds of SATs the prospective player has. Also, I show them how well students did here and how well they are doing on the Pro circuit. This reassures them that they can make the adjustment to Stanford and from Stanford make the adjustment to the Pros.

Another recurring question is: How well have our players done on the Pro tour? Well, it is obvious that coming to Stanford has not hurt them, though perhaps this was more of an issue when I first started at Stanford.

SEEING THINGS FROM THE STUDENT'S PERSPECTIVE

In order to be as effective as possible as a recruiter, I have always found it helpful to think as well in terms of the prospective student, imagining and anticipating the key points he or she should be considering when looking at the coach and the program.

Most coaches are very positive people. We can find something good about almost any situation (and often need to in our coaching careers). As a coach addressing a prospective student, it makes sense to emphasize the strengths of your tennis program and of the school itself, particularly those elements that are not obvious to the casual observer, but that might be of great importance to the student and his or her family, and may make the difference in the final decision as to which school to attend.

It is important for the coach to realize that the student and student's family will be making a judgment about you both as a tennis coach and also as a person. Whether through correspondence or over the telephone or during a personal visit, the way in which you relate to the student and his or her family will reveal a great deal about your relationship with the players on your team and also about your general outlook concerning academics and athletics. The impression which you personally make with the prospective student will greatly influence his or her decision.

TIPS FOR CREATING A GOOD FEELING FOR YOUR SCHOOL AND PROGRAM

Little details will often make a great difference, such as whether or not you return a call quickly, whether you answer letters promptly, and whether in your correspondence you show personal interest and concern and take the time to write the letters yourself.

Your feelings about your tennis program and your school will be reflected in a variety of ways when you talk with the student and his or her family and, possibly, his or her high school tennis coach. It is important that you be as honest as possible and also as enthusiastic as possible. One of the obligations incumbent on the coach in talking with families and prospective students is to be forthright about your own outlook so that there are as few ambiguities as possible. The more explicit you can be in articulating your beliefs about coaching and academics, the more helpful for the family in making their college decision.

Another way in which you can provide useful information is to make sure that during the visit of the student, he or she has the chance to talk with members of the tennis team off the court and away from your own supervision. If possible, it is a good idea to arrange for the student to stay overnight in the dorm, with a chance to go to classes, meet students who are not on the team, and get a sense of the school apart from your own vision as the tennis coach. The more information that the prospective student and family can receive about the school and program, the better. It is to your own benefit to help the student learn as much as possible about your school.

Similarly, it is important to arrange for the visiting student to watch your team at practice. The impression which you create during this team practice will often determine whether the prospective student feels that he or she would be comfortable as a member of your team. While you do not want to stage your practice to create a false impression, it is impossible to ignore the fact that you and your team are to some degree on show during the visit of the student and family. It makes sense to approach this situation as enthusiastically as possible, so that both the student and the members of your team feel good about this experience. Once again, as a coach displaying your program to the student and family, it is important to make sure that you take plenty of time to show the student the facilities and explain your schedule and your philosophy of how you organize and coach your team. There are many things which as a coach you tend to take for granted but which are not obvious to visitors to the school. The greater the effort which you make to anticipate the questions and concerns of the prospective student and his or her family and to cover these during the visit, the more effective you will be in your recruiting effort.

Also, I have discovered over the years that it is very important to be positive, not only about your own program as a coach, but also about tennis programs at other schools. There are many good tennis programs in our country and many excellent coaches. The more you communicate a positive sense about other coaches and programs, the more a student and his or her family will look positively toward your program as well. And there is no surer way to create instant suspicion and questions about your own sincerity as to downgrade other coaches and programs. Here, the old maxim is very true that if you have nothing good to say it is better to say nothing. The impression which you create with the student in terms of your own confidence and image of yourself is reflected in the way in which you see other coaches and programs. Just as you would not want other coaches to denigrate your own program or abilities you must be equally fair and considerate in describing their programs, and in doing so, everyone benefits.

DECIDING THE SCHOLARSHIP QUESTION

Concerning scholarships, if I have the option I go on proven results rather than potential. In my situation I look at national rankings. There is usually a reason a player has been winning in the twelve's, in the fourteen's and so on. Now you get two kids who are exactly equal who want scholarships, then you go with the player who you think has the most potential. At Stanford I would consider someone ranked nationally among the top five high school seniors for a full scholarship, someone ranked nationally in the second five for a half scholarship. I wouldn't consider someone for financial aid unless that person had had a very successful senior year.

Ideally, if you could pick, you'd like your top four guys on full scholarship and your fifth and sixth guy on half-scholarships. (This applies to Men's NCAA Division I tennis; women in Division I are permitted eight full scholarships.) I've never promised more aid to someone than what they have when they come in, although over the last seven or eight years there have probably been twelve or thirteen players at Stanford, many of them All Americans, who came in with no aid, like Peter Rennert and Jim Gurfein, who reached the NCAA finals, or Jeff Arons, who was an All American. Last year, Jim Grabb and Eric Rosenfeld were on fulls; they had been on halfs their first three years. I never promised them more aid than when they started, as I said, but I did try to help them once they were doing very well. This is just my own policy, however. Many coaches have different approaches concerning scholarships which also work well for them.

Realistically, when you look at the top five in the eighteen's, only one and one-half on the average are candidates for admission at a school like Stanford. Maybe in a good year there are two kids in the top five who should apply to Stanford. We have been lucky in that there have probably over the past fifteen years been only three guys in the country who have turned down full scholarships to Stanford. Our get ratio has been extremely good. John Ross was one who turned us down; Vitas Gerulaitis would have been admitted, but he did not apply.

The recruiting game can be a funny and unpredictable one. Take, for example, Roscoe Tanner. Back in 1970, he was set on going to Tennessee. So I said: "Good luck," and I didn't hear from him in about two months. He did come to JDC camp for one or two years, and he did have a good time, which is why he considered Stanford in the first place. All of a sudden in August, he called me and asked if he could still come to Stanford. Well, at Stanford you have to let them know by May 15th, but they agreed to accept Roscoe. Room assignments had already been made. His call came completely out of the blue. I had just assumed Tennessee was a foregone conclusion and I can't remember why he changed his mind at the last minute.

In the case of Scott Davis, he was seriously considering UCLA or USC because he had grown up in Southern California. I was surprised too when he decided on Stanford. He was no lead pipe cinch to be admitted to Stanford, and he knew it would be hard; so his back-up had to assume more importance. It was a little gutsy to wait for Stanford, since we do not let you know early, when you have other schools as definites. We have no Early Decision or Early Action. But I did keep in touch with Scott, and finally he decided to come here.

If a kid is definitely set on Stanford, I won't fly him out or go back to visit his parents, but I do like to visit a boy's home, especially if the kid lives far away. I think it's very important that his parents know me, because I'm the person their child will be spending probably the most time with once he's at Stanford. I don't do this a lot, maybe two or three visits a year, and only with kids whom I'm confident will be admitted.

John McEnroe was an exception to my rule. I had never seen John play while I was recruiting him. I knew he was a serious student who could meet the academic requirements, and he was the best player who also had the qualifications to get into Stanford. I never met John's parents or visited him. He knew Peter Rennert very well and visited the campus. I handled him like most of the other players. I talked to him and his parents on the phone a couple of times but didn't do anything unusual in recruiting John for Stanford.

In conclusion, recruiting can be an extremely positive experience. Many times the student athlete is afforded special opportunities to find out how he or she might fit in to a particular school. Many lasting friendships are formed between recruits and their families and team members and coaches whether or not the recruit enrolls at that particular school. It is the responsibility of the coach to communicate to the prospective student the special qualities of the school and tennis program and help the student and his or her family to make as informed and intelligent a decision as possible.

CHAPTER·2

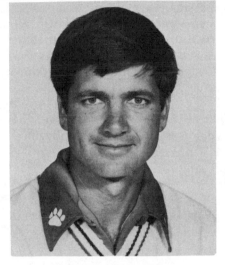

Chuck Kriese
Men's Tennis Coach
Clemson University

Since coming to Clemson University as men's head tennis coach in 1979, Chuck Kriese has established his team as a collegiate power. In the past eight years, Clemson has been to the NCAA Tournament eight times, a feat only five teams in the nation can claim. Additionally, Clemson was ranked in the top ten in the nation each of those seasons, won the ACC regular season seven times, captured the tournament title six times, and had thirteen players reach All America status a number of times. Three of his players have been named as ITCA Senior Player of the Year: Mike Gandolfo in 1980, Mark Dickson in 1982, and Jean Desdunes in 1983. In 1984 Rick Rudeen received the prestigious Rafael Osuna Sportsmanship Award and set an NCAA career singles victory mark with 173 victories. Freshman Lawson Duncan was voted ITCA Rookie Player of the Year after setting a regular season record of 69 wins and reaching the finals of the NCAA singles championships. In 1986 Richard Matuszewski received the John Van Nostrand Memorial Award, given to that player who has performed well during his collegiate career and shows great promise to make it as a professional. In 1987, Matt Frooman became the NCAA Men's Division I recipient of the ITCA Graduate Scholarship Award, given for outstanding academic achievement to a varsity tennis player who is going on to graduate school.

Over the last eight years, Kriese's record is an incredible 220–67, a 76.7 winning percentage. Ten of Kriese's former players are currently in the pro ranks, with Mark Dickson and Lawson Duncan ranked among the world's top fifty. At the end of the 1981 season, Kriese was honored as the ITCA Wilson Coach of the Year by his peers.

In 1982 Kriese was chosen to coach the U.S. Junior Davis Cup team at the French Open and was also asked by the USTA to coach the U.S. Sunshine Cup Team that finished second of twenty-four teams in international competition. In November 1983, Kriese was inducted into the South Carolina Tennis Hall of Fame as its second charter member. He has been a guest lecturer on training and motivation on numerous occasions at USTA seminars and conventions and has also appeared recently on ESPN's instructional series, "Play Your Best Tennis."

A former captain and most valuable player on the Tennessee Tech tennis team, he was inducted into the Tennessee Tech Hall of Fame in 1985, the first tennis player to be so honored. After graduation from Tennessee Tech in 1972, Kriese ventured to the Port Washington, N.Y., Tennis Academy, where he earned his professional training under the legendary Harry Hopman. A year later, Kriese returned to his alma mater and completed his master's degree in health and physical education.

In addition to coaching, Kriese is very active in college tennis administration, having served in a number of positions for the Intercollegiate Tennis Coaches Association, as well as on its Board of Directors.

AN APPROACH TO TRAINING AND CONDITIONING

Chuck Kriese, Men's Tennis Coach, Clemson University

PLANNING YOUR TRAINING AND CONDITIONING PROGRAM

Unfortunately, the best training efforts of a player or a coach are often undermined by the lack of careful organization. Possibly even more important than the strength of the training program itself is the effectiveness of the overall plan. A high school or college coach must construct a thoroughly detailed specific plan and then stick to it. Successful coaches do not have a secret plan. They merely understand the basic principles of developing a sound program and staying with it from start to finish.

PEPP (Preparation, Enthusiasm, Poise, and Perseverance) is the acronym for a plan that will provide this direction and be a guide for the coach in athletic training. PEPP actually can be used for any job, whether it is in the training of an athlete for a specific event or work in any other occupation or job that takes discipline and direction. Yet PEPP is only a guide. It is up to the individual to implement this program.

P—Preparation

Bobby Knight, the well known Indiana basketball coach, said it best once in an interview: "More importantly than an athlete's needing the will to win, he or she needs the will to **Prepare** to win." Without preparation and planning in both physical and mental areas, the athlete has little or no hope for success in his or her sport.

Preparation must be detailed and thorough, and inclusive of complete programs of training for not only the body, but the mind and spirit as well. The coach must develop this program from start to finish so that the athlete is ready mentally, physically, and emotionally for the job he has to do. There are five important steps in Preparation:

Step 1: Create a Sense of Burning Desire

Nearly every person involved in athletics will state that he or she has a desire to be successful, but having a burning desire is very different from merely wanting to do something. It is this intangible difference that distinguishes between good and great, between just another day at the ballpark and one that is remembered for years. A burning desire cannot be manufactured by a coach, it must come from within the athlete.

Step 2: Set Specific Goals

Setting goals is very important to the success of anyone in competitive sports. Some goals are never realized. Others are always reached. Some are set too high, while others set too low. What then is the key for the coach in setting these goals?

Achieving an athlete's maximum success does not depend on merely the setting of goals but rather the setting of the right goals. The problem in goal setting is that if all of our goals are set too idealistically, few might ever be reached, but if goals are set too realistically, all may be reached but performance remains far from potential.

The key for the coach is to set goals that will help an athlete strive for the maximum use of his or her gifts while still being able to reach a moderate number of these objectives. If set properly, goals should be reached only about 50–60 percent of the time.

A coach should constantly reset and redirect a player's goals. It is best to have three types of goals: a long-range ultimate goal; an intermediate goal that is a year or so away (to keep us on course toward the main goal); and short-range goals that constantly provide smaller successes and failures to keep our enthusiasm and learning stimulated for what we are trying to achieve.

The coach should also set goals for a player in more than just one area. An athlete cannot hope to reach great heights if all emphasis is only put on one area of his or her life. There is a very high correlation between athletic success, intellectual success, and social success. Goals should be set in other areas of interest, including academic areas, social areas, family areas, career planning areas, financial areas, and also spiritual areas. Success in each of these areas supports and aids the development of the others.

Step 3: Make Your Player's Work Constructive and Positive

Being a hard worker is not a guarantee of success. People have to work hard to achieve their goals, but hard work is never a guarantee of success, it merely improves the chances of success. Hard work will give our athletes the confidence of knowing that they have done everything possible to ready themselves for the task at hand. Unfortunately, many people train hard for negative reasons and often these preparations end up as nonproductive.

As a coach, it is vital to have your players work hard, sacrifice, pay the price, but do so positively and for the right reasons.

Step 4: Take Care of Details

A high school or college coach may have a player with the greatest burning desire, have him or her set the most specific and appropriate goals, and also work in the most dedicated fashion imaginable in preparing for a game, match, or event, but all of this can be wasted through the neglect of seemingly insignificant details—simple yet vital items such as eating and sleeping properly, keeping equipment in good condition and in adequate supply at courtside, or scheduling a good warmup in order to start the match in the right physical and mental frame. A coach must make sure that a match is never lost for any other reason besides the mechanics of the game itself.

Step 5: Acknowledge Fear

It is imperative that a coach succeed in having his or her player face the fact that there is usually going to be some nervousness and even fear before and during the event.

Courage is an emotion that can only occur in the presence of fear. Without fear, there can be no courage. It is critical for an athlete to understand this and when fear is present, to deal with it in a courageous fashion.

There are instances when fear in competition might not exist. Young children usually aren't susceptible to the negative effects of fear until they reach 10–12 years of age. This is about the age when pressure starts to become noticeable and both direct and indirect outside pressures can then make the situation more than the youngster is capable of handling. The pressures involved in competitive sports should be a gradual thing relative to the ability of the young athlete to understand and deal with them.

Another non-fear situation occurs when an athlete completely ignores the pressure of the event by remaining indifferent to the outcome. This way they do not risk losing, yet they diminish their chance to gain at the same time. Many athletes would rather have success come their way by good fortune or chance rather than take an active role in making it happen.

Fear should be looked at as a prelude to a positive emotion. If it is used by the athlete in a productive way, good performances on the court will occur time after time. Fear needs to be acknowledged directly, by both coach and player, so it can be dealt with and overcome.

E—Enthusiasm

The word *enthusiasm* itself comes from the Greek *Ev enos* (pronounced hen theos), which translate as "the spirit of God within." The meaning of the word itself describes its essence and importance to the athlete. To be inspired from within is very different from trying to force or fake the emotion.

Athletics is one of the purest and most expressionist of all art forms. Through sports, one's inner self can be totally released in a creative manner. But often athletes inhibit this inner creativity and restrain their self-expression. This is a shame because the benefits of enthusiasm are many and great and give athletes the opportunity to express their inner selves through their performance.

Enthusiasm projects the athlete's confidence and this helps overcome any fear that may exist toward the opponent. Conversely, true enthusiasm often makes one's opposition fearful of the situation.

A coach must understand that enthusiasm is difficult to generate as one's job becomes more routine. Even the most exciting event or experience has a tendency to lose its edge after it is done a number of times. The true test for the coach, therefore, becomes his or her ability to remain enthusiastic and keep his or her player equally enthusiastic after the novelty of the situation has worn off. The great coaches and players can do this. They handle their jobs each year with the same eagerness and enthusiasm as they did their first. It is crucial for the veteran coach and athletes to have the enthusiasm of rookies.

P—Poise

Just as it is important for the experienced athlete to maintain enthusiasm, it is equally important for the coach to teach the inexperienced
athlete to have poise in pressure situations. Poise is the ability to
execute one's skills on the court or playing field regardless of any
situation, adverse or favorable. Great athletes perform under pressure
time and time again regardless of outside elements.

Poise is learned through the experience of facing pressure situations
in many athletic contests. The poised athlete is invaluable. Calm under
the heat of the battle is a contagious quality that rubs off on others. It is
hard to teach poise, but there are ways for a coach to help an athlete
develop a sense of poise:

  a. The athlete should know that when there is adversity and the contest
      is close, growth occurs in sporting events. Actually, athletes should
      train themselves to look forward to these situations. Every experi-
      ence that the athlete has under pressure will only better prepare him
      or her for more important matches or games in the future. The more
      pressure an athlete faces, the less he or she will fear the situation at a
      later, more important time.
  b. The athlete should know that creativity in any area of life only occurs
      when a person is in a relaxed state.
  c. Treating success and failure in the same way helps an athlete develop
      poise and confidence. The tendency after a success is to let emotions
      run sky high with no boundary. Conversely, the tendency after a
      setback is for the emotions to bottom out in grief, anxiety, and even
      discouragement. The key to continuous growth in athletics, regard-
      less of a winning or losing experience, is to handle each in the same
      manner. A coach must remind his or her players never to get too high
      over a win, and never to let emotions run too low over a loss.

P—Perseverance

The greatest athletes in the history of sport became great primarily due
to this one simple single trait. They would never give up, or quit.

Most people only see the glory and glamour of the star athlete after he
or she has achieved greatness. But the coach is witness and partner to
the struggle at every level necessary to outstanding achievement. It is
the hardship and the setbacks that mold great athletes. The confidence
that is obtained from those struggles is what propels them to greater

CHART 1

Put PEPP Into All Areas of Your Life!

To reach Goals, set them
half-way between idealistic
and realistic expectations.

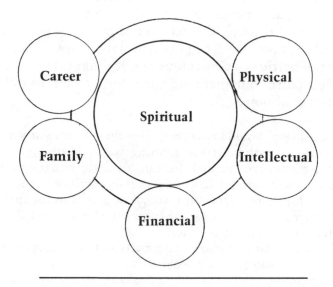

PREPARATION

6 Steps of Preparation:

Burning Desire

Goals

Constructive Work

Details

Acknowledge Fear

Assertive, Take Action,
Have Courage to do your best

OR

Doubt, Worry, Anxiety, Choking

ENTHUSIASM

From Greek word (e v enos) meaning: *THE SPIRIT OF GOD WITHIN*
              hen theos

- Total release performance
- *ENTHUSIASM* can make opposition fearful and builds your confidence!
- *CONFIDENCE* in your abilities will always overcome the fear you may have for the opposition.
- True enthusiasm is inspired; False enthusiasm is forced.
- Be a Go-Giver, rather than a Go-Getter.
- Compete to express, not to impress.
- Veterans must have enthusiasm of rookies.

MAINTAIN A BALANCE BETWEEN
THESE THROUGH PRACTICING CONCENTRATION!!

POISE

- Rookies must have the poise of veterans
- Love, adversity and close situations; That is when the GROWTH occurs.
- Remember #2 level of arousal under the heat of the battle.
- Creativity only occurs in poised and relaxed state.
- Most growth occurs when success and failure are handled in the same way.

    REMEMBER, pressure makes diamonds or doo-doo, it's up to you!

PERSEVERANCE

- Break downs always happen before break throughs.
- Set-backs are the key to the molding of any great man.
- Be disappointed, *NEVER* discouraged.
- Learning and personal growth are the keys.
- Every person has their unique timetable for success.
- NEVER, NEVER, NEVER GIVE UP . . . *BELIEVE IN YOURSELF.*

FOLLOW THROUGH!!

and greater heights. They fear little because they have faced and conquered much. Perseverance in all situations, the ability to face all adversity and to keep trying, is the final quality all great athletes must have.

In developing your player's perseverance, a few reminders might be helpful:

a. Remember that breakdowns always happen before breakthroughs.
b. Setbacks are the key to the molding of all great men and women.
c. Every person has his or her unique timetable for success. Never compare your own successes with another person's. It can only lead to frustration. Keep working at your own rate.
d. Another person's accomplishments never make you look bad. Jealousy is a negative emotion and nothing positive can be gained by showing it. Be happy for others' successes, and you will find all of your creative talents working for you in a positive way instead of being wasted in jealousy for another's accomplishments.
e. Be disappointed but never discouraged.
f. Know the difference between quitting and changing directions. Quitting is running away from a threatening situation and avoiding the responsibility involved. Changing directions is moving in a direction that will enhance the situation and be a benefit for one's life. One might change direction in a field a hundred times during his or her lifetime, but should never quit.

THE SEVEN BENEFITS OF A COMPREHENSIVE PHYSICAL TRAINING PROGRAM

There are seven reasons why a comprehensive and thorough physical training program will enhance performance on the tennis court:

1. A rigorous and consistent program of physical training increases confidence in match situations. If a person is prepared physically for a match, he or she will also be prepared mentally. The physical training that athletes go through in preparation for match play makes them very aware that their bodies are ready. Therefore, they will have the attitude, "I have done all that I can do and am now ready to play." This will enable an athlete to compete without pressing, rushing or being tentative with his play throughout the match.
2. A rigorous and consistent program of physical training improves technique and power. It is obvious in watching the top pros today that tennis is becoming more and more a strength event. All of the top

players are great athletes. Unless a person develops his athletic abilities to the maximum, it is impossible to compete at this level.

3. A rigorous and consistent program of physical training reduces the number and severity of injuries. As we know, the grind of the circuit is so strenuous now, even on the collegiate and high school levels, that the body undergoes more strain from tennis competition than ever before. A tough program of physical training will not only reduce injuries but often totally eliminate them. Such a program must follow strict guidelines of flexibility and strength training, as well as a very good running program.

4. A rigorous and consistent program of physical training delays fatigue in competition. The development of muscular endurance through physical training enables the athlete to participate at a higher intensity for longer periods of time. This helps him or her become a strong finisher in all events.

5. A rigorous and consistent program of physical training enhances fast recovery. Once again, muscular endurance developed through a good physical training program enables the body to recover much faster after a strenuous match. Thus, the athlete can compete day after day throughout the competition with the same level of excellence in all of his or her performances. Most athletes can compete early in the competition very well, but as the fourth and fifth days of the competition come around, the body tends to break down under stress. But a well-conditioned athlete can go all out many days in a row and recover quickly after each performance.

6. A rigorous and consistent program of physical training reduces the number of tired hours after training. For a high school or college athlete there exists evening hours where study and other activities have to take place after the training is over. An athlete in top condition can recover very quickly from work out sessions no matter how strenuous they are and be ready to undergo study or other activities that evening.

7. A rigorous and consistent program of physical training makes the tennis player a better athlete. Overall athletic ability is very important. Through a strict training program, a tennis player will see his or her strength, speed, power, agility, flexibility and other motor skills drastically improve. Through the improvement of all of these, a player's overall performance will improve dramatically, improving his or her confidence and enhancing performance on the tennis court.

There are many additional benefits in developing a rigorous and consistent program of physical training. Being specific with one's physical training is essential to gain maximum benefit from the program. Chart No. 2 structures the balance of physical training that a tennis player should undergo in a period of a week, including a daily flexibility program which is essential for the athlete. Flexibility not only relaxes the body of the athlete before he or she steps out on the court, but also guards against the possibility of any injuries during the match and also alleviates any soreness from previous performances. It is essential to remember that only static or nonmoving type stretching exercise should be done. Ballistic training or any type of bouncing stretch exercises are not recommended in a flexibility program.

It is also recommended that from three to a maximum of four days a week an anaerobic program of training should be undertaken, as well as one day per week of aerobic training.

In order to be fit on the tennis court, one must pursue some form of running program off the court. Those players who improve their fitness through extra training are almost always more likely to prevail in a long, grueling match.

Many junior players run great distances to achieve the level of fitness which will enhance their performances in match play, spending countless hours doing miles of distance work. Distance running has been accepted for a long time as a way for tennis players to train. The fallacy of its importance has only been brought out on a few occasions, and even many highly ranked players run long distances religiously.

It has been shown, however, according to Fox and Mathews' *Interval Training*, that 70 to 90 percent of the energy expended by a tennis player must be derived from his anaerobic (without oxygen) system. This means that the body, in order to produce energy to play tennis, uses the stored up energy of the muscles, which have the chemical names of adenosine triphosphate (ATP) and phosphocreatine (PC), as well as glucose, which is broken down to lactic acid. However, in distance running, the aerobic (oxygen) system, an entirely different energy source, is used.

The big problem in distance training is that at no time in an actual distance run does one's system function at the same intensity that it does when a point of tennis is being played. Each point is an all-out explosive type of exercise; in order to gain maximum results, a training session should simulate the playing of a point as closely as possible. Actually, a tennis player could run five or six miles a day and still be out of shape to play tennis. It would be like a 100-yard or a 220-yard dash man getting ready for his season by running distances instead of training his system at the maximum intensity for shorter amounts of time with rest intervals between each of his efforts.

Often, the question is asked: "What about the endurance needed for playing a long match? Doesn't distance running help this?'' But the type of endurance one needs in tennis is completely different from that of a distance runner—a top-level tennis player must have the capacity to replenish his anaerobic (without oxygen) system time after time following several high intensity work periods. This is contrary to having the capacity to withstand a continuous low intensity work load for a long period of time, which is what one receives when he or she runs distance. Long distance running is fine at different times for losing weight, breaking the monotony of a training routine, general cardio-respiratory care or for just plain enjoyment, but if one is looking for the best type of physical training for tennis, short, explosive types of exercises are far superior.

SAMPLE 7-WEEK PROGRAM INTERVAL TRAINING PROGRAM FOR THE TENNIS PLAYER

Chart 3 is a sample 7-week program of an interval training program for the tennis player: Monday, Wednesday, and Friday of each week are the strenuous anaerobic training programs. There is very light activity on Tuesday and Thursday. One day on the weekend, either Saturday or Sunday, can be used for an overdistance aerobic run. One day of the weekend also should be used for rest to let the body recuperate from the workouts. The workouts start out at the moderate rate of predominantly long sprints and middle distance-type work. This gives a good base and also gets the system ready for higher intensity workouts later in the 7-week program. As the program develops in the 5th, 6th, and 7th weeks, you will notice there are still some long aerobic workouts, but the majority of the workouts become shorter, very high intensity anaerobic workouts in trying to help the athlete peak in his conditioning for a tournament or competition.

INTERVAL TRAINING EXERCISES

Some good interval-type training exercises that can be used to train the anaerobic system are the following:

    I. Running Drills
        (a) Sprint 50 yds 8–10 times with 1 1/2 to 2 minutes rest between each sprint.
        (b) Sprint 100 yds 6–8 times with 2 to 2 1/2 minutes rest between each sprint.

PHYSICAL TRAINING FOR TENNIS

Chuck Kriese, Director of Tennis, Clemson University

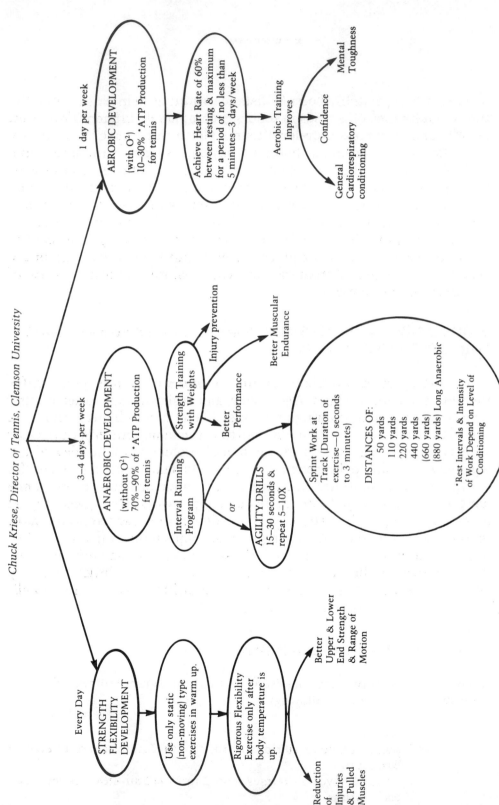

1 day per week

AEROBIC DEVELOPMENT (with O^2) 10–30% *ATP Production for tennis → Achieve Heart Rate of 60% between resting & maximum for a period of no less than 5 minutes–3 days/week → Aerobic Training Improves → Mental Toughness / Confidence / General Cardiorespiratory conditioning

3–4 days per week

ANAEROBIC DEVELOPMENT (without O^2) 70%–90% of *ATP Production for tennis

Strength Training with Weights → Injury prevention / Better Muscular Endurance / Better Performance

Interval Running Program or **AGILITY DRILLS** 15–30 seconds & repeat 5–10X

Sprint Work at Track (Duration of exercise—0 seconds to 3 minutes)

DISTANCES OF:
50 yards
110 yards
220 yards
440 yards
(660 yards)
(880 yards) Long Anaerobic

*Rest Intervals & Intensity of Work Depend on Level of Conditioning

Every Day

STRENGTH FLEXIBILITY DEVELOPMENT → Use only static (non-moving) type exercises in warm up. → Rigorous Flexibility Exercise only after body temperature is up. → Better Upper & Lower End Strength & Range of Motion / Reduction of Injuries & Pulled Muscles

Chart 2

*ATP—(Adenosine Triphosphate)—is the energy reserve of the muscle.

CHART 3

Sunday	Monday	Tuesday	Wednesday	Thursday	Friday	Saturday
Rest	Flexibilities 2 × 440 @ 75 sec 2 × 220 @ 30 sec 3 min. rest intervals	6 agility drills	Flexibilities 1 × 440 @ 75 sec 4 × 220 @ 30 sec 3 min. rest intervals	6 agilities	Flexibilities 6 × 220 @ 35 2 min. rest	overdistance 1–3 miles
	Flexibilities 2 × 220 @ 32 2 × 110 @ 15	6 agilities	Flexibilities 1 × 880 @ 2:50 1 × 440 @ 70 sec 1 × 220 at 33 3 min. rest	6 agilities	Flexibilities 8 × 110 @ 16 sec 1 min rest	overdistance 1–3 miles
	Flexibilities 1 × mile for time	6 agilities	Flexibilities 2 × 440 @ 70 2 × 220 @ 31 3 min. rest	6 agilities	Flexibilities 3 × 220 @ 31 3 × 110 @ 15 2 min rest	overdistance 2–5 miles
	Flexibilities 880 for time Rest 5 minutes 440 for time	6 agilities	Flexibilities 4 × 220 @ 30 2 min rest	6 agilities	Flexibilities 2 × 220 @ 30 6 × 110 @ 14.5 2 min rest	overdistance 2–5 miles
	Flexibilities 1 × 440 for time 5 min. rest 1 × 440 for time	6 agilities	Flexibilities 6 × 220 @ 30 2 min rest	6 agilities	Flexibilities 10 × 110 @ 15 1:30 rest	overdistance 3 miles
	Flexibilities mile for time	6 agilities	Flexibilities 4 × 220 @ 30 4 × 110 @ 14 1:30 rest	6 agilities	Flexibilities 5 × 110 @ 15 5 × 50 @ full speed 1 min rest	overdistance 3 miles
	Flexibilities 880 for time 5 minutes rest 440 for time	6 agilities	Flexibilities 4 × 110 @ full 4 × 50 @ full 1 min rest	6 agilities	Flexibilities 12 × 50 @ full :45 sec rest	overdistance 3 miles

(c) Sprint 220 yds 4–5 times with 3 to 5 minutes rest between each sprint.

(d) Sprint 440 yds 2–3 times 6 to 8 minutes rest between each sprint.

II. Agility Drills

(a) The Service Box Drill:

Start in the center of the service box, facing the net and run as quickly as possible from one side to the other side touching the center service line and the singles side line. You can also run forward and backward or at angles to get a variety of movement. (Do this drill for 20 seconds at a maximum rate and then repeat up to five times.) Take approximately one minute between each execution.

(b) The Suicide Drill:

Start at the doubles sideline and sprint first to the singles sideline and back, and then to the center service line and back, then to the opposite singles sideline and back, and finally, to the opposite doubles sideline and back again to the starting position. (Do this drill up to five times with approximately one minute rest between each execution.)

(c) The Ball Drill:

Two people are needed for this drill. Your partner kneels down with two balls and rolls them, one at a time, to one side and then to the other. You must retrieve them one at a time and toss them back to him, remembering always to face him and to use good tennis footwork. Use the same hand in which you hold your racquet to pick up every ball so that you will be forced to put your body weight forward to the correct foot as if you were playing a shot.

III. Jumping Exercises

(a) Bench Blasts:

Place one foot on a bench while the other remains on the ground. Push off as hard as possible using the bench leg and come back down, and then push off immediately again. Repeat 20–25 times on each leg. (Do three sets of exercise on each leg and rest up to one minute between each set.)

(b) The Australian Double-Knee Jump:

The Famous Australian Double Knee Jump, in which the individual jumps high enough into the air to touch the knees to the cheek and then back to the ground, should be done at maximum intensity for up to 20–30 repetitions. The exercise should be repeated up to three times with a 45-second to 1-minute rest between each exercise.

CHAPTER · 3

Allen Fox
Men's Tennis Coach
Pepperdine University

Following the 1986 season, head Pepperdine men's tennis coach, Allen Fox, improved his record to 200–57. Fox led the Waves to a 22–8 mark in 1986, and Pepperdine advanced to the championship match of the NCAA Tournament before falling to Stanford 5–2. Pepperdine also finished second in 1982. Since taking over the reigns of the Pepperdine program in 1978, Fox has led the Waves to the NCAA Tournament nine times—only UCLA and USC can make similar boasts. His teams have never ranked lower than seventh in the final ITCA collegiate rankings, and five teams have ranked among the Top Four. In the last five seasons, Fox has coached sixteen ITCA All Americans. No less than a dozen of his former players are active on the professional tour, with Brad Gilbert and Eddie Edwards being the most noteworthy. In 1988 his #1 player, Robby Weiss, won the NCAA singles title and was selected as the Volvo Tennis/*Tennis* magazine Men's College Player of the Year.

A former NCAA singles and doubles champion in UCLA, Fox brings a wealth of knowledge and experience to his coaching. A doctor of psychology, Fox has an international reputation as a sports psychologist. His book, *If I'm the Better Player, Why Can't I Win?*, was so successful in the United Sates that it was translated into French, German, Italian and Japanese.

Fox was a three time member of the U.S. Davis Cup team and ranked among the top 10 in singles. In addition to advancing to the quarterfinals at Wimbledon in 1965, Fox also won several premier tournaments, including the Canadian National, U.S. National Hardcourt and Pacific Southwest Championships.

In addition to coaching, Fox has recently become the expert tennis analyst for the Prime Ticket Network in Los Angeles. Fox has also shared his coaching strategies and techniques with the Israeli Davis Cup Team, serving as the team's adviser the past two years.

THE PSYCHOLOGY OF COACHING TENNIS

Allen Fox, Men's Tennis Coach, Pepperdine University

The first problem you run into in coaching high school and college tennis is addressing the needs of the individual against the needs of the team as a whole. The conflict can come when a player wants one thing but has to give in on that thing so that the group as a whole benefits.

FOSTERING TEAM PURPOSE

As a coach, you are basically the psychological head of a tennis family and you must foster a coherent team feeling; there are centrifugal forces on a team that tend to make it want to break apart. The coach has to pull everything together and check these forces. For example, practice is sometimes a great difficulty with individuals versus the group. A player may be having trouble with his forehand and want to work on that, but your practice plan is to have the team as a unit work on the volley. The individual's need has to be sublimated to the good of the group.

I think everyone wants to see the team win and the way you pull together is with an outside threat. In this case, it is the teams you play against. It is a question of pride in winning, of pride in your school. If you set up group goals, the team will be more willing to give of themselves to achieve these goals for the good of the team and not just focus on their individual goals.

As a coach, I try to create this sense of team purpose by building up pride in our school and in our tennis program. We talk about accomplishments of past players and the things that the current players will try to live up to. I try to explain why our program is important to Pepperdine as a school. We have at least one team dinner at the President's house and our players develop pride in accomplishing something for Pepperdine University. We talk about the level we want to reach, specifically, winning the NCAA and ITCA Team Championships. This is what we shoot for in our practice sessions.

In addition I set up specific goals for our team on a short-term basis—like an upcoming tournament. I try to set up an atmosphere where the guys will handle themselves like mature individuals, like champions, so each player can be proud of the other. Everyone should want the feed-back about Pepperdine to be positive from the other teams and players.

MAKING EVERYONE FEEL LIKE A WINNER

As a coach, you want all of your players to feel that they are winners. It is important if you decide to move a player down a position that the player understand that he or she is still a winner, but the player moving up in his place is playing better at that moment. You should not emphasize a person's weaknesses or inadequacies; you would emphasize that you have a strong team with a lot of good players and a certain player who is performing well is justified in moving into a higher position. This is very tricky to handle, however, because you have to give a player hope that he can again move up and take his former spot in the lineup, and that you have confidence that the problem is temporary and can be fixed.

In doubles the psychological make up of your players is a major factor. Players vary in their degree of stability and things can happen in tennis matches that are emotionally unpleasant. Some players react well to this and some react badly. I want at least one stable individual on a doubles team so that when things are going badly, the team doesn't fall apart as a whole. The stable person can hold the doubles team together for awhile, while the more emotional partner gets himself or herself back together.

Overall, I think some people feel more pressure in a team situation than they do individually, because they have the whole team riding on their results; even the existence of a line up may create pressure. I don't have any magic formula for coping with this situation. I try to relieve the pressure by getting away from winning and placing more stress on the achievement of personal goals. For instance, I'll say, "The NCAA's are our goal. It we don't win the NCAA's, we're still going to survive; but we're going to work intensively and this will make everyone better and stronger for the future."

I don't come down on players if they lose a tennis match. I come down on them if they get upset and lose their heads. I try to find good things to say if someone has lost but handled himself well throughout the match.

In terms of a team captain you want somebody that is a productive person and a solid individual, someone the others can look up to—a person who can work with the coach to help pull the team together, even if sometimes this role may place the captain in opposition to the rest of the team. That can be difficult for a player, and the captain has to be able to take that pressure.

There is a natural antagonism that goes on between a coach and a team. It is the nature of the beast that the team should be antagonistic to the coach because the coach represents authority and must tell players things that they don't want to hear or do. Sooner or later, as a coach you are going to have a conflict with each player. You may have to punish them, and somewhere along the line everyone is going to experience this situation. As much as they might like you, the personal relationship with a player gets much better only after the four playing years are over because finally, there is no more risk that as a coach you are going to do something to them at that point, and conversely, there is no further risk that they might do something of which you might disapprove.

YOUR PERSONAL RELATIONSHIP WITH YOUR PLAYERS

I really believe that a coach makes a big mistake if he or she tries to be friends with the players. This is often hard to accept because there is a natural tendency to want to be friends. Usually, you like the players. In fact, you might identify with them and like to be one of them. But a coach makes a mistake if this urge wins out. The players already have plenty of friends and it is important to remember that what they need is a coach, not another friend. You have to draw firm guidelines and stick to them. The players might get upset and mad, but a coach has to have good judgment as to when and where to make a stand, to know what is really important.

Often as a coach I wonder how pervasive I have to be in the lives of my players. With some guys, I find myself watching their studies, even worrying about what they eat! I try to keep myself out of this whenever possible, though, because you can generate real antagonism if you interfere with their lives too much. I have a couple of study rules, but sometimes I don't stick to them. When we travel, for instance, everybody brings their books and they study on the plane. Generally, I'll have one study hall on an away trip, and we do have study hall every night during the year from 7 to 10 pm for those players who haven't proven that they know how to study on their own. All the freshmen and anyone with grade problems after that first year has to participate in study hall.

I also send out notices to their teachers to see if they have been attending class and to see how they are doing, if I have any doubts. But away trips are hard, and I don't want to force our players to study all the time.

When we are traveling during a team tournament, I want my players to concentrate on tennis. In my heart of hearts, I wish they had no desires other than to play tennis and study, but I know that is rarely the case. So I set a curfew and within this time frame they can do as they wish. Usually the curfew is about 11:30 PM, but some players don't know what enough is. In my early coaching years, I had a lot of mature, older guys on our team, and they knew what enough was, so I didn't have to set curfews for them, but then younger guys came in who didn't know how to set their own limits. However, I don't want my players to be uptight about this and associate me primarily with telling them not to do things they really want to do all the time.

Before the match itself, I want my players to relax, calm down and focus their thinking before starting to play. We do a systematic set of stretches for about ten minutes, some close their eyes to relax. We do this preferably in a private place somewhere or on the court if necessary. Then we discuss the match ahead.

HOW AND WHEN TO USE DISCIPLINE

Discipline is somewhat difficult in tennis than in other sports because you are dealing with well educated and strong minded individuals, and it is impossible to deal with them on a totally authoritarian basis. In most team sports, such as football or basketball, a coach can afford to be more authoritarian; in fact, the team expects this. There are so many players on the team, and the coach cannot take the time to reason with each one of them. In tennis you do have the time to reason with each player and you need to. And you have to give them more leeway.

As a coach, I clash sometimes with my players. Occasionally, I have heavy clashes. There was one individual with whom I clashed often because he was so undisciplined. Over a period of time we worked out an arrangement where I would give him more flexibility, yet I would expect him to abide by certain rules and do specific things which were required. The player was a very compulsive sort of person who would say things like, "I can't warm up four on a court." Now a coach could force him to do this anyway or tell him he cannot warm up. However, with this player, I felt I could not order him around like that. It just would not have been productive. Instead, we would discuss the situation and I would make some concessions if he would agree to other, more important requests. You cannot pull the leash too tight with highly strung players. The other players on the team may not like the fact that one player is being treated differently, but you have to handle each situation to get the optimum results, and other players have to understand that this is your prerogative as the coach.

On the other hand, there are certain absolutes—curfews, trying hard in matches, and showing up for and working hard in practice unless there are extenuating circumstances.

Brad Gilbert is a good example of a player whom I coached recently where I had to make certain exceptions. Brad had gone to a junior college before entering Pepperdine. There I think they tried to make him tow the line very hard and disciplined him very strictly. When Brad came to Pepperdine, I realized that he was the kind of person who gets a fixed idea in his mind of how he wants to do something and doesn't want to budge and gets very nervous if he is forced to do something different. We talked and I said, "If you're willing to bend some, then I'll go out of my way to bend some with you. I'll give you more leeway than the others, but you'll have to do things you don't want to do sometimes." I helped him realize that this was in his best interest as well as the team's. He understood our agreement and knew that it would be in both our interests to keep to it. With Brad's temperament, I couldn't be too authoritarian. And as a result, Brad was very supportive while he was on our team and still remains very loyal. He calls from all over the world and keeps in touch. Brad was very team oriented in his own way. He would always cheer on his teammates and seemed to try even harder in team matches.

How you coach players depends on the psychological make up of the individual. The players who want to win and are secure are easy to coach and are very receptive to your ideas. The worst individuals to coach are those that are looking for a way to lose. Sometimes they will even resent your coaching them during a match because they want to flip out, and you are there encouraging them to stay with it. The player is on the verge of losing it and often he will use what you say as another reason to lose and then blame you. "I'm confused now . . . You've told me the wrong thing," etc.

I probably coach more on the court now than I used to. I'm not afraid to go out and grab a guy by the neck even if he says, "I don't want to talk now." A player has to learn to listen to the coach even if he would rather not. A coach should not be passive if a player starts to get out of control. The coach must be firm and the players should know this when they see you coming. Never let a player manipulate you. Some players I'll leave pretty much alone and others I need to be on top of, especially during a tight match. Some players need motivational help, others need technical advice.

HOW TO HELP YOUR PLAYERS OVERCOME MATCH FEAR

The psychological struggle going on within a player during any match is fear versus desire to win. Anything that will reduce fear is going to be a positive. If you have a good program at your school and build pride in this program and pride in the team uniform and pride in past team results, a player will feel stronger: "I'm part of the Pepperdine tradition. Our teams are historically strong." On his own, the same player might not feel so strong. The Stanford teams are a great example of this pride. Stanford has won the NCAA title so often that each team has this sense of pride, of accomplishment and strength from wearing the Stanford uniform.

There is always a fear of the unknown. Once you have won a major title, such as the NCAA's or the ITCA/Rolex National Indoor Championships, you know the feeling of winning; you don't have a psychological barrier of fear as you get close to winning again. Most players get very nervous as they get closer to the finish. Having won a major championship once can help a player get through a tight match or situation—experience always counts. In addition, the sense of playing for the team and the school—outside of one's own personal identity—can provide support and inspiration.

Team unity is something that cannot be stressed enough—the idea of cohesion of individuals, friendships and personal feelings. It is very important for a team to try to get along. If someone does not like a fellow team member, I minimize this as best I can. Usually the reason is not that significant, it is simply a matter of behaving differently from the player in question. A player who is a team member will give up selfishness voluntarily for the group's benefit.

One of our team rules is that nobody leaves a team match before the last match is finished. Sometimes this is not easy—maybe it is cold, or the players have other things to do, but I explain that it is more important to pull for each other because one day they will be the last match and they will want to have the team there rooting for them. For similar reasons I try to discourage socializing during practices and matches, because it tends to deflect from our team unity.

There are no books that really can teach coaches how to cope psychologically with their players. Most psychology books are useless. The only answer is experience. Everyone who lives is a psychologist, and the really good coaches are the best ones. They understand instinctively how to deal effectively with a team. John Wooden with basketball was successful in this area because he appeared to be a "boy scout." In fact, he wasn't—he was tough as nails, but he had his pyramid of success. Responsibility, unselfishness, all the catch words that made up this pyramid of success were higher ideals for players to aspire to.

The real killer is selfishness—the team versus the individual. Selfishness makes it harder for the team to win. Team spirit deflects some of the pressure. Wooden never said, "You've got to win this game." He would say, "You've got to have higher ideals. You've got to have character, morals. You've got to support your team, you've got to do your best for the team." The more you try to protect yourself, the more pressure you feel because it is impossible ever to do this.

KEEPING YOUR PLAYERS FOCUSED

During the individual match, the narrower the focus of the player, the better. The coach will give the player a game plan to start out with, which will be reviewed between games and adjusted if necessary. But the main focus always should be the ball itself. I want my players to work on their emotional state. Good play follows from this; a player should be excited, but not overexcited; positive and optimistic; strong and powerful. The shots will come if you focus on what you are doing from point to point. The game is all played by habit patterns and reflex, so the coach needs to set good emotional tone and the reactions will be as good as they are going to be.

One difficulty for the coach is how to create within a player a ferocity to win, yet at the same time a sense of control and limits. This is not easy. You try to give the players a moral system, and you keep emphasizing this all the time whenever you talk with them. One way to achieve this is to use players they know as an example of good sportsmanship and excellent court conduct—ones who have very high moral values. Guys get very bored when you talk morals, so it is better to do it by anecdote. Winning cannot be the only thing. If you're going to act like a jerk, cheat and misbehave, you will not be allowed to play in a lot of events, and your peers will eventually ostracize you.

However, sometimes when you try to calm a player down, the first thing that happens is that they play worse and suppress everything, so that they start to lose games because they are playing at a lower energy level than before. But following that, they learn to raise it better, in a more controlled way, after they have been disciplined a few times and learn to reorient themselves in a more positive way.

As a coach you really have to distance yourself from your players. The younger you are, the more you may want to be a friend of the players. Some coaches are just a couple of years older than the members of the team. But as you get older, it becomes easier to keep some distance. The ideal goal is for your players to respect you, but also to have some fear of you—just a little bit. So perhaps you have to blow up once in a while; otherwise, they may not have any fear of what you might do.

There are a lot of decisions the players will have to make. If they get to a place and you are not around, they will have to decide whether they will do what they want to do or what they know you want them to do. If you are their buddy, they are likely to do what they want to do to the detriment of the team and themselves. But if an element of fear exists, it might prevent them from acting badly. You are not afraid of your friends, so if a coach becomes a friend to the players, then he or she might ultimately lose control and this could become a serious problem. Most of the time you will have some conflict with a couple of players, not the whole team—this situation may occur over and over. If you don't set up good team rules, though, then everyone is gone. The coach creates a sense of the team, naturally, not by whipping everyone, but by coming down hard when someone has broken a rule. You must always be firm.

Another psychological nuance unique to college tennis is the impact of our scoring system. No Ad scoring is a sprint, really. With regular scoring, you can use the deuce/ad situation as a little perch, where you can hide out and work around it. But there is no hiding place in No Ad. Every point is important and concentration is vital. I let players figure it out, rather than try to prepare them for it. On a 3-all point, I coach them to get their first serves in at all costs, even if they have to take something off it; they should play the point aggressively, yet not wildly. What you don't want to have happen is for your player to miss the first serve because his opponent then goes on the offensive. A first serve allows the server to take the offense. The 3-all point is a pressure point, so both you and your opponent are nervous. Your opponent is less likely to come up with a great shot if he's nervous, so it is not necessary for the server to take a wild chance on a 3-all point. If you miss your first serve, then an opponent can hurt you. So get the first serve in, and then come in to the net, attack.

There is a curve of effectiveness in a match. Early in a match, when there is relatively little pressure, you get a little pumped up and you are likely to be very effective. If a player goes to the net, you raise your level of excitement and can respond. But late in the match you are pretty high in tension and away from the ultimate place in the curve of effectiveness. You are more likely to make a mistake at that stage—you have to make a great passing shot on the guy coming in to the net.

Now with the player on the receiving end of a 3-all point, I would not go for the winning return but would go deep and solid, looking to attack if possible. If the server has attacked and come into the net, I would go low to the feet on a return. I would not try to hit a clean passing shot winner. On the second serve, I coach my player to attack it and take the offensive. I would not try something drastically different from before, however; but I would try to resist being too defensive, which is what people do under extreme pressure. The trick is to be deliberately aggressive, not wildly aggressive. Go for your shots but make them solid ones. In No Ad, there is no room to work your way into a match if you are playing badly; if you are playing well, though, it gives you an edge on those big 3-all points. All in all, there is no question that the No Ad system changes somewhat the psychological complexion of a tennis match, and is an important factor for the coach to focus on with a player, in practice drills and in talks. Often the fate of the entire team match comes down to that last 3-all point. The way in which a player handles this pressure situation is thus a microcosm of the way the entire match is handled by both the individual player and the team as a unit and ends up reflecting rather vividly the philosophy and effectiveness of the coach.

Carol Plunkett

Carol Plunkett
Women's Tennis Coach
San Diego State University

Entering her tenth season in charge of the San Diego State Aztec women's tennis, Carol Plunkett has been the driving force behind SDSU's ascendancy among the perennial national women's tennis powers.

Eight times in the past nine seasons, the Aztecs have been ranked among the top ten schools in the country. Each year since the inception of the NCAA Championships for women in 1982, San Diego State has advanced to at least the quarterfinals of the tournament. In 1984, the Aztecs achieved their highest placing ever with a fourth place finish. In 1985 Plunkett was voted Division I Wilson Women's Coach of the Year by the ITCA.

Since 1977, San Diego State has won more than .70 of its matches, compiling a 186–75–1 record in the past nine years. Six Aztec players have earned ITCA All-America honors in that span, including Micki Schillig, a singles finalist in the first NCAA Women's Championship in 1982.

Plunkett graduated from Oregon State in 1965, having earned a bachelor's degree in physical education and received a master's degree from the University of North Carolina in 1967, also in physical education. She came to San Diego State after serving as an instructor at Colorado State University from 1974–76. Prior to that, she taught at North Carolina, the University of Rhode Island and Eastern Oregon State College.

The 42-year-old Plunkett has served on the Intercollegiate Tennis Coaches Association's Board of Directors and as Assistant Chair of the Women's Operating Committee of the ITCA; the NCAA Executive Tennis Committee and has been NCAA Western Regional Advisory chairperson. In addition, she has been active in the San Diego area in community tennis, serving as Workshop Director for San Diego Children Centers, San Diego Cities coach and Adidas Sports Development Clinic guest instructor. Plunkett has been very active on the Aztec Athletic Foundation, the fundraising arm of the SDSU Athletic Department.

CHAPTER·4

DEVELOPING AN INTENSIVE TENNIS PRACTICE

**Carol Plunkett, Women's Tennis Coach,
San Diego State**

The development of a daily practice session for high school or college that is intensive and of high quality requires an analysis of program objectives and a solid understanding of not only personal coaching philosophy but also the philosophy of the particular program. If the shared commitment of the team members, school, and coach is that (1) each player selected for the team should have the opportunity, motivation, and instruction to become the very best player possible and (2) winning will result from this commitment, then planning practices becomes a very simple procedure.

HOW TO MAKE SURE TEAM OBJECTIVES ARE SHARED

The intensity or quality of the practice is not determined by the level or ability of the players as much as it is by their commitment and desire. When selecting players for a team, whether recruits or walk-ons, it is important to focus on the team objectives and make certain that these objectives are shared by all. The more similar the players are in ability, the easier it is to build team unity and good practices. If twelve players are on the team, but players eleven and twelve are not capable of drilling with the top ten players, these two players will have difficulty enjoying practice and/or feeling part of the team without additional special drills planned with them in mind. A compensatory drill might include feeding of balls with the entire team with an emphasis on stroke techniques. After reviewing the team objectives, you might decide to drop players eleven and twelve and carry only ten players, or perhaps have entire team practices two days a week and grouped individual practices on the other days. If the number one and two players are so much more advanced than the rest of the team that they get no practice and are bored or practicing lazily, again the planning of practices becomes more of a challenge. It might be necessary to allow the number one and two players to practice at clubs with a professional or with the men's team or perhaps with the coach during private mini practices. Games can also be structured with the score being used to equalize the opponents. The possibilities are endless and specific to each situation.

ADJUSTING PRACTICE SCHEDULES TO THE COMPETITIVE SEASON

With the reality of year round competition, practices will differ depending on the phase of the competitive season. Although it is difficult to divide the tennis season into a pre-season and competitive season, such a division should be made in order to plan peaking for major tournaments and to allow time for game changes to take place. If the coach and the players plan the competitions for the year, it will be easier to plan practices for these two seasons. It should also be noted that with teams composed of several nationally ranked players, what will be a pre-season for one might be a competitive season for the other, and practices will be more individually planned.

FOUR PRE-SEASON PRACTICE OBJECTIVES

Perhaps the most important season for practice is the pre-season. During this period, the athlete must attain four objectives: (1) an optimum level of conditioning, (2) comprehensive skill development training, (3) applied strategies, and (4) point plans that will be used during the competitive season.

To accomplish the four objectives in the pre-season practices, coaches must have very specific day by day objectives to be accomplished by both the team and each player. A good practice session has four basic components: (1) physical preparation which includes stretching, conditioning and warm-ups, (2) instructional/skill development, (3) point plans, (4) scrimmage or competition.

Since most injuries that occur at the more competitive levels of the game are due to overuse or high stress, the physical preparation period of the daily practice should be designed not only to bring about a higher playing level but also to reduce injuries during the season. The stretching exercises described in the book *Stretching* (Anderson, 1981) are excellent and could be supplemented with other specific stretches given to those athletes who show a particularly limited range of motion in the movements necessary for their game.

CONDITIONING ACTIVITIES

Scheduling conditioning activities is influenced by the availability of weights, courts, equipment and other facilities. If there is a time limit on the weight room, one might consider lifting weights for the upper body on M-W-F and the lower body on T-Th, or doing a complete body workout M-W-F using a 30-second timed station and rotation period. As the athletes in the latter workout program would be lifting lighter weights with an emphasis on more repetitions, this workout model brings about greater muscle endurance with a minimum of soreness.

If the players have an adequate aerobic base, you might consider interval running two days a week with perhaps one day of distance. If the players are not aerobically sound, their conditioning should start with medium distances to establish a base from which more intensive anaerobic training can commence. Generally interval work can be limited to short bursts that will total no more than two miles. If the speed bursts are less than 220 yards, the recovery jog should be approximately twice as far as the speed burst. If the speed burst is more than 220 yards, the recovery jog should approximate the distance of the speed burst. As with all training, increases should be made gradually over a period of 6 to 12 weeks. Depending on the amount of court conditioning, the anaerobic conditioning can be done as few times as twice a week or as many as five.

BALL DRILLS AND AGILITY DRILLS

To make the physical preparation part of practice even more specific to the goals of the program and individuals, a majority of this part of the practice time is spent on court conditioning. These will be referred to as ball drills and agility drills. Agility drills are performed on one court by the entire team and are a series of footwork patterns used during match play such as: Running, stopping, starting, sliding, skipping, cross

Figure 1

stepping, lunging, scissor kicking, and many combined footwork patterns involving all of these (Figure 1). The emphases of these drills are speed, oxygen debt, overload, rapid change of direction, quick first steps, leg strength, and proper footwork for the stroke being mimicked.

A progressive building up of physical preparation time, especially during the pre-season, to a 25-minute maximum with 15–20 second rests between each bout is more than adequate. A coach can expect a significant number of blisters to be developed during these drills if precautions are not taken. With proper skin lubrication and taping procedures at the beginning of practice, feet become calloused sufficiently to avoid blister problems throughout the season.

One of the more creative and efficient methods of on court conditioning is the use of ball drills. You have the opportunity to create situations to evaluate performance errors. These activities are a concentrated means to develop footwork, muscle and cardiopulmonary endurance, and quickness: With a large quantity of balls, a coach may intensely drill six players on one court in a 30-minute time span. Drills may include, but are not limited to, moving wide for either the forehand or backhand and returning to the center with a slide (Diagram 1), running side to side and driving both the forehand and backhand strokes (Diagram 2), high and low forehand and backhand volleys (Figure 2), and balls tossed anywhere on the court with the player always returning to the center (Diagram 3). It can be assumed that a high degree of physical fitness promotes confidence and mental toughness on the court.

As you move into the instruction or skill development phase of practice, it is important to know individual player strengths and weaknesses, or how each player is winning and losing points. In addition to general note taking during play, a system of statistics should be developed to show you and the player exactly how points are being won in a match. Two such examples are included, although any system could be developed by you, not to mention the highly sophisticated computer print outs available now through several dealers. The first chart records where each ball that is hit by one player lands throughout an entire set (Diagram 4). As the ball lands, a symbol is placed where the ball bounces. When the player changes sides of the net the symbols are placed on the opposite side of the net. When the set is completed, both the coach and the player can immediately see where more practice is needed. For example in Diagram 5 the player is having difficulty serving the ball to the center of the service court. This finding would indicate the need for developing more topspin on the serve.

In Diagram 5, a running tally is again kept for one player that indicates weak returns, forced errors, unforced errors, winners and basic returns. A weak serve is considered a weak return. The player in Diagram 5 needs further development of the backhand and perhaps should be encouraged to go to the net more often.

After each player has been evaluated, initiate drills that will develop

Figure 2

**Ground
Stroking &
Conditioning**

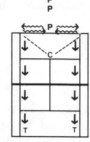

Coach alternates tossing forehand/backhand balls.
Player moves and hits ball.
Coach establishes targets (cross-court or line)

Diagram 1

**Ground
Strokes &
Conditioning**

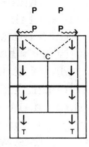

Two players will alternate hitting tossed balls from coach, returning to center court after playing ball.
Usually the same players can stay in for 6 - 18 tosses.
Fatigue will determine length of drill.

Diagram 2

**Suicide
Drill**

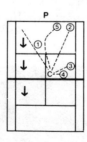

Coach tosses 8 - 18 balls in various court placements.
Player's objective is to make a play of the ball and recover to center before the next ball.

Diagram 3

T – Target	----- – Direction of tossed ball
P – Player	➔ – Direction of hit ball
C – Coach	⌁➔ – Player movement

Player _____ Sue _____   Date _____ 9/19 _____   **To compute percentage of error**

Opponent _____ Jackie _____   Competition _____ 8 game pro-set _____

Example: $\dfrac{\text{Total backhand errors}}{\text{Total backhands}}$ = % of error

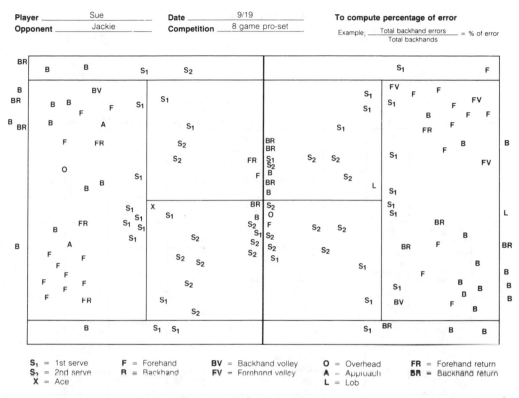

S₁	=	1st serve	F	=	Forehand	BV	=	Backhand volley	O	=	Overhead	FR	=	Forehand return
S₂	=	2nd serve	R	=	Backhand	FV	=	Forehand volley	A	=	Approach	BR	=	Backhand return
X	=	Ace							L	=	Lob			

Diagram 4

each player's game to a maximum. Any stroke that the player will be called upon to execute in a match should be thoroughly instructed as to its execution and purpose in a point. How frustrating for a player to have a coach tell a player to hit short and bring her opponent to the net when the only thing she has worked on in practice is hitting deep!

When you watch a player and think of new dimensions you would like to add to the player's game, it is important for both the player and you to realize that a great deal of time is necessary in order for changes to become a natural part of the game, often more time than either the coach or the player is willing to put in. In that case, perhaps helping the player to do what she does best would be most prudent. Because of variations of grip, speed, strength, and height, the same strokes or point plans will be different for different players. Stroke techniques or point

8 Game Pro-Set

Player _____Sandy_____ **Opponent** _____Judy_____ **Date** _____9/20_____

Game	Serves	Return F	Return B	Forehand	Backhand	Volleys	Approaches	Overhead	Score
1	✓○○○⊘			✓✓✓ X	○✓○	✓ W			0 - 1
2		○✓	✓ X X	✓✓✓✓	✓✓○	✓	✓		0 - 2
3	✓⊘✓✓W ○✓			✓✓✓✓	✓✓	W			1 - 2
4		✓	○✓ ✓	✓✓ ⊘X	○⊘X				1 - 3
5	W✓○✓ ✓○⊘				✓○○	○X			1 - 4
6		✓W X	X⊘ ○	✓✓	X		✓	W	1 - 5
7	○○✓○✓ ✓			✓✓	✓○	✓○	✓	✓○	1 - 6
8		✓✓	X○ ✓	✓✓W✓	○✓✓X				1 - 7
9	✓✓✓○✓ ✓○⊘			✓✓✓ ✓	○✓✓○✓	✓X○	✓	✓	1 - 8

Legend   ✓ = Return   ○ = Unforced error   W = Winner
⊘ = Weak Return   X = Forced error

Diagram 5

plan drills should be planned for each individual on the team. For example, the drive approach for some players might be preferable to the chip approach.

As a coach it is tempting to structure too many drills that are meant to overcome weaknesses and yet not enough to develop strengths. Some players left to their own devices will work only on their strengths; others will concentrate primarily on weaknesses. It is important in planning a practice to strike a balance. To help ensure that all aspects of practice are included, a helpful tool to use is the weekly workout schedule. On this form, the daily workouts can be planned for the team or for each player as in Diagram 6. This schedule enables a coach to be certain that each area of the game is being practiced sufficiently by each player. Any number of drills may be added according to the needs of the players. The example being presented is a beginning one that can be made more advanced by either adding drills, more pace, more specific placement, or more concentrated time. Drills using two on one or three on one are not only tremendously effective in practicing strokes and physical conditioning, but also present the opportunity to build team camaraderie, leadership and team coaching efforts.

CONSISTENCY DRILL

Very few practices should go by without intensive drilling for consistency. Not only do these drills groove each stroke but the repetition of driving a ball 20, 30, or 40 times without an error tremendously increases the player's ability to concentrate for long periods of time. It has often been said that in tennis one's ability to win is directly related to the ability to tolerate boredom. The coach should facilitate a player's ability (1) to focus on the ball and each hit as often as is necessary to win the point, and (2) to keep playing the type of point plan that is winning points, rather than trying something new because of boredom. Change of pace, ball spin, ball placement, and consistency should be worked into drills for all strokes as often as is necessary for the player to feel somewhat comfortable integrating them into her game.

While every stroke should be practiced numerous times during the week, rarely should a day go by that the serve and return are not drilled. While it is important to use targets with many drills so that both the coach and players have immediate feedback as to their success with placement, it is critical that targets be used for both the serve and return (Figure 3).

Weekly Tennis Workouts

	Monday	Tuesday	Wednesday	Thursday	Friday
Practice Partner	*Ann*				
I. Baseline consistencies					
1. FH crosscourts deep	5 min.				
2. FH crosscourts short					
3. BH crosscourts deep	5 min.				
4. BH crosscourts short					
5. FH down line	5 min.				
6. BH down line	5 min.				
7. Crosscourt-down line exchange	5 min.				
8. Inside baseline on rise					
9. No pace/defensive	5 min.				
10. Full pace	5 min.				
II. Serving					
1. Slice/Spin	10 min.				
2. Flat	10 min.				
3. Topspin	10 min.				
4. Forehand placement	10 min.				
5. Backhand placement	10 min.				
6. From service line					
7. Serve/return/volley	5 min.				
8. Serve/return/inside baseline					
III. Service return					
1. Deep forehand	15 min.				
2. Deep backhand	15 min.				
3. Inside baseline	15 min.				
4. Short slice					
5. Lob					
6. Deep slice/approach					
7. To backhands					
8. High bouncers					
IV. Volley					
1. FH flat	5 min.				
2. FH slice	5 min.				
3. BH slice	5 min.				
4. High/low	5 min.				
5. Service line-up					
6. Put always					
7. Volley off					
8. Volley lob					

V. Overheads
1. Front court/fly/bounce — 5 min.
2. Back court/spin
3. Approach
4. Deep
5. Angles
6. ½ pace

VI. Approach
1. Short ball
2. Serve
3. Lob
4. Service return
5. Crosscourt
6. Down the line

VII. Passing shots
1. Short topspin
2. Lob — 5 min.
3. Down line — 5 min.
4. Crosscourt

VIII. Drop shot
1. Short ball
2. Volley
3. Crosscourt
4. Down line

IX. Game modifications
1. No serve
2. 1 serve
3. First one in
4. Ball crosses net ___ times
5. Point from baseline
6. Point from net — 8-game pro set
7. Ball behind service line
8. Server starts down in score
9. Point with forehand
10. Point with backhand

Diagram 6

Figure 3

While point plans were listed as a separate segment of practice, the best teaching/learning occurs when point plans are actually taught with each stroke. For example, teach the player the option of coming to the net following a nice topspin lob to the backhand. Instruction should include the safest percentage shot with each stroke as well as a means to set up an aggressive attack on the ball. It is also helpful to have players fill out regulation score cards for each other. This experience will often reveal point patterns such as perhaps missing their first serve on every first point of a game, consistently losing every 2-all point, winning a majority of points in the deuce court, or double faulting more often in the ad court. Once players begin to be aware of how critical certain points are, or their own tendencies to play certain points certain ways, it becomes more apparent to them that they need to have point plans. Point plans keep the player's attention to the hit at hand and prevent the mind from wandering. The player will no longer just react to the ball but rather will control the point.

SCRIMMAGING

The last segment of practice consists of some form of scrimmage or competition. This may take many forms such as matches, pro-sets, challenges, or what can be called match modifications. A match modification is designed to have players practice a particular aspect of their game. For example, if a player has a tendency to go for winners before setting up a point, a match modification might be to play a Pro set in which the ball must cross the net seven or eight times before the point can end. If the ball becomes dead prior to the seventh or eighth hit, the point mut be replayed. If a player tends to hit for lines, a match modification might be to have the player play on a smaller court by using chalk lines to reduce the width of the court.

Regardless of the form of competition, it is important that this be a regular and substantive part of practice. It is in this segment of practice that the coach can see not only the physical but also the psychological readiness of the player for competitive play. It is necessary to determine early the optimum arousal level of each player and to have a thorough understanding of when, how, or if a player will choke. It is beneficial for each player to recognize an ideal performance state and work toward producing it whenever possible, including during drills and practice.

Drills or competition that stress self-competition, or an improvement of the player's past performance, as compared to an emphasis on winning or losing, work toward minimizing inappropriate arousal levels or choking. If the goal of the drill is to improve the number of first serves from the last service game, to have fewer unforced errors, and so on, the player should concentrate more on the control she has of the match and less on her opponent.

As with any sport, daily practices for months on end can become a boring and tedious routine. Changing the time, place, content, surfaces, balls, or stations can add variety and fun. The use of a video machine is not only one of the finest learning tools of the game but can also add a great deal of interest and spark to any practice.

Once the competition season starts, the emphasis in practice changes. The competitive season will be controlled to some extent by the number of competitions per week as well as the necessary travel. The most important learning which occurs during this phase is the actual mental and match toughness from competitive experience. Practices should compliment this experience. One day a week of intensive physical conditioning to maintain the fitness level that was attained through pre-season training is recommended. A thorough practice twice a week directed at a player's strong and weak strokes would be adequate, but the emphasis of practice should actually be setting up and carrying out specific point, game, and match plans. All too often, players are able to hit the ball back and forth indefinitely but have no concept of how to win the point.

If the coach has the necessary skills, she should provide each player with the opportunity for one on one instruction on all segments of the player's game. Even if the coach has no changes to make, the motivation garnered by the athlete more than justifies a coach's time. However, perhaps the most critical outcome of one-on-one instruction is the coach's and player's ability to communicate quickly and efficiently regarding any stroke or game change. As coaching is allowed on a 90-second change over, there is little time for lengthy discussion of techniques. If the coach knows what phrase, cue, image, or feeling the player needs to perform more successfully, her coaching becomes more efficient and comfortable during competition.

The final design of tennis practice is obviously influenced by factors such as the number of available courts, the amount of practice time available, the caliber of the players, etc. However, the concepts discussed in this paper can be applied to any coaching situation. By incorporating these concepts into the planning of practices, coaches will be able to maximize the development and increase the level of enjoyment and success of the players.

REFERENCES

Anderson, Bob. 1981. *Stretching.* Palmer Lake, CO.: Stretching, Inc.

CHAPTER · 5

David A Benjamin
Men's Tennis Coach
Princeton University

David A Benjamin, a former Harvard University tennis and squash star and nationally recognized teaching professional, became head coach of varsity tennis and squash at Princeton University in 1974 and led both programs to national prominence during his first four years. While head squash coach, his Princeton teams won four national titles, with a record of 39–1, and his tennis teams were ranked among the top ten in the country. In 1978, he relinquished his squash duties to devote his full energies to Princeton's tennis program, and also took on the responsibility of Chair of the Men's NCAA Tennis Committee.

Benjamin began his career at Harvard as the captain and No. 1 player on the undefeated freshman team of 1963. He played No. 2 on the varsity as a sophomore and junior and moved up to the No. 1 singles spot as a senior in 1966, when he captained the Crimson to an undefeated season and the Ivy League Championship.

Phi Beta Kappa and a finalist in the Rhodes Scholarship competition, he was graduated from Harvard in 1966 with a B.A. degree in American History and Literature, magna cum laude, and received the Charles Henry Fiske Fellowship for study at Trinity College in Cambridge, England. Benjamin received an honors B.A. and M.A. in English in 1968 from Cambridge University, where he also played on the Varsity Lawn Tennis Team and the Varsity Real Court Tennis Squad. In the fall of 1968, he returned to Harvard to begin his doctoral studies in the History of American Civilization. He completed his thesis and was awarded his doctorate in 1977.

In 1979 Benjamin wrote *Competitive Tennis: A Guide for Parents and Young Players*, published by J. B. Lippincott. He also taught as a member of the English Department at Princeton, as he had at Harvard.

Along with his academic pursuits, Benjamin has been actively involved in tennis instruction, both at home and abroad. In 1964, he was selected to coach the national tennis team of Togo in Western Africa, and in 1970 was the Director of the International Tennis-Ski Camp in St. Moritz, Switzerland. He was chosen by the State Department in 1973 as a short term American grantee for a tennis project in Western Africa, and from 1974–1976 he was the Coordinator for the Joint International Tennis Teaching Project of the USTA's Center for Education and Recreational Tennis.

Respected by players, fellow coaches and administrators, Benjamin was elected President of the Intercollegiate Tennis Coaches Association in June of 1979 and re-elected in 1981. Since 1983, he has served as Executive Director of the ITCA.

An innovative and imaginative tennis administrator, Benjamin helped create the ITCA national ranking system for intercollegiate singles players and doubles teams and also was responsible for establishing the Volvo Tennis All American Tennis Championships and the Rolex Regional and Rolex National Indoor Intercollegiate Tennis Championships. During his years with the ITCA, this not-for-profit tennis coaches association has expanded to include over 1000 coaches from NCAA Divisions I, II, and III, the NAIA (National Association of Intercollegiate Athletics) and junior and community colleges.

A native of Great Neck, N.Y., Benjamin is married to the former Martine Rafat of Le Vesinet, France. They have two sons, Alexander David, born on August 3, 1976, and Nicholas Henry, born on June 26, 1980. The family resides currently in Princeton Junction, N.J.

CHAPTER · 5

ANATOMY OF THE TEAM LINE-UP

David A Benjamin, Men's Tennis Coach,
Princeton University

INTRODUCTION

Tennis is one of the most individualistic of all sports. From a very young age, tennis players are encouraged by teaching pros, their parents and tournament experience to do everything possible to improve their own games and to think exclusively in terms of their own success. By the very nature of the competition, this success is achieved at the expense of one's opponents. Tennis players as a group are therefore extremely egocentric, and the better players are often those athletes who believe most deeply in themselves and focus their attention and energies on competing successfully against everyone else.

Due to the solipsistic nature of tennis, the experience of competing on a team, whether at high school or in college, usually creates a certain degree of initial confusion. It is the responsibility of the coach is to develop a structure which enables the players to learn how to work together, practice with each other and yet at the same time compete for positions on the team in much the same way that they would normally be competing for trophies in a tournament. The goal of the coach is to help instill in the players a common sense of purpose which is ultimately channeled into performing well in a team situation, both in singles and doubles.

The team line-up is the metaphorical vertebral column of tennis team competition, and much like the spine itself, is composed of a series of individual components which must remain healthy, operate independently and at the same time function together as an organic whole.

In many ways, the method and the manner in which the tennis coach decides who will play what position on the team will have a dramatic and long-term effect on the attitude of each of the players towards the coach, their teammates and the team itself. At the same time the way in which a coach determines the team line-up will very often end up defining the coach and his or her vision of competition. If handled correctly, the process of creating the team line-up will not only help the members of the team develop their own skills as players but also forge a larger sense of the team itself, helping the players to approach team match competition in as positive a manner as possible.

THREE WAYS TO DETERMINE TEAM POSITIONS

The rules of the Intercollegiate Tennis Coaches Association concerning the team line-up are intentionally flexible as to the method by which the coach may determine the positions on the team. The one overriding stricture is simply that the team line-up must always represent the players' order of ability. In other words, the coach must have his or her best player at the number one position, the next best player at the number two position, and so on down through the top six singles spots, as well as the three doubles positions. However, the ITCA rules leave to the coaches' discretion as to how he or she determines the matter of order of ability, and throughout college tennis there is a great deal of variation as to the systems used by coaches to set up the team line-ups. All in all, there are three basic methods employed by coaches to determine the positions played on the team:

The first is to go almost exclusively by the results achieved by the players on the team in tournament competition (both summer and noncollegiate tournament play, as well as ITCA sanctioned tournament play) and team match results. Here the coach is letting objective results determine the order of the team, relying upon match competition apart from inter-squad results. Obviously, the coach still needs to interpret the actual tournament play of his or her players, and this does often create a subjective element to the process, but it is usually clear through the match experience of the players on the team who has done better, whether through ATP points accumulated over summer play or outstanding wins in tournaments. Obviously, a coach whose team is comprised of players who are competing a great deal in the summer and in other types of tennis competition can more easily rely on these results than can a coach whose players are not involved in much match competition other than team play itself.

The second method of setting up a team line-up is based on seniority and the subjective judgment of the coach as to how the players on his or her team compare to one another. There are many coaches who feel strongly that incoming freshmen should never have either the opportunity or the obligation to play high on the team but should spend their first year, no matter how talented, on a lower spot on the team where they can acquire match experience and build up their confidence. At the same time, this system provides an opportunity to players who have worked their way up the ladder over the past several years to compete at the higher spots, enjoying the privilege of seniority and benefitting from their greater collegiate match experience.

But the disadvantage of this seniority system is that if an incoming player is extremely talented he or she might chafe at the lack of opportunity of competing at a higher spot on the team that first year. Carried to an extreme, this system could create an imbalance in the order of ability of the team which could be construed as not following the ITCA rule of order of ability. Still, there are many coaches who feel that it is not fair to rely exclusively on tournament and match results over the summer or during the academic year apart from the team, and who also for a variety of reasons prefer not to have players compete among themselves for positions on the team. These coaches argue that they should be the final judge of who should play what spot on the team, based on their understanding of the players' games and match abilities, and that it is essential to attach a certain amount of importance to past experience and seniority.

The third system for setting up the team line-up, and without doubt the system preferred by the largest number of college tennis coaches, is the challenge match system. There are a variety of ways in which challenges can be set up by the coach; much depends on the variables of the composition of the team as to how this is handled. One traditional way of structuring challenge matches is by starting off with an all-inclusive round-robin tournament and then using these results to set up a ladder for the team. There are many other variations, including a straightforward elimination tournament, a tournament with play-backs or a combination of all of the above systems. But no matter how the actual challenge matches are set up, the basic principle governing the challenge system is that the players on the team are competing against each other directly for position, establishing their tennis abilities by defeating their fellow teammates.

Many coaches rely exclusively on challenge matches to decide positions on the team, feeling that this is by far the fairest and most objective way to set up the team line-up. In fact, certain conferences have even mandated challenge matches as the only acceptable method of setting up the team line-up or making changes once the line-up has been established at the beginning of the season. In general, however, most coaches who rely upon challenge matches still use a great deal of flexibility and judgment within the challenge system. This will often depend upon such factors as the age of the players on the team, their past experience, and their overall ability. The challenge match system offers the coach the opportunity not only to have an objective method of measuring the relative abilities of the players but also a chance to watch each player compete under a great deal of pressure in a tough match situation. This enables the coach to learn more about each player's particular strengths and weaknesses, and this can then be worked on in subsequent practices, better preparing players for the even tougher pressure of team match competition.

At the present time most college teams are restricted as to the number of team matches which they can play over the stretch of a season, both by NCAA rules governing dates of competition as well as conference rules. In general, most teams will play somewhere between 18 to 25 team matches. Since the academic year stretches over a nine-month period and most teams practice throughout the year, the percentage of days of actual team competition is actually very small relative to the overall number of practice days. Challenge matches can offer the coach an opportunity to have the team compete in a situation which often is nearly as intense as a team match itself without adding to the expense and time demands of an actual dual meet match. This is another advantage of the challenge match system.

The coach may pick and choose among these three systems in setting up the team and create variations which involve all three methods. It is critical to realize that a system which works well for one team one year may not work well for a different team another year. In college tennis there is almost always turnover in the composition of the team from year to year; one year a team might consist primarily of young freshmen who need a great deal of match experience, yet several years later the same players will now be elder statesmen with three years of collegiate match experience.

In all cases, what is very important is that the coach explain to his or her team at the beginning of the year the system that will be used that year for establishing positions on the team and make sure that the team understands without any possibility of confusion the way in which the team will be structured. It is vital that the coach communicate this information early and remain as consistent as possible in implementing this system throughout the year.

INVOLVING TEAM CAPTAINS WITH THE LINE-UP

One way the coach can avoid misunderstandings is to establish a close working relationship with the captain or captains of the team and have the captains involved as much as possible in the variety of issues dealing with the line-up. Captains can also help in emphasizing verbally and by example the importance of working together for the sake of the team over achieving the ego recognition of playing high on the team. Everyone would like to be the #1 player on the tennis team, and if the team consists of twelve players, all will want to be starters, although only six may do so in any one singles match.

Once the coach has explained the system which will be used to set up the team line-up, it is important that all of the players accept this system, and in practice each day encourage each other positively to improve their games and to work for the greater good of the team, even though they might have to compete against each other for spots on the team. The well-coached college tennis teams always display a sense of solidarity and mutual support during the team matches, which is the result of the way in which they have trained day after day during the system. This sense of team spirit often is responsible for the team's achieving a successful season.

DEALING WITH TEAM LINE-UP PROBLEMS

Once the coach has decided upon a system for setting the team line-up, has explained it in detail to the team and implemented it during the season, it is still important for the coach to realize that no matter which system is used, there will inevitably be problems which may arise and which will demand a great deal of responsive flexibility. There is probably no better test of the successful tennis coach than whether he or she reacts constructively and intelligently to the complications which arise concerning the team's line-up over the stretch of the season. These problems are not limited to any particular spot on the team; often the greatest agonizing occurs in determining the sixth and last singles position rather than over who should be the #1 player—although the latter is also a major source of concern for the coach, since the #1 spot is the most glamorous position on the team.

There are several specific situations which I would like to use to illustrate the variations which can occur in terms of challenge situations. The first occurred early in my own coaching experience at Princeton, when I had two players on my team who were both juniors and of equal ability, Bob Fisher and Bill Dutton. Bill had won the 1974 Fall ECAC Championships at #1, but in the Spring had played #2 behind Bob Fisher, and both remained undefeated. Prior to the last match of the year against our archrival, Harvard, we agreed that Bob and Bill would play a challenge match to see who would play #1. Bill Dutton played two very sharp sets but Bob seemed very distracted and played nowhere near his normal ability. After the match, Bill Dutton, who at the time was captain of the team (the following year Bill and Bob would be co-captains) came up to me and said that he felt Bob hadn't tried his hardest because the two were such good friends and that possibly Bob would have a better chance of winning at #1 against Harvard, and that for this reason he would rather stay at #2. I was impressed by Bill Dutton's offer to make a personal sacrifice for the sake of the team and agreed with his interpretation as to what would work out best for us. As captain of the team Bill acted in a way that made a great difference for myself, as coach, and the rest of the team. The example he set in that particular situation helped foster even greater team unity in our final match for the league title.

In 1978 at Trinity University in San Antonio, Texas, Coach Bob McKinley had a different type of problem with four freshmen on his team, who all were junior superstars and could play #1 on any of the top ten college teams. His solution to this dilemma was to alternate his top four players (Ben McKeown, Larry Gottfried, Sammy Giammalva and Erick Eskersky) at the #1 spot, giving all a chance to compete as the team's top player at different moments during the span of the season.

A different dilemma, yet one which also involved the #1 position, was faced by Dick Gould of Stanford, when he had John McEnroe arrive in the fall of 1977 as a freshman just off an extraordinary summer of tennis achievements, including reaching the semi-finals of Wimbledon and the round of 16 at the U.S. Open. But Matt Mitchell was a returning member of Stanford's 1977 NCAA Championship Team, along with several other top collegiate players. Dick Gould decided to set up a round robin challenge situation for McEnroe, Mitchell, Billy Maze and

Perry Wright and let the results determine the final line-up, even though the year before he had avoided challenges and kept the line-up with Mitchell at #1 throughout the year. In 1978 Dick felt that Matt Mitchell deserved the chance to play #1 on his team, yet John McEnroe also merited a chance based on his outstanding summer achievements. The only fair way to determine the line-up would be head to head challenges. So the four top players competed for the #1 spot, and ironically, at one point in the season, Matt Mitchell, defending NCAA singles champion, was actually #4 on the Stanford team.

A still different type of problem occurs if a player wins his or her challenge matches but does not do as well in team competition. There are some players who compete better against their teammates in a challenge situation than in a team match situation. Sometimes this is because the players know their teammates' games very well and know how to play effectively against them, but are not as good competing for the first time against players with whom they are less familiar. Other times, it is simply the factor that some players do not like to play against their own teammates. When this situation occurs and a coach realizes that during the team matches a player is not doing as well as he or she should but is still winning the challenge matches, the coach faces the difficult situation of having to move a player down or even off the team despite a successful challenge record. Naturally, it can be very painful for a coach to demote a player who is trying hard but losing matches, but for the sake of the team it is necessary to do this. The one important thing for a coach to remember is that it is a team competition and that the interest of any one individual on the team must not be put ahead of the team as a whole. On the other hand the coach owes it to the player to explain as sensitively as possible why such a decision is necessary and try to encourage this player not to think negatively about his or her game, but to work harder and look forward to a chance later in the season to play up again.

Another type of variation occurred on our Princeton team in the late 1970s with a player who was clearly not playing up to his ability in challenge matches. As a freshman, Tom Brightfield had arrived at Princeton as one of the better junior players in the country and had a good season playing at #5. But during his sophomore year, Tom began losing a number of challenge matches; even though he was playing #1 doubles he had moved down to #9 on our team in singles and never competed that season among the top six in singles. In his junior year Tom continued to have difficulty in defeating our top eight singles players, and it became obvious that he was not able to focus competitively during these matches. Tom was clearly more talented than the teammates to whom he was losing and he had the capability of winning matches for us high on the team that other players couldn't win.

About midway through our season, I decided to gamble and arbitrarily put Tom into a challenge situation for the #2 spot on our team, leapfrogging him ahead of six other players. I explained to the rest of the team that this was an experiment, one which I felt would benefit our team as a whole, given Tom's obvious talent and our need to have someone of his ability winning matches high on the team. Tom responded with a streak of brilliant tennis which began that winter at the ITCA National Indoor Team Championships with straight set wins at #2 singles against some of the top players in the country and he continued through the rest of his junior and senior year with consistently outstanding tennis. In this particular case, the initial challenge system did not function well for either Tom individually or the team overall, and it was necessary to take an unusual measure to give Tom the opportunity to compete at the level which brought out his real talent and his best tennis.

A coach needs to set up guidelines and rules for the team line-up and challenge matches which are fair to everyone, but at the same time a coach has to realize that all rules might not work as well as possible and at the right moment some of the best decisions made by coaches involve breaking their own rules, which were set up with the best of intentions but simply were not working out as they should.

WHEN TO BREAK YOUR OWN RULES

Yet it is often very difficult to be sure that the rules which one has set up should, in fact, be broken. In my own experience as a coach, a situation occurred in the fall of 1979 which best illustrates this type of dilemma. The spring before, our Princeton tennis team had been ranked eighth in the country. The following fall we had all of our players returning, including one player, Jay Lapidus, who in his junior year was ranked #1 in the ITCA Intercollegiate Tennis Rankings and already #90 in the world on the ATP computer. Leif Shiras was undefeated at #2 on our team that previous spring and co-captain, Steve Meister, was undefeated at the #3 spot. Jay was clearly then at a level above everyone else, and there was no question that he would be our #1 player. Not only had he reached the semi-finals of several Grand Prix events and participated on the Junior Davis Cup Team, but over the first several years on our team he had only once or twice lost even one set in practice. However, Leif Shiras and Steve Meister were another case entirely. Both were outstanding players who had had superb seasons the year before and both were capable of winning at #2 on our team. Leif as a junior at Princeton with a great record his sophomore year had little desire to relinquish the #2 spot nor to have to prove that he deserved to retain it through a head to head challenge with Steve Meister. Steve, on the other hand, as co-captain of the team and as a senior, wished to have the chance to play #2 and felt that he deserved to challenge Leif to see who was the stronger player.

From Leif's point of view such a challenge was problematic and one which he wished to avoid. He felt that his undefeated season at #2 against strong national competition the year before had clearly established his ability to win for the team and this should be the bottom line. But Steve felt that he too would have won at #2 the year before; this was a new year and he deserved to have the chance to move up. As a coach, I could see the validity of both of their arguments but finally felt that Steve's perspective was more valid than Leif's and that a challenge match was, in fact, the only fair way to determine who should have the #2 position. I explained to Leif that if he was truly better than Steve then he could certainly prove this through the challenge matches and that if Steve were able to beat him in two out of three challenge matches (which is the way we set up this particular challenge, given its importance), then he deserved the opportunity to have the #2 spot and would most likely do as well or better than Leif competing behind Jay.

Leif disagreed but went ahead with the challenges, which he lost in a very close and tightly contested series of matches. Accordingly, for most of our 1979-80 season Steve Meister played #2 on our team and Leif played #3; but in retrospect, neither player seemed to play up to his potential through most of that year. Even though Steve Meister was extremely talented, the extra pressure of playing ahead of Leif and right behind Jay seemed at times to take an edge off of his match ability. Leif, on the other had, clearly lost some of his former zest in the team matches, playing two spots behind Jay, his doubles partner.

With hindsight, I would have done better to keep the line-up exactly it had been the year before, where all three players had had such marvelous undefeated seasons, but hindsight is always perfect, and at the time I felt that on both a personal and a team level having Leif and

Steve play off for the #2 spot was the fairest and wisest thing to do. As a team we still had a very good year. At the end of the season Leif went on in the 1980 NCAA Singles Championships to reach the semifinals, so obviously, his playing #3 on the team created no lasting damage, and in fact after college all three of our players had very successful careers on the pro circuit, both in singles and doubles.

It is clear then that there are never any magic formulas, and all that a coach can do is to try to stay as flexible and responsive as possible, to try to learn from the players and, at the same time, have the players try to learn from the great variety of experiences offered, both through the challenge system and team match competition.

CHAPTER · 6

Richard N. Leach

Dick Leach
Men's Tennis Coach
University of Southern California

When Dick Leach became the USC men's tennis coach in March 1980, he had a formidable task ahead of him. It was already seven matches into the season and he was replacing George Toley, who had guided USC for 26 years to a remarkable 430–92–4 dual match record (an .821 winning percentage) and more NCAA team titles (10) than any other tennis coach.

But Leach wasted little time establishing his own winning tradition. Under him, USC won 22 of its final 27 matches (.815) and finished 27–7 overall in his rookie year. USC beat UCLA twice, including its first win on UCLA's courts since 1972. USC finished tied for first in the PAC-10 and was third in the NCAA tournament. That year, his top player, Robert Van't Hof, won the NCAA Singles title.

In 1981 Leach guided the Trojans to a fourth-place finish in the NCAA tournament and 28–10 mark. USC handed eventual NCAA champion Stanford one of just two of its dual match losses, 5–4. In 1982,

USC placed second in the conference with a 7–3 record behind NCAA champion UCLA, finished 30–5 overall and received another bid to the NCAA championships.

In 1984, USC won the PAC-10 title with a 9–1 mark and finished 32–4 overall. USC made it to the quarter-finals of the NCAA Championships. For his achievements in 1984, Leach was elected ITCA Wilson Coach of the Year.

In 1985, USC lost in the NCAA semi-finals to eventual team champions, the University of Georgia, having finished the dual match season with a 34–4 record, 8–2 in PAC-10 competition. At the end of 1986, Leach's record stood at 200–40 for a .833 wining percentage and USC entered 1987 as the No. 1 ranked collegiate team in the country.

Leach coached tennis at Arcadia High School from 1965 to 1969, collecting a 93–19 record and was the U.S. Junior Davis Cup coach from 1966 to 1968. He was the pro at the San Marino Tennis Club from 1969 to 1976 and since 1971 has been the general partner and owner of four tennis clubs—Big Bear Tennis Ranch, Westlake Tennis and Swim Club, Ojai Valley Racquet Club, and Racquet Club of Irvine. In the summer of 1984, Leach coached the U.S. team in the Galea Cup, the equivalent of the Davis Cup for players twenty years old and under.

Leach's son, Rick, was a member of the Trojan tennis team and an outstanding collegiate player, who in 1986 was ranked No. 1 in both singles and doubles competition, becoming the first player to do so since John McEnroe at Stanford in 1978. As a doubles duo, father and son have won a number of tournaments and titles. In 1988, Rick Leach won a Grand Slam Doubles title, taking the Australian Open Doubles Championship with partner Jimmy Pugh.

CHAPTER · 6

COACHING DOUBLES

Dick Leach, Men's Tennis Coach,
U. of Southern California

Today there seems to be an overemphasis on singles play at all levels except for college tennis. At the high school level very few teams stay together through the 12- and 14 and under divisions on into the 16- and 18 and under divisions. Many of the players who team up together don't live in the same geographical area, let alone the same town, and consequently, only play three or four times a year together—hardly enough time to form a true partnership. Another problem is that many junior tournaments have become so large they have been forced to drop all doubles events because of limited facilities! Meanwhile, on the pro tour doubles remains the poor cousin to singles with many of the best players not even bothering to enter the doubles events. Over the past fifteen years, only John McEnroe has showed as much interest in doubles as he did singles.

But under our college format of six singles matches followed by three doubles matches, the match outcome is usually determined by the results of these three doubles matches, with most close college matches going 3–3 into the doubles. Since they play after the singles, the pressure of the match usually rides on the three doubles teams, but often so does the excitement and glory of winning for the team. It is no accident that in college all the best players play doubles as well as singles.

THE TWO KEY CONSIDERATIONS IN COACHING DOUBLES

There are two key considerations in coaching doubles: the players' personalities and their style of play.

In doubles pairings, it is vital to consider the personality of each player. If possible, never put two dominant personalities together. They will probably spend more time arguing over who should do what than trying to implement each other's style of play. The ideal situation with a doubles team is to have one player who is the stronger take-charge character, with the partner more ready to follow.

Communication is all important in doubles, and both partners must be able to talk to each other before, during and after every match. A team that will "bleed" for each other and is always communicating will often defeat a much more talented pair of tennis players. It is also important that doubles players respect each other's abilities. If one member of a doubles team loses confidence in his partner, he will begin to look for negatives instead of positives, and the mutual support that is so mandatory will disappear. I had the unfortunate experience in college of playing with a partner who shook his head everytime I missed a shot. This hardly helped my confidence or improved our teamwork.

In general, it helps if both players are good friends. As a coach I like doubles teams to be roommates on our road trips, and this compatibility translates usually into on-court communication and camaraderie. The team that has fun together often wins together.

In addition to the question of the players' temperaments, their style of play is also important. You need a wedge and a hammer. The wedge is the steady player who sets up the openings, the hammer is the player who has the shots and power to put the ball away. Most of the time the steady player (wedge) will play the deuce court, trying to minimize the number of errors on the service return by keeping the ball low for easy poaches by his partner. The ad-court player (hammer) has to be able to put a lot of pressure on the server with strong returns of service. In regular scoring (college tennis is now played with no ad scoring) he takes all the ad points and has to be able to handle the added pressure of these game points (in No Ad tennis, the receiving team has the right to decide which player will return the 3-all point).

But if you should end up with either two dominant personalities or two passive personalities playing together despite your best efforts as a coach to arrange otherwise, then you, as a coach might have to play the role of mediator of the dominant combination and motivator of the passive team.

In my seven years as men's varsity tennis coach at USC, I have worked with some outstanding doubles teams.* Probably, my best teams were Rich Leach and Tim Pawsat, the 1986 NCAA champions; Jorge Lozano and Todd Witsken, the number two collegiate team in the

---

Note: Dick Leach has had ten different players become All Americans in doubles since he began coaching at USC in 1980.

nation in 1985; and Robert Van't Hof and Doug Adler, semifinalists in the 1980 NCAA championships. I also have had several other teams that through hard work and great team spirit achieved a great deal. Among them were Roger Knapp and Billy Nealon, 9–0 in Pac-10 competition at number two doubles; and Matt Anger and Antony Emerson, Pac 10 champions in 1984 at number three doubles. Knapp and Nealon were not great doubles players but had so much spirit and teamwork that they thought they could beat anyone, and often did. Matt Anger came to USC admitting that he was a limited doubles player and not even sure that he deserved to be in the starting doubles line-up. But Matt was always willing to listen and learn, and in 1984 he finished the season as the Pac 10 doubles champion and was ranked number fifteen in the Intercollegiate Tennis Coaches Association final rankings. As a coach I always knew that any player who could return serve and compete like Matt Anger could learn how to be an effective doubles player.

Robert Van't Hof and Doug Adler were not a team when I took over at USC in March 1980. Adler was my smartest doubles player, though only average in singles, and Van't Hof was my number one singles player. I suggested the use of hand signals to encourage Robert to poach more, and had Doug learn to complement Van't Hof's strengths and weaknesses; that spring they went 8–1 in the Pac 10 and reached the semi-finals of the 1980 NCAA Doubles Championships, and demonstrated continuously the way in which a team which worked well together could often beat players more talented yet less determined.

Todd Witsken and Jorge Lozano were both extremely talented players; Lozano particularly had great doubles instincts before coming to USC, having already starred in Davis Cup play for Mexico. Witsken's problem was that he was capable of making so many different types of shots that often he tried the more difficult (and lower percentage) shots instead of a more mundane winner. But in both his junior and senior years Todd became a fabulous doubles player, perfecting his shot selection and using his great control and touch when needed.

The combination of Rick Leach and Tim Pawsat is an example of a team that played many years together (since the 14 and under division) and had great feel for the doubles game along with never ending teamwork, spirit and determination. Tim's four-year doubles record at USC was 119–30 (78–17 with Rick Leach). He was a four-year All American in doubles. In junior tennis, Rick and Tim won eight national championships, including all four national championships (Hardcourt,

Claycourt, Indoor, and Nationals) in 1982 without losing a set–a first in USTA history!

In my own career I always preferred doubles over singles because of the team concept. My highest national ranking in men's open play was number five with Robert Potthast in 1966 and again with Sherwood Stewart in 1967. In 1968 at the Newport Casino I played with Dick Dell to set the all time record for the longest match in tennis history, defeating Len Schloss and Tom Mozur of the University of Tennessee 3–6, 49–47, 22–20! More recently I have teamed with Horst Ritter, an All American of USC in 1963, to win the over forty senior doubles titles, including the number one ranking in the U.S. in Men's 35 and over division in 1977 and 1978. Horst and I stayed back while returning serve even before some of the top pro teams used this strategy to offset the strong serve and poach games. This also took advantage of Ritter's tremendous groundstrokes which he had developed while growing up on the clay courts of West Germany. We were a better team when I compromised my net rushing instincts to compliment his backcourt style of play.

THE TECHNICAL ELEMENTS OF DOUBLES PLAY

To move from the critical areas of pairing your teams to the equally important aspect of teaching your players how to play solid doubles, it is important to examine the technical elements of the doubles game: serve, return of serve, poaching, first volley, overhead, lob, second shot after the return of serve, and vertical movement. I myself feel that the serve, overhead, first volley, and lob are the most basic parts of a sound doubles game, but the service return, poach, second follow-up shot and vertical movement are also very important.

Serve

A big serve never hurts. However, a consistent first serve is more important, one that will enable you to get into the net where you have the advantage. Statistics have proven that in doubles the percentages favor tremendously the team which gets its first serve in. In addition, a player must develop a deep second serve, so that the receiver can't run around and tee off on it. As a coach, I try to teach my players to serve to both the forehand and backhand corners of both serves, with the same motion; this helps prevent the receiver from reading your serve and attacking it.

Overhead

Good doubles players learn to cover their own overheads and then quickly regain the net. The overhead placement should be at the opposing net player if you are inside the court and deep to the opposing player in front of your partner if both players are back at the baseline. Meanwhile, the partner of the player hitting the overhead should be moving close into the net position for a possible poach off the return.

First Volley

A good doubles player must have a steady first volley. Since you will be hitting few winners off this shot, you should also make very few errors. The first volley should be hit down the middle of your opponent's half of the court, whenever possible, since this reduces the angles your opponents will have on their second shots. If you are facing a strong return that is consistently low, you have to try to hit low and soft to either alley.

Lob

The lob is by far the most unused shot by most high school and college players. A large part of this stems from the great confidence our players have in their ground strokes. They feel they can hit the ball through or past anyone, and part of the reluctance to lob more is the result of sheer naivete or stubbornness, or both. However, if your opponents are climbing all over the net, you simply must move them back. There are also times when your opponents are simply overpowering you and here you have to try a defensive strategy, with both players staying back when returning serve. This type of play demands good defensive lobbing techniques, and should be practiced extensively by your players in drilling and scrimmages. It is important to determine which opponent has a weaker overhead or gets too close to the net and to use the sun with your lob. Also, teach your players to lob offensively into the wind, and lob high with the wind.

At this point, I would like to discuss briefly the more difficult and finer points of doubles: service return, second shot (after the return), poaching (lateral movement) and vertical movement.

Service Return

In coaching doubles, it is important to teach a good doubles player when to chip the return and when to hit with topspin and power. A hard first serve that stays low is usually easier to hit back hard with topspin. A second serve that kicks high requires the returner to move in and take the ball on the rise. I always remind my players to aim for the center strap on hard returns and slightly wider on chip or soft returns. It is vital to have your players learn to follow their returns to the net on their opponents' second serves. Also, if their opponents tend to poach a lot, have your team hit a few returns down the line to keep them off guard and honest.

Second Shot

Only an experienced player can keep the second and third shots in play and low to set up his partner. Your players must know which opponent is closing (lobable) and which opponent hangs back and is vulnerable to low shots to set up their partners. It helps to realize that most players are creatures of habit and move the same way almost everytime. Have your team study their moves at the net so they can anticipate where there will be openings on the second and third shots.

Poaching

There are several opportunities to poach or move laterally and cut off a shot for a winner. The most common is when your team is serving. There are two standard methods: freelance poach or using signals. If your players have a very good feel for doubles, they can probably do fine freelancing. However, if your team does not have big serves and you want to make sure they are covering for each other, a hand signal is strongly recommended. Your players can use a simple open or closed fist to signal a move or a more sophisticated set of signals that include poaching on the first serve, second serve, both serves, and placement and speed of serve. For example, use the thumb and little finger for placement and speed (have your player wiggle his or her finger for a kick serve) and the first finger for poaching on the first serve only; first and second fingers for your second serve only and first three fingers for both serves. In all cases, your players must be sure to fake the poach when not going to draw easy shots to the alley, and to keep the other team always guessing.

It is also possible to have your doubles team poach off the service return. The key here is for your player to move directly forward toward the server and only move laterally at the last second. By doing this, he or she can cover both the alley and the middle of the court. Whereas if your player moves only laterally along the service line, the alley is left wide open and often the player cannot put away the poach because he or she is so far from the net.

You should also teach your players to poach off their partners' overheads. This takes good timing as your team's opponents are usually very deep. Have your team learn to anticipate their partner's shots so they will be moving at the most opportune times and faking when poaching could get your team into trouble.

Vertical Movement

A good doubles player is always trying to move forward and take the net with his partner. In fact, you should teach your players that anytime one player has an easy shot, the other player must move way in to the net, anticipating the chance to attack and poach.

I believe this covers in brief most of the different parts of the doubles game to be mastered, whether at the high school or college level. Yet there are still some small subtleties that have to be learned. Anticipation and moving without the ball are maybe the last big steps to being a good doubles player. These take good coaching and many years to master. You must have your doubles players practice their doubles techniques regularly.

We try to do several doubles drills or play doubles during every team practice at USC. Due mainly to the influence of Bjorn Borg, many players have developed extreme grips (Western) on their forehands and backhands. But to be a good doubles player you must be a good volleyer, which requires learning a continental grip, a grip very foreign to most players today. By making young players play more doubles, you will be helping their singles game because they will be exposed to the serve and volley and the net on almost every point and will be forced to learn skills which otherwise they might avoid.

Doubles Drills

On these two pages, I have illustrated three of my favorite doubles drills, which our team uses in practice on almost a daily basis. I deeply believe that drilling is a vital process in developing the necessary doubles skills and having your teams improve; as a coach you should schedule these drill sessions as often as possible and make sure they are taken very seriously by your players.

POACHING AND DEFENDING DRILL

Players A and B are practicing a two step poach towards the net center strap. They hit their poaches between the center service line and players C and D like in a match situation (A hits to D and B hits to C). Players C and D should practice covering the center, staying low and making reflex volleys (see reflex volley drill). If C or D is able to make a save, the four players then play the point out working on their reflex volleys and horizontal sliding to help cover for their partner when they are pulled wide. Note: The coach hits the first ball each time, simulating the service return, alternating balls to A and B. After about 10 minutes, players should trade positions.

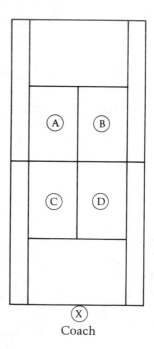

Coach

NET REACTION DRILL

We have three players on each side with one net player and two backcourt players. The net player is the only person that can volley a ball out of the air. After every five points, have the three players on each side rotate clockwise. The coach starts each point from the far sideline. Play to 21 points. Note: This drill teaches the net player to be bold and move a lot, because he is always covered by his two partners. He also learns to move forward (when the ball is deep to his opponents) and back to the service line (when his partners are deep). The deep players learn how to play the angles and defend against them.

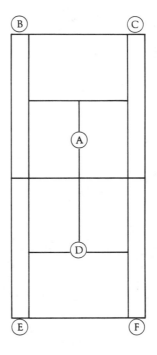

Coach

REFLEX VOLLEY DRILL

Line up players A, B, C, and D along the service line. The coach should stand about ten feet from the net and hit very hard volleys at the players. Hit continually to one player until they miss and then immediately proceed to the next player. Note: The key to this drill is the low ready position the players should start in anticipating hard and low shots.

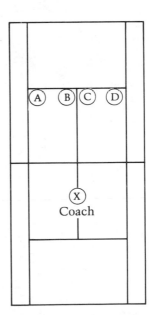

Bernard "Tut" Bartzen
Men's Tennis Coach
Texas Christian U.

When Tut Bartzen became men's tennis coach at TCU in 1974, he inherited a tennis program that had finished last in the Southwest Conference in six of its previous seven seasons. Accepting that challenge, Bartzen moved the Frogs into a position of respectability, not only in the Southwest Conference, but in national ITCA rankings and NCAA championship tournaments as well.

Since that shaky start, Bartzen has fashioned ten consecutive winning seasons at TCU, including back-to-back 20-win seasons in 1977 and 1978 and again in 1983 and 1984. Such team accomplishments along with his influence on TCU's NCAA Doubles champions, David Pate and Karl Richter (Pate also won the ITCA National Indoor Intercollegiate Singles Championship in 1982), have earned the 58-year-old Frog mentor numerous coaching honors, including the 1982 ITCA Wilson Coach of the Year, the Dallas All-Sports Associa-

tion's College Coach of the Year and the Johnston Award.

A 1948 graduate of William & Mary College, Bartzen was unbeaten in 50 singles matches as a collegian. He captained his squad during both his junior and senior years and twice paced the Indians to the NCAA Championships.

Breaking into the nation's top ten singles list in 1953, Bartzen served as a member and assistant playing captain of the U.S. Davis Cup team in 1959 and never lost in 15 matches as a representative of his country. Remaining among the top ten for nine years before becoming a professional, the TCU coach logged amateur victories over such leading contenders as Rod Laver, Rafael Osuna, Tony Trabert, Roy Emerson and Charles Pasarell.

Bartzen's pro career brought him similar success and in 1961 he became only the third person in history to win the men's National Clay Court title four times, a feat equalled only by Bill Tilden, Frank Parker, and since Bartzen, Jimmy Connors.

Married to the former Sara Ledbetter, the Bartzens have four children: Tut, Jr., Angela, Fred, and Tommy. Tut Jr. and Angela played collegiate tennis at TCU.

CHAPTER·7

THE ALL COURT GAME VS. SERVE AND VOLLEY

Bernard "Tut" Bartzen, Men's Tennis Coach, Texas
Christian Univ.

In tennis, as in all other sports and fields of endeavor, people tend to imitate the champions or leaders, not only their style and tactics, but also their mannerisms. Every new champion reminds us of someone out of the past. However, they usually have some traits of their own which make their style of play unique.

In view of this, all champions fit into three basic categories: all-court, serve and volley, or baseliner. We can recognize one of these three styles in every high school or college player. As coaches, it is our responsibility to make this player as successful as possible, based on the skills he or she possesses and the additional abilities we can help him or her attain.

But first, we need to define the all-court, baseline, and serve and volley game and to identify the great players of the past who exemplified these styles. Then, we need to find a way to help our players, in whichever category they find themselves, to become more skillful.

An all-court player possesses all the shots and feels comfortable on any surface under all conditions. He or she has no apparent weaknesses, and frequently has one or more outstanding shots.

A baseliner has outstanding groundstrokes, but rarely approaches the net, preferring to wear down the opponent off the ground. Ivan Lendl in men's tennis and Chris Evert in women's tennis exemplify this approach.

A serve and volley player is one who thrives on rushing the net at every opportunity. By nature the serve and volleyer is aggressive and wants to get points over as quickly as possible. Patience is not one of this player's virtues. Rather, this individual epitomizes the concept that the best defense is a good offense.

It would probably be accurate to assume that most players, if they had their choice, would be all-court players. In that way, it would not matter whom they played or under what conditions. They would always be equipped to meet the challenge, since they would have the necessary shots to implement any tactic, execute any shot from anywhere on the court. As coaches, we would all love to have six all-court players on our team.

If the all-court game is the goal of all players, why do so few achieve it? To answer this question, it might help to examine the only two players to win the Grand Slam, which includes the Australian Open on grass, the French Open on clay, Wimbledon on grass, and the U.S. Open (now on hard courts at Flushing Meadows, but previously on grass and for a few years, Har-Tru, at Forest Hills). Don Budge accomplished this feat in 1938, which was the first time ever. Obviously, it requires exceptional talent and a well rounded game to achieve the Grand Slam under such varied circumstances and conditions over the stretch of a full calendar year. Budge was a perfect example of such a player and even today is praised as the player with the best backhand ever. Even a serve and volleyer as great as Pancho Gonzales at the height of his professional career, playing Budge indoors on canvas in the twilight of his career in the 1950's, found it prudent not to serve and volley against Budge's return of serve.

During his first trip East, Don Budge learned that his Western style forehand would be a problem on grass because of the low bounces. When he went back to California, he changed his grip to an Eastern one. This enabled him to improve his forehand to the extent that low bouncing balls were no longer a problem. Budge's serve and volley were first rate, and he completely dominated the game during his era, which was cut short by World War II. Wayne Sabin, a first tenner from that era, said all the best players conceded first place to Budge and played instead for second place. An interesting side-note on Don Budge is the fact that he used a heavy racket with a 4 and 7/8" handle without a leather grip. He had an ideal build, great timing, which produced heavy shots that all players agreed felt like shot puts when they made contact.

While Don Budge will be remembered as an awesome backcourt player, he could also force very effectively by coming in to volley very powerfully, as evidenced by two U.S. Open Doubles and two Wimbledon Doubles titles. It is easy to see how such a player would be effective on any surface.

The second, and only other male player to win the Grand Slam, was Rod Laver. He did this as an amateur in 1962 before the era of Open Tennis, and then repeated this feat as a Pro in 1969. Winning the Grand

Slam twice in the span of eight years is a very impressive accomplishment, and if Rod had not turned Pro in 1962, one can only speculate as to how many more times he might have won the Grand Slam.

Rod Laver was appropriately nicknamed the Rocket, for he could hit winners from any place on the court. His backhand was his best ground stroke, but in contrast to Budge, he could hit this shot either over or under with pronounced spin. With a continental forehand grip, his quickness allowed him to take the ball early, so he was strong on this side as well. Being left handed helped the effectiveness of his serve, which was enhanced even more by his quickness and the decisiveness of his volleys. He could defend with good lobs and passing shots, but he much preferred to attack. My own first encounter with the Rocket was in 1956 in the National Clay Court Championships, just before he won the U.S. National Junior Championship at Kalamazoo. Even though I won the match, it was very evident to me that Laver had all the tools to become a champion. He just had not yet attained the consistency necessary to play on clay. However, winning the French Championships twice made it obvious that he soon gained that quality to supplement his great attacking game.

In analyzing the only two male Grand Slam champions (Margaret Court Smith and Martina Navratilova have also achieved Grand Slams), it is interesting to compare them. In stature, they were very different— Budge tall and athletic looking; Laver smaller and almost awkward in appearance. Budge was tremendous off the ground, and with all his other assets, was good enough to win five major titles on grass. Laver had a great attacking game, yet was good enough off the ground to win two French Championships on clay. The point is clear that the great players, though their games may be more suited for one surface than another, can bridge the gap and win regardless of the conditions or surface, making whatever adjustments in their games may be necessary.

There are, of course, many other outstanding examples of all-court players, even if these champions did not win the Grand Slam.

Bjorn Borg, having won six French titles, would, in my opinion, have to be classified as the greatest clay court player. Borg had the ideal arsenal for clay court tennis: great ground strokes, super temperament, exceptional endurance, ability to cover the court, plus awesome passing shots, topspin lobs and an excellent serve. His volleying in comparison to other parts of his game was mediocre, and except on grass, Borg seldom ventured up to the net.

For any player to win Wimbledon five consecutive times is almost unbelievable. However, in 1976 to 1980 Borg did just that with a game which most people thought was perfect only for clay. How did he do it? In addition to his clay court strengths, Borg improved his serve, not only in velocity but also in variety and placement. Also, he improved his volleys by effectively dumping short volleys, which are very effective on grass. Naturally, he had to come to the net more on his own serve, which on clay he rarely did, and of course, his return of serve was still better than anyone else's, so he put pressure on the server at all times. Borg was the rare player who appeared to be the consummate baseliner, but who, through resourcefulness and an outstanding serve, also produced the ultimate achievement by winning the premier event of the world on grass, a surface which is usually a graveyard for good clay court players, as I can personally attest. In fact, many good clay court players often do not play Wimbledon because the change to grass is so traumatic and unyielding.

The next player who comes to mind as a great all-court player, but who still never won the Grand Slam, is Ken Rosewall. I always loved to watch Ken play, especially to see the mechanics of his game. From the first time I saw him at the Italian Open, when he was seventeen, he was poetry in motion, never off balance, never an off center hit. Any players who thought Rosewall was just a good, steady hitter never had played against him, because his shots carried a lot of pace and were taken early from his position near the baseline. Even in 1953, I thought he was an excellent volleyer, but he did not volley that much early in his career. I suppose he felt that he could win from the baseline. In fact, he defeated Vic Seixas, one of the U.S. greats on grass, something like thirteen consecutive times, and most of these wins were on grass, with Rosewall playing from the backcourt.

After Ken turned Pro, he became a very strong volleyer. In fact, he began to come to the net on everything: serves, returns of serve, even in the middle of a baseline rally he would often decide to attack the net. Rosewall seldom made volley errors. To appreciate Rosewall as an all-court player, you must look at his record and its longevity. He won the U.S. Open in 1970 and was runner-up in 1955 and 1974, a span of nineteen years. He was runner-up at Wimbledon in 1954, 1956, 1970, and 1974, a twenty-year span. He won the French Open in 1953 and 1968, a fifteen-year span; and he won the Australian Open in 1953, 1955, 1971, and 1972—a nineteen-year span. I do not know of any other player who competed at such a high level on different surfaces for such a long period of time. In doing so, Rosewall demonstrated what a complete player he was. The only criticism leveled at Kenny most often related to his serve. How well can a player 5'8" and 145 pounds serve? The answer is simple. His trajectory was flat, so his serve went deep in the court, and it stayed low. He also mixed it up effectively. The clincher was that his follow-up shot was so tough, whether a volley or ground stroke taken on the rise, that he always had you in trouble. In addition, his return of serve was amazing. I saw him many times take Gonzales' first serve indoors on carpet, return it and follow it into the net and volley Pancho's first volley! So, even if you did break Ken in a set, he was so tough, he generally broke you twice!

Tony Trabert has to be included with the best of the all-court players who did not win the Grand Slam. A single word could describe Tony's game, solid. Every phase of his game was well balanced with good pace. His shots carried the trademark of heavy as a result of the heavy racket which he used with a 5 inch grip. Trabert was an excellent match player who always knew what was happening, and he had the ability and know how to take advantage of this trait. It is noteworthy that he was the last American to win the French Open in 1954 and 1955. He won the U.S. Open in 1953 and 1955, as well as Wimbledon in 1955. It was the Australian Open that eluded him the year he won the three others.

Now to take note of some of the best serve and volley players who were products of the 1940's through today. Jack Kramer won the United States Open in 1946 and 1947, Wimbledon in 1947. Kramer popularized percentage tennis based on the net rushing tactic. After he turned Pro in 1947, he ruled the Pros with an iron hand, using a great serve, sure, penetrating volleys and a forehand that most felt was only surpassed by the great forehand of Pancho Segura. Jack Kramer's game plan was very predictable. He hit deep and forcefully to the corners and finished the point by hitting into the opening which inevitably appeared.

The player who succeeded Kramer was Gonzales, who won the U.S. Open in 1948, 1949. After an initial tour loss to Kramer, Gonzales went on to dominate Pro tennis in the 1950s. Pancho had a deceptively simple service motion, but nevertheless, his serve was awesome, especially on crucial points. Though his volleys were less penetrating than Kramer's, he made much more use of finesse and was much faster on his feet.

John Newcombe was another classic serve and volley player, who won the U.S. Open Championship in 1967 and 1973; Wimbledon in 1967, 1970, and 1971; the Australian Open in 1973 and 1975. Newcombe had a super first and second serve, a very penetrating volley, especially on the forehand side. Off the ground, Newcombe also had a very good forehand, as well as excellent execution of the lob.

Of course, John McEnroe belongs in the serve and volley group because he has a superior serve and incredible reflexes at the net. John won the U.S. Open in 1979, 1980, 1981 and 1984; Wimbledon in 1981, 1983, 1984. He differs from the others in that he is left-handed, which makes him more effective, and it would be hard to surpass him in the area of reflexes. His racket preparation on the volley is truly unique.

CHARACTERISTICS OF SERVE AND VOLLEYERS

Common characteristics of all these serve and volleyers are outstanding first and second serves. The first volley is extremely reliable and effective. Serve and volleyers are deadly overhead and have excellent mid-court games, which sets up their good finishing volleys. All were gifted athletes, and with the exception of McEnroe, all were over six feet tall.

After reviewing the two types of players who have achieved ultimate success in the game, what can we learn from their playing styles to help our players reach their full potential?

Perhaps we would all prefer to have a well-rounded player who is reasonably good in all departments and use that as a foundation on which to build. Many collegiate tennis players aspire to trying to make it as a Pro after graduation. To be reasonably successful, they need a well-rounded game. Assuming they apply themselves totally to the effort, they can improve immensely over their college years, thanks to the tough collegiate competition now available through the Volvo Tennis/Collegiate series. In addition, the summer satellite competition will reinforce the areas where our players need the most work.

When I recruited David Pate for TCU, he was ranked in the 70's in the 18 and under boys. He had a good serve, forehand and overhead. His volley and backhand were average. His strength and speed were outstanding. In the next three years his volley and backhand improved immensely; however, he continued to win matches with his serve and forehand. He worked hard to continue to improve his strengths, and we kept drilling him on the volley and backhand trying to help him gain more confidence and become less vulnerable. Dave became an outstanding collegiate player, gaining All America status three years. With more confidence in his backhand and volley, David learned to be a little more patient and develop the points more effectively. As a collegiate player, Pate's game became an all-court one, which gave him many advantages. As a result, whether he played indoors or on a fast court, he felt comfortable with his serve and volley. If he played on a slow court or against a player with an excellent return of serve, he could serve and stay back, then work his way into the net. This did not mean that he always won, but we felt that tactically he had a chance to win in any given match situation. If you are not an all-court player, then under certain circumstances and against certain opponents you are at a definite disadvantage. David is in his fourth year as a Pro and is currently ranked among the top 30 in singles and doing well in doubles, as well.

DEVELOPING SERVE AND VOLLEYERS

Most people probably think of me as a coach who favors either the baseline game or the all-court game, because I was basically a back court player. However, near the end of my active playing years, I became much more comfortable at the net, and was surprised to find that I did not get passed as many times as I expected. While there was no question that I was a backcourt player, I feel that I know a great deal about serve and volley players, as most of my opponents elected to play me that way and I had a healthy respect for them. If you have a player coming into the net with a very good serve and volley, I think you can get excellent results from him probably sooner than any other type of player, because his tactics are relatively simple—get to the net as soon as possible. Since he is working in only two areas, his progress will probably be more rapid, because his area of concentration is more centralized. His tactics are concerned with how to serve to his opponent to set up the best volley situation and from there to analyze what type and in which direction the passing shots will go. Does the opponent lob frequently, is it high and defensive or is it an offensive topspinner? In most cases the college players do not lob that much or that well off both sides. When the opponent is serving, our return might be a chip-and-charge and just let the percentages work, figuring the server will miss a few and the net man will guess, or know, where most of the passes are going and make winning volleys. Remember, you only have to get four out of seven points!

For the serve and volleyer to be highly successful, he should:

1. have a very good serve;
2. be strong enough physically to hit the big serve and cover the net with relative ease;
3. be good overhead;
4. be an aggressive volleyer.

The serve and volley players who have won the NCAAs in the past ten years are: Bill Scanlon, Trinity University (TX); Robert Van't Hof, USC; Matt Mitchell, Dan Goldie, John McEnroe, and Tim Mayotte, all from Stanford; and Mike Leach, Michigan. They fit the category well, and they have all made their marks on the professional tour after college.

If a coach is fortunate to have gifted athletes with whom to work, keep them working on their basic styles of play and try to expand their areas of expertise gradually, so that you do not detract from their main strengths. I would begin by working on improving your player's return of serve, as this will either pave the way to the net for a winning volley or will produce a defensive volley from the server, which will then give your player an easy passing shot.

Next, a shot which we sometimes forget to work on is the lob, which is always a helpful shot against a good volleyer, and a bit easier to produce than a pin point passing shot. In this area I teach my players the high defensive lob which provides a lot of recovery time and gives the opponent plenty of time to think about the consequences of less than a clean placement overhead.

Finally, I drill my players on passing shots, starting with the backhand, as most players' games seem to be programmed to approach on the backhand.

As coaches, our primary job is to match a player's personality and talents to the type or style of game that he is best suited to play. When you do this, you are working in harmony with the player's natural talent, thereby increasing his chances to succeed in competition. Players who are aggressive by nature will not be content to hit twenty or thirty balls a point. They want to get on with the game and attack. They will be well suited temperamentally for a serve and volley game style. But other players, who are more passive and easy going, will probably like to work in a deliberate, patterned environment and will be better suited for an all-court game. I am sure that most people thought I developed my game for clay courts, but as a matter of fact, I never played on clay until I attended William and Mary College, where

I then played on clay regularly. It just happened that the game which I had developed under the coaching of George Richey, the father of Cliff and Nancy, adapted very easily to clay.

Rather than developing one's game for a certain surface, I think a player should work on developing the style of game completely comfortable for him or her. Then, he or she can use that style, with slight variations, to play on any given surface successfully.

Also, we should bear in mind that by the time most players get to college, they have probably played at least eight years of competitive tennis and many of their habits and tennis mechanics are well set. One thing is for certain, their personalities are not going to change. It is up to us as coaches to guide them in the best direction for strengthening, smoothing and polishing their strokes, and we need to give our players a realistic insight on how to progress towards their maximum potential within the framework of their talents and personalities.

For who knows, one of us may have the next World Champion right under our nose!

Glenn Bassett

Glenn Bassett
Men's Tennis Coach
UCLA

Of the 452 matches which Glenn Bassett has coached, he has won 398 for a winning percentage of .883. Few coaches in any sport can boast that kind of record, and Bassett, with his seven NCAA team titles and ten conference championships, is regarded as one of the game's finest teachers. Of UCLA's 15 team championships, Bassett has been involved in 13, either as a player, assistant coach or head coach.

No. 1 rankings, All Americans, and championship titles have been the norm at UCLA since Bassett led the Bruins to their first NCAA championship in any sport almost 36 years ago as a co-captain under coach Bill Ackerman. Since then, he has assisted in the winning of five NCAA championships (under the late J. D. Morgan) and brought home seven of his own (1970, '71, '75, '76, '79, '82, '84).

The 1986 squad won Bassett's 10th conference title, defeating USC twice in league play and Stanford once en route to a 9-1 record. Overall, the Bruins posted a fine 31-4 mark, finished second nationally in the ITCA rankings, and tied the single season UCLA record for victories set the previous year.

A three-year letterman at UCLA from 1948–50, Bassett was the nation's No. 5 ranked singles player and scored a tremendous upset over top-seeded Dick Savitt of Cornell in the quarterfinals of the 1950 NCAA championships. Savitt later went on to claim the Wimbledon singles crown. Bassett played in three Wimbledon tournaments, defeating such notables as Savitt, Ham Richardson, Rafael Osuna and Alex Olmedo.

Bassett began his head coaching career at his alma mater, Santa Monica High School, where his teams won a record five consecutive Southern California CIF titles, losing only two matches in six years. As a player at Santa Monica High, he won the SoCal Junior Championship and later took the Junior College crown at Santa Monica City College.

CHAPTER · 8

ON COURT COACHING OF PLAYERS IN A MATCH

Glenn Bassett, Men's Tennis Coach, UCLA

College tennis is unique in permitting the coaching of players throughout the actual match. The on court coaching of players during a match starts with practicing properly. If you have good practice habits, coaching during the match is made much easier.

During practice try to relieve your players of a lot of mental and physical problems. If they practice properly, then you have them in a ready frame of mind, physically and mentally. Physically, they must know that they are in at least as good condition, preferably better, than their opponents. Mentally, through drilling, they must know that they are able to hit any shot, which will give them positive feelings rather than negative feelings created by lack of preparation, which will become obvious, even if one tries to cover it up.

Practice enables you to develop the rapport you must have with your player during the match. It enables you to develop a game plan with your players according to their strengths and their opponents' weaknesses. Develop this rapport through constantly working with your players, and know exactly what your players can and cannot do. You and your players must be on the same wave length so that you can adapt to that individual during a match.

Also, you must have the confidence of your player during a match; otherwise, you will just be spinning your wheels. This confidence is developed during practice by discussing all aspects of your player's game with your player and working in a variety of ways to strengthen your player's game within the ability of that player. Never try to push a player beyond the possible (for example, making a serve and volley player out of Harold Solomon).

Once the day of the match arrives, make sure you are around during the warm ups to reenforce each player's game plan and confidence. Your physical presence will enable your players to draw on your own strengths (knowledge, caring, confidence, spirit).

Before the start of the match, go over your game plan with your players so that the two of you understand what must be done to win the match. Usually, winning the match is, purely and simply, playing up to one's potential—you can ask no more. In fact, if you do, the player will feel too much pressure.

Once the match is in progress, stay calm, keep your head, and concentrate so that your player will pick this up. The player on the court has so much pressure on him that you can relieve this with your demeanor. Some players will need you a lot, some very little. Some need yelling at, others don't. Get to know your players and coach them differently according to their individual needs.

A good coach is the one who can take a player when he is in trouble, and bring him back to victory. Be resilient and get your player to be resilient. Too many coaches do an artificial job. They show up for matches but they don't put in the necessary hard work in practices and drills where you really get to know your players in depth. That is where coaching on the court really starts.

TWO COURT COACHING FUNDAMENTALS

There are two fundamentals you should adhere to on the court:

> Pick up, immediately, any weakness which you spot in the opponent in order to relay these during the match to your player. This may provide the winning edge. Try to pick up these weaknesses during warm ups, earlier matches, or the ongoing match.

> If your player is winning, be sure he or she does not lose concentration. Also, if the game plan is working well, make sure they keep using it. If your player is losing, work with him to find some way to come back. This is the fun part of coaching!

At UCLA we start psyching up for a team match, preparing for it mentally, a few days beforehand. I'll work with my players individually in the mornings on their strengths and weaknesses, so once the match starts, I feel they'll believe in me and realize I know their particular games.

We have a meeting the day before the match and go over our game plan; this is reiterated the day of the match. We scout a lot. We have a game plan for every match so that our players know what they must do to win. "What can I do to win?" is the idea. I want the players to say: "I'm going to win if I do this." We practice the morning of the match; I think that is very important. The length of this practice depends on how tired we are. If the players have had a match the day before, I'll let them sleep in and we'll practice a bit later, then shower and have lunch before they come back before the match for a warm up practice.

Usually, we drill and play a few points and go over things I want them to do in a match. If an opponent has a big serve, I'll have a player practice his return of serve. If someone lobs a lot, I'll have a player practice overheads, that kind of thing. The morning is just touching up, however, since we've gone over these things earlier in the week.

Before the start of a match, I like to walk around during the warm up so our players can see I'm on their side and perhaps draw strength from me. Players need that. Everyone is little scared out there, I don't care how good he is, even someone like Jimmy Connors. I've seen Jimmy during many moments of weakness, just like everyone else. As I walk around the courts before the start of the match, I'm keying in on a lot of things, maybe even sometimes on things that I shouldn't. I key in on our opponents' strengths and weaknesses, of course. A lot of times coaches will say, "Okay, just worry about yourself." I'm not that kind of coach . . . I like to get a sense of an opponent's traits. I don't think my guys do a good job with that. I don't think they understand what's happening on the other side of the court, and that's where my observations can really help them. It amazes me how bad my players are in picking up strengths and weaknesses, even in the warm ups.

I watch my players to see if they are following our game plans and if they're breaking down in anything—movement, concentration, whatever it might be. That is more important to me than the score of the match. Sometimes I have to ask what the score is because I don't know. That is not always good, because sometimes I might be too late. I spend a game or two with each player and continue to go around covering each match. This way, I know something of the trend in each situation, at the expense of knowing completely how a particular match is going. I can't be tied down to one match at the expense of all the matches going on.

Once the dual match begins, I go around to each court again, to see what is happening and if our game plan is being followed. I don't stay on the courts very long, but again, it's very important that each player sees me and knows I'm aware of him out there. I continue to do this until I see someone getting into a little trouble. I'll spend some time with this player seeing what we can do to make him more resilient, able to bounce back. I try to keep moving all the time. As the singles matches thin out, then I'll start staying with a match that's in trouble.

After the singles matches are over, we always have a team meeting to go over the weaknesses and strengths of the opposing doubles teams. Again, the idea is for each team to get an idea of how they are going to win that doubles match. During the doubles, my coaching technique is the same. I keep moving, letting my players know I am available and aware and on their side, always encouraging them and giving constructive criticism, even sometimes chewing them out if I think they need this—a little like throwing cold water on them to wake them up! But I don't scream and yell at my players very often. Occasionally, I feel it necessary, however. Most of the time I try to stay calm because the situation is tight out there and reason should prevail. When players are ahead, I try to keep their concentration level up so they don't slack off. You want to make sure they keep up their game plan, since it is winning for them. Sometimes when players get ahead, they want to end the match fast, so they change their winning game plan. Maybe it's nerves or anticipation, or they want to get off the court quickly to tell their friends about the match. Maybe they're physically tired—a lot of things happen out there and a coach has to pinpoint it and help the player make an adjustment. Basically, however, I want them to take their time, but keep up the same tempo with which they're winning. You've got to watch out for a player who begins to rush when ahead.

I try to have the players take a point at a time, instead of focusing on the consequences of winning or losing—have them think of playing each point the best they can according to the game plan set up. Once players start thinking about the consequences of the entire situation, they might get scared, or nervous and tight.

During a dual meet team match, the players have a job to do. We think of a dual meet match as having a first and second half, like football or basketball—singles and doubles. If you have a second half to play, your job isn't done. I see so many people win their singles matches, and then think the match is over. I encourage our players to root their teammates on; camaraderie is important in college tennis. But they have another job to do in the doubles, and so they have to collect themselves, think about what they have to do, and get their minds attuned to what's ahead instead of what's going on in the singles matches still being played. In doubles, if you are sloppy from not concentrating on what you have to do, you can get into trouble very quickly. I want a fast start in doubles, and everyone has to have their heads into what's going on. Rooting for the rest of the team after a singles match is fine for a bit, but then I like those playing doubles to back off, do a little hitting and prepare for their doubles matches.

STICKING TO YOUR GAME PLAN

In a major individual championship, such as the ITCA Rolex Intercollegiate Indoor Championships or the NCAAs, we have a game plan as we do in dual meet matches. I like being able to dig my teeth into one match right from the start, and have my finger on the pulse of a match throughout. I talk with my players about the progress of the match at each changeover, which is not often the case in a dual meet situation. I can encourage a player and project myself into the match along with the player, which brings our heads together more.

If you're going to sit on the court with a player you have to have your head into the head of your player. Otherwise, you should not be on the court. It is tougher to coach some players than others, but you have to talk to them and make them believe in you if you're going to be out there.

In 1971 Jimmy Connors was a Freshman at UCLA and faced Roscoe Tanner, then at Stanford, in the finals of the NCAA's. Before that match, we had a long talk. Jimmy had a sore shoulder so I rubbed him down. The two of us were very close for that match. The game plan was strength against strength. Tanner's serve against Jimmy's return. Our plan was to return that serve. Luckily, I had a player who could do it. Not very many people could return Tanner's serve, especially his last year at Stanford, when he was playing extremely well. Jimmy was a Freshman, but he knew what to do with Tanner's serve. He kept the ball low to Tanner, and Tanner's hands were not as good as they should have been down on a low volley, particularly on his forehand volley. I didn't think we'd have much of a problem holding serve. I just wanted Jimmy to get a good percentage of his serves in and keep Tanner on the move, come in once in a while and keep Tanner off balance so that he couldn't come in himself.

Jimmy won that match in four sets. We stuck to our game plan throughout. Jimmy served the best I've ever seen him serve, but his return of serve won the match for him. I didn't want Jimmy to get tricky. The win was special for Jimmy because it took place at Notre Dame, where his father had gone to school.

A different type of NCAA finals took place in 1975 at Corpus Christi where Billy Martin, also a Freshman at UCLA, struggled against George Hardy of SMU—and also maybe with trying to match Connors's earlier feat. Billy went into that match extremely tired; he was not a very strong player physically, and he had had a tough match against Freddy DeJesus of Michigan in the semis. At breakfast the morning Billy had to play Hardy, Billy was like a zombie. He could hardly eat he was so nervous and tired. I've never seen a player so tired, except possibly for Peter Fleming in 1976, and I knew we were in real trouble, because Billy wasn't eating at all. The day was very warm, and it was extremely windy, well over 25 miles per hour. The wind tires you because you feel like you are fighting it all the time.

Billy used to put an incredible amount of energy into every point, and would perspire more than anyone I have ever seen. When he was playing matches, the sweat would go down into his shoes (he had on adidas shoes then without any airholes). You could see his footprints like he was coming out of the shower. Billy was slipping all over the place, so we were punching holes with ice picks all over these leather shoes to try to get some ventilation. We had to change shoes several times during the match. Sweating as much as Billy did drains you. He had nothing left at the start of the match. He lost the first two sets 6–0, 6–1, and I started throwing sodas into him for the sugar. We also iced his neck. He was like a punch drunk prize fighter sitting in his corner.

For the first two sets, I told him to hit his return as hard as he could to try to avoid getting into long points. But this wasn't working because he didn't have the strength at that point. When we got the third set, which was the key to turning the match around, Billy began to show some signs of life. It might have been from the soda, although I wouldn't recommend pouring sugar into a player in most situations. We were desperate, however! Billy began to return balls very hard. Hardy kept coming in so this tactic worked. But we didn't want any long rallies. Then, when Billy got some energy back, his mental toughness just came out. He just had a tremendous, tremendous will to win and willingness to pay the price, however much it cost in pain and emotion. Finally, this made the difference, and Billy took the last three sets and the championship, 6–3, 6–3, 6–3.

In 1977, when Eliot Teltscher came to UCLA, I thought I might have a lot of trouble after hearing what others had told me, but Eliot was one of the best practice players and one of the easiest guys to get along with. He really helped the team out and did what we said. But sometimes in matches he would get too uptight. In the 1978 NCAA's when he played John Sadri in the quarters, Eliot was beaten partly because he lost his composure and his will to win. This was unusual for Teltscher because he was such a great competitor. Eliot was fun to have on court because you knew you were going to get 30 or 40 miles to the gallon out of him everytime he played.

Maybe one of our most memorable matches ever was against Stanford at UCLA in 1978, a big match, large crowd, and we all knew how well McEnroe performed in front of a crowd . . . Teltscher had him 6–3, was ripping his return of serve and had McEnroe afraid. It was in the second set 5–3, 3 all on Teltscher's serve—match point for UCLA. We were trying to go down the center to McEnroe, not give him any angles. Teltscher hit a good serve down the middle, and McEnroe hit a pretty good return back, which started a backcourt rally. Finally, Teltscher made a short backhand approach to McEnroe's backhand down the line. McEnroe ran way across the court, and just got the ball before it bounced twice and flicked his wrist with a backhand crosscourt that just dropped an inch inside the alley line. We couldn't believe he got to that shot! Our players were all standing by the court at that point, ready to charge on the court and congratulate Eliot—he had the match won, we thought! Eliot just stood there in shock—and so were we. McEnroe went on to win, and Stanford beat us 5–4.

Fritz Buehning was a tremendous team player. He had that body language that said, "I'm not going to lose and I'm going to lead my team to victory." The guys saw him walk with a purpose on the court and drew strength from him. He was a great big guy and very easy to talk to, but I had to yell and scream at him a little more than some players to get something out of him. I got after him to try to fire him up. He never got tired, even though he wasn't in the best of condition. I never had to calm him down, like I did with other players.

With Blaine Willenborg, I had to calm him down a lot, but I enjoyed coaching Blaine because he really liked having you on the court. He'd call me, "Coach, Coach, come on over! What should I do?" I felt we had good rapport. Tactically, we had to try to cover up his backhand. I wanted him to get in his first serve in as much as possible, a knuckleball type high above the net and deep—a big quick twister, so he could get into the net. He was a pretty good serve and volleyer, but he tried to drop shot and drop volley too much. Still, he was very successful at this, and disoriented people, perhaps more than anyone else I've ever coached as far as the up and back game. He got someone on a YoYo and would exhaust them and drive them crazy, out of sync. In singles or in doubles, people would hate to play Fritz and Blaine. Fritz would slap a ball for a winner, or slap a ball into the fence. He never got into a groove. He would really mix up his shots and no one knew how to play these guys.

Another guy who I really enjoyed, but who never did as well in the Pros as I thought he would, was Jeff Borowiak. Jeff was the best athlete I ever had. He was a gymnast and could walk and tumble—could walk on our railing and do back flips. Great basketball player. He won the NCAA's as a Junior in 1970. In his Senior year he played ahead of Jimmy Connors all year but Connors still won the NCAAs.

Another fun player I worked with was Brian Teacher, who had a unique element to his game that very few people had. When he got to the net he was like a spider; players just couldn't get the ball by him. Brian could just sense where the ball was going on passing shots. He would blanket that net and players would get very discouraged. Brian would act very nonchalant about his volleys, and this would further demoralize his opponents. The pressure of playing Teacher was too much for most players, and they never could figure out how to cope.

In conclusion, I would like to repeat that the challenge of coaching all players in a match situation, whether a Connors or Teltscher, or someone less talented, is finding the best ways to motivate them and help them to get the most out of their games under the pressure of a match. Because, as college coaches, we are allowed to coach continuously during a match, we are in a unique position to help our players and participate actively with them on the court.

CHAPTER · 9

Steve Wilkinson

Steve Wilkinson
Director
Tennis and Life Camps

Steve Wilkinson is the director of Tennis and Life Camps, a holistic tennis experience for adults and juniors. Participants learn relaxation techniques, nutrition, and sportsmanship, as well as strategy and strokes. Also he coaches the Gustavus Adolphus College tennis team, NCAA III champions in 1980 and 1982. Three times he has been named ITCA Wilson coach of the year. Steve has served on the national executive committee of the U.S. Professional Tennis Association since 1977 and the Intercollegiate Tennis Coaches Association since 1981. As a player he has won more than thirty national titles in the open, 35's, and 45's events of USPTA, USTA, and National Public Parks tournaments. Steve has taught college classes in accounting, economics, religion, Asian studies, and coaching theory. He has a Ph.D. in world religions from the University of Iowa. Articles by and about him have appeared in *Tennis, World Tennis, Tennis USA,* and *Tennis, a Professional Guide.*

CHAPTER · 9

SPORTSMANSHIP TRAINING FOR TENNIS

Steve Wilkinson

SPORTSMANSHIP OR WINNING—WHICH IS MORE IMPORTANT?

Tennis competition involves choices. Picture a hard fought battle between two outstanding players. It is going down to the wire in the third set. There is a solo umpire in the chair who has been instructed to overrule in case of obvious mistakes. The player from Kalamazoo College, Tim Corwin, has received a couple of questionable calls from his opponent. Now the score is 5–6 in the set and 3–3 in the game. It is match point for Corwin. The opponent serves wide into the add court. Tim returns the serve softly at the feet of the incoming server. He hits a brilliant half volley into the open court, down the line. Corwin races to the far side line and hits a passing shot down the line for an apparent winner. The player at the net did not see where it landed. Neither did the umpire in the chair, located on the opposite side of the court. Only Corwin saw that his passing shot was clearly out. "Out," he called. Instead of winning the match, he was now facing the prospect of a third set tie-breaker. The USTA Code requires players to call their own balls out in this situation. Tennis competition can involve difficult choices.

Consider another situation: It is set point in the finals of the U.S. Open Doubles Championship at Flushing Meadows. Two promising young players from the United States have won the first set, but they are down set point at this moment. The opponents from Europe are formidable, two of the best players in the world at the time. A victory for the Americans would mean a certain Davis Cup berth, more than $20,000, and their first title. In a fast exchange at the net, one of the Europeans drills a ball through one of the Americans. The ball goes long. The umpire does not see the ball hit the American, and so he makes no call. The Europeans are furious. They know the ball hit him. The American is confused. He felt the ball possibly nicked him, but he is not sure. What should he do? Tennis competition involves hard choices. If he had been sure, the rules require him to call it on himself. If there had been no umpire and he was unsure, benefit of the doubt goes to the opponent, and again he would have lost the point. But there was an umpire and he was unsure. He said nothing. The point and eventually the set went to the Americans. They won the title, and later played Davis Cup for the United States.

It was Januray 16, 1982, and a rising young star, Eliot Teltscher, was pitted against the veteran Vitas Gerulaitus in the finals of a major Grand Prix tournament. What an opportunity, and Teltscher was playing well! He had gone up a break in the third, only to have that lead slip away. Now the score was 5–6, 30–40 with Teltscher serving. The serve was placed wide, taking Gerulaitus out of court. Teltscher moved in close to the net and volleyed firmly into the open court. Apparently the score was now deuce, but for some reason Teltscher was extending an outstretched hand to Vitas. Teltscher indicated that he had touched the net. The umpire had not noticed it. Gerulaitus had not observed the infraction. However, Teltscher knew that he had committed an infraction and was not entitled to the point. That act of integrity cost him ten thousand dollars and his first major title. Gerulaitus commented in a television interview after the match when asked if he had seen the infraction. "No! I didn't see it; the umpire didn't see it; the net cord judge didn't see it. Only Eliot could have made that call and it cost him $10,000. Eliot Teltscher was the best man out there today."

Tennis is an exciting, fast moving sport, played for big stakes. A single call, one way or the other, can be the difference between winning and losing, between a national championship and an early round loss, between several thousand dollars, and nothing. Many spectators are surprised to learn that the players themselves are required to make difficult calls against themselves. They assume that if the umpire makes a mistake against you, then protest—but don't reverse the good fortunes that may come your way. Indeed, the sportsmanship code undergirding tennis is an anamoly.

The unique Code of tennis is even more important in nonumpired matches. This is the case in more than ninety percent of all matches in USTA tournaments and ITCA dual matches. The Code requires every doubtful call to go in favor of the opponent. If you reach a ball as it bounces twice, but you are only 99 percent sure you reached it on one bounce, the point goes to the opponent. If a ball hits near your baseline and you are 99 percent sure it was out, you are required by the Code to play the ball. If you delay making a call, but then realize that it was out, the Code requires the ball to be good. Indeed, most newcomers to tennis are shocked to discover that competitors, striving to win important national titles, bend over backwards in favor of their opponents. This generous position is maintained, even if you are convinced that your opponent is not doing the same.

Choosing between sportsmanship and winning is a difficult decision, given the rewards and recognition associated with winning. Mark Kruger, an outstanding tennis competitor for Gustavus Adolphus College, faced this choice. For three years he won All American honors based on his collegiate record. Also, he was twice a finalist for the prestigious ITCA Head/Arthur Ashe Award, an honor that recognizes playing accomplishments, sportsmanship, scholarship, and humanitarian concerns. In an essay required for that award, Mark wrote that his relationships with teammates and opponents were more important to him than winning. This could be observed in his cordial manner of competing and practicing. For example, not once during his four years of competing did I, his coach, observe him challenge an opponent's or teammate's line call, either through words or body language. Mark was being honest when he claimed that people come first. When people and sportsmanship come first in competition, one can honestly say that tennis begins with love.

For many other competitors winning is paramount and sportsmanship is conditional. If the opponent is sportsmanlike, if the officials make correct rulings, and if the level of play is up to expectations, then sportsmanship is feasible. The bottom line, however, is winning. "Winning isn't the most important thing. It's the only thing," said one famous coach. "Show me a good loser, and I'll show you a loser" said a controversial tennis competitor, known for both his fighting, championship play and his obnoxious behavior. When winning becomes the overwhelming obsession, one can honestly say that in tennis, love means nothing.

ATTITUDES THAT FACILITATE SPORTSMANSHIP

Most of you do not have such an exaggerated emphasis on winning. Every competitor tries to win, but most of you do not think it is proper to neglect sportsmanship. Even many poor sports would like to do better, but the pressures of competition cause them to waiver and fall short. However, it is not the competition itself which produces the pressure, but the individual attitudes which you bring to the competition. By examining common attitudes which tend to build pressure and frustration, the problem of poor sportsmanship can be better understood. When alternative attitudes are substituted, sportsmanship immediately becomes a more achievable goal.

First, you need to focus on those things over which you have control and to hang loose upon things lying outside your control. For example, winning lies outside your control. A fantastic performance by an opponent, sickness, cheating, officiating errors, luck, or a number of other factors, all outside your control, can decide the outcome of a closely contested match. Also, playing well is an equally frustrating goal. It is so easy to play great for a while, and then absolutely stink for the next few games. There is no easy explanation for the difference. Sometimes you grow anguished and yell, "I can't believe I'm playing so poorly. This is a joke! Even my grandfather could have made that shot. And he is in a wheelchair!" The more you lament, the longer the poor play lasts. Good play often returns as quickly as it went if you ignore the reasons for the poor play (over which you have no control) and center on controllable elements in the game.

So what is controllable? Your full effort toward victory can be achieved every time. Near the end of a tie-breaker, in a closely contested match, neither you nor your opponent can honestly be certain of victory. You cannot be certain you will play each point well. However, you can be certain that you will try your hardest. You can both know that you will leave the contest with pride, with your heads held high, knowing that you expended full effort. It is within the control of both of you.

Reinhold Niebuhr put this distinction between the controllable and the uncontrollable into perspective when he formulated the Serenity Prayer. He said, "God, grant me the serenity to accept the things I cannot change; the strength to change the things I can; and the wisdom to know the difference."

How perceptive! Often the wisdom to know the difference is missing. You think you can control winning, but you cannot. You assume that playing well is your right, if you have practiced hard, but it is not. You can grow frustrated, thinking you should be able to control these things, and consequently abandon the elements of your game which you can control. Thoughts like these may creep into your mind. What is the point in trying if I am playing like this? or There is no use in trying. I am down two breaks. There is no way for me to come back now. The ability to try is always within your control, until you lose your will to try. So frequently the will is lost when you reach despair over things outside your control, which sometimes you mistakenly assume you should be able to control. When you reach despair, sportsmanship becomes difficult or impossible.

Another essential attitude for sportsmanship is renouncing the expectation that everything will work out fairly. It won't. Never lose your resolve to treat others fairly; that is something within your control. You will not always achieve your goal, but you can always try. When others are unfair (not within your control), your commitment to fairness (within your control) can waiver. Sportsmanship always suffers when your commitment to fairness decreases. At its most basic level, sportsmanship rests on the Golden Rule—Do unto others as you would have them do unto you. This is the ultimate principle of fairness.

Fairness is not the expectation that your opponent will always give you the benefit of the doubt on a line call, because you have done the same for him or her. Fairness is not the expectation that you will win an equal number of let-cord shots or 3–3 points when you are using no-ad scoring; that you will win against an equal opponent if you have spent more time practicing; that you should not have to play with an injury or sickness when your friends are healthy. The next time you start feeling sorry for yourself and getting depressed, reflect on the good fortune you have, being able to enjoy the sport of tennis. Is it fair that you can run and play when many people must devote their full energies to finding their next meal? Play with the knowledge that you are fortunately blessed, and sportsmanship becomes much easier.

Third, you need to reject retaliation or revenge as a valid response to injustice. An eye for an eye, and a tooth for a tooth approach makes sportsmanship unlikely. With this approach, you are not the one who controls your actions. You are like a reed, blown by the wind. If the winds are pleasant, you are in luck, but forget sportsmanship when the foul winds are blowing.

People who justify retaliation fear intimidation or exploitation. If competitors know you will not retaliate, they will certainly take advantage of you. Therefore, you must be firm and unrelenting. Fight fire with fire. If you get a bad call, give it right back to them. Let them know you will not tolerate any nonsense.

This position brings you back to the bottom line in competition. If winning—with or without sportsmanship—is the bottom line, retaliation can be a valid response. If sportsmanship needs to be present in the struggle to win, then retaliation has no place. Indeed, you are not taken advantage of when someone treats you unjustly and you turn the other cheek. Instead, you are compromised when a competitor gets your goat and entices you to sacrifice your principles of sportsmanship in order to get even. If you cheat because your opponent has cheated, you also become a cheater.

So frequently a sense of righteous indignation rises up within a competitor. Did you see what they did? That is the worst I have ever seen! Coach, don't talk to me until you say something to them! I don't feel the least bit sorry for my actions. Sportsmanship can never flourish when retaliation is justified.

Fourth, reject the expectation that you are entitled to play at a certain level. No matter how simple a shot might be, it is unrealistic to assume you should never miss. However, how many times have you found yourself thinking, How could anyone miss that set-up? Instead you need to remember that everyone misses easy shots. You should visualize a successful shot every time you hit the ball, but you need to realize after the point is over that errors are part of the game. So are losses to players who are not normally as good as you. Poor sportsmanship often festers and then bursts open when competitors forget or deny this fundamental reality.

Fifth, sportsmanship is facilitated when you identify personal goals for each match which are not threatened by the accomplishments of your opponent. If your sole goal is winning, you will find it difficult to appreciate either the skill or the luck of your opponent. You have created a win/lose situation in which either you or your opponent is successful. Consequently, sportsmanship, which is based on a charitable attitude toward your opponent, is difficult. Instead, if two of your most important goals are watching the ball into the strings and hitting high percentage shots, they can be accomplished even when your opponent is winning. You are focusing on goals within your control. They assist you in playing your best tennis and leave you in a better frame of mind to be sportsmanlike. The opponent is perceived as a partner, working together with you, enhancing both of your skills.

ACTIONS THAT BUILD SPORTSMANSHIP

Sportsmanship should begin before you and your opponent step on the court. Introduce yourself, shake hands, and establish eye contact. Show a personal interest in your opponent. Learn something about him or her as a person. Avoid pre-match excuses. Poor court conditions, an unfavorable time of day, lack of practice time, injuries, or a thousand other reasons are all inappropriate. They are used to preserve your ego, but they unintentionally detract from your opponent's accomplishments. If your opponent is not as good as you, be certain you communicate that you take your opponent and the match seriously. Refusing to warm up with your opponent, joking with your doubles partner or spectators, and creating the impression that you are only preparing casually, all need to be avoided.

Once the match begins, you can do many things which continue to build sportsmanship. In nonumpired matches, begin by calling the score before every point. Needless confusion and hard feelings resulting from controversies over the score can be avoided. The server should call the score, but if he or she forgets, do not be bashful about asking. Never assume that you both know the score. If you do lose track of the score or disagree, then go to the point where you both remember or agree. When trying to reconstruct the score, interact aimably in a nonaccusatory fashion. Never assume that the other person is at fault. Either of you can avoid the problem by carefully calling the score.

Next, give your opponent the benefit of the doubt on all your calls. If there is a one percent chance that the ball was good, then call it good. Never waiver from this approach, even if it appears that your opponent is not reciprocating. Also, if your opponent has a better view at the ball, offer to change your call if he or she saw it differently. After all, Vic Braden has shown that people are legally blind when trying to make line calls on the run. Sometimes you are moving and your opponent is standing still, looking straight down your line. If you are interested in the most accurate call possible, then the opponent's judgment is critical.

Also, out and let calls must be made immediately. Particularly aggravating is the practice of calling the ball out after you have missed the shot. This happens frequently on the return of serve. The returner takes a swing at the ball, misses, and then calls it out. You sometimes get the impression that the opponent is waiting to see if his or her return is good before making the service call. Another problem is asking for a let after the point has ended. That familiar question, Did you hear a let?, is completely inappropriate. For example, you may hear a let on your own serve, but make no call, thinking it is the receiver's responsibility to call the let. The receiver may hit the return for a winner, but you make no attempt to play it. In this case, you lose the point, because you made no let call. A ball is not a let until it is called, and it must be called immediately by anyone who hears it.

Another important area of sportsmanship is avoiding the temptation to challenge your opponent's line call. The USTA Code stipulates that all such challenges are inappropriate, even if your opponent has made a series of bad calls. Also, be careful to avoid nonverbal challenges which depend on body language. A stare, with your hands on your hips, or a shaking of your head, accompanied by laughter, can be equally offensive. Instead, you should summon an umpire in a low key manner, during the ninety seconds allowed for the change over. However, there is an exception to this rule. ITCA rules require a challenge before a solo umpire can overrule a bad call. Therefore, in ITCA, solo umpired matches, polite challenges are permissible.

Next, the sportsmanship code requires you to call your own balls out, on the other side of the net, when you are positive that you missed. Even if your opponent plays the ball, you are obligated to stop play and to call the ball out. The one exception to this rule is on the first serve, where a winning service return by your opponent could be nullified by an out call.

The final point relating to line calls involves a disagreement between you and your doubles partner. If you are certain that your partner made a mistaken out call, even if he or she had the better view, you are obligated to contradict your partner. To stand by your partner's call, when you know it was wrong, leaves you guilty of cheating. However, you lose the point when you contradict your partner. When you and your partner disagree, doubt certainly exists. When there is any doubt, the ball is good. When an out call is made on a good shot, the team making the erroneous call loses the point. Currently USTA rules permit the offender to play the point over if he or she returns the ball. However, most officials believe this exception should be eliminated. ITCA rules clearly prohibit the point being replayed.

Traditionally most people associate sportsmanship with good court behavior. Certainly you need to avoid profanity, racket or ball abuse, and other forms of poor sportsmanship. It is degrading to you. Also, you unintentionally put your opponent down. You are saying that your poor play, not your opponent's good play, accounts for your frustration. By viewing yourself as your own best friend, try treating yourself the same way you would treat a good friend. You would probably not swear at a good friend or throw your racket when he or she made a mistake. Then treat yourself the same way, avoid making others around you feel uncomfortable, and give credit to your opponent.

If you are a sportsmanlike competitor, you will go further than avoiding negative behavior. You will sincerely compliment your practice partner or opponent when he or she has made an outstanding shot. Furthermore, you will acknowledge, with a smile and a thank you, compliments paid to you. It is so easy to brush compliments aside, particularly when you are being hard on yourself and developing the idea that nothing you are doing is right. Instead, act confidently, even if you don't feel that way. Your actions and gestures can cause your feelings to change. The better you feel about yourself, the more positive and sportsmanlike your actions toward your opponents will be.

When the match is over you should shake your opponent's hand and offer a compliment. Identify at least one thing which your opponent did well. This is hardest when you have lost to someone you thought you would beat, and you have played very poorly. You may be convinced at the time that your opponent has done nothing well. It was entirely your poor play that caused the loss. However, think harder, and come up with at least one compliment you can offer sincerely. Another difficult time to offer a compliment is after a match in which you have destroyed your opponent. Still, there may have been some strong elements in his or her game. Do not overlook the mental attitude or the fact that he or she continued to try. Everyone needs and usually appreciates genuine words of encouragement from a better player.

Again, after the match, avoid the temptation to make excuses. Remember, any reason, no matter how valid it may be, is an excuse when it is used to explain a loss. Bite your tongue, avoid explanations, and silently prepare for your next encounter. Let your racket do the explaining when you play later. In the meantime, give your opponent full credit for what he or she has accomplished. Remember, sometimes a gracious winner will offer excuses for you. Be polite, but counter each excuse with something he or she has done well. Not even a polite winner should deter you from your goal of giving full credit to your opponent.

SPORTSMANSHIP TRAINING PROGRAM FOR TEAMS

Early in the season, you, the coach, need to make it clear that you are serious about sportsmanship. A pre-season meeting is valuable. Include all your players and their parents, if your players are living at home. Require everyone to sign sportsmanship pledges. This is a basic prerequisite for participation. Sportsmanship comes before anything else, including winning. Players or parents not wanting this emphasis are forced to evaluate their priorities and decide accordingly. On the following pages are three sportsmanship pledge cards: for players, parents, and coaches. They cover similar topics, from the perspective of each group. The pledges apply to any athletic team—not just tennis players.

After the pledge cards are signed, the stage is set for sportsmanship being taken seriously. Parents sometimes can set a terrible example and be a very negative influence on the players. Usually they are not aware of what they are doing. The pledge heightens awareness. Also, the parents' expectations for their child to win can put excessive pressure on their child. Sometimes that pressure helps produce emotional outbursts and terrible displays of temper. Poor sportsmanship becomes an escape mechanism from the pressures of competition. The pledge card helps remove some of these pressures. Emphasis is placed on the things which lie within the players' control.

With the expectations for coaches, players, and parents layed out so clearly, all three parties can work together more efficiently. For example, if the parent should step out of line, the child is there as a reminder. Each group is a check on the other. Everyone is working toward a common goal. Corrections can be more easily appreciated when everyone is both correcting and being corrected.

Pledge cards are valuable, but more is necessary in order to integrate sportsmanship training into a tennis program. Various important aspects of tennis sportsmanship need to be outlined. Differing levels of performance are possible. Players set daily goals and then measure performance. Coaches often recommend this approach for improving physical conditioning, stroke development, and other areas of tennis training. A similar plan does work for sportsmanship.

The following sportsmanship training program was developed for use by the Gustavus Adolphus College varsity tennis teams. It is part of a larger training program which includes mental training, diet training, and a number of other areas. A top score of four is possible in each area, for a truly outstanding performance. A three means you did it most of the time; a two designates average success; a one means you accomplished it occasionally; and a zero points to a poor day with virtually no success. Since there are ten areas, a perfect score is forty. Each day, after a match or practice, a total score is calculated. There may be a couple of areas on which you are concentrating. Those would merit additional attention in your journal. Those areas, plus your total score, need to be

PARENT'S PLEDGE

I, _____, parent of _____, will do the following things during the (year) season in (sport) at (school).

SUPPORT YOU, MY CHILD'S COACH. I appreciate your willingness to coach my child and to take a personal interest in his/her development. I will support you, even when I disagree with your decisions, and even when it appears you are slighting my child.

PROMISE TO LOVE YOU, MY CHILD. My love does not depend on your athletic performance. I love you always, just because you are you. I take pride in your being a member of the team. You do not need to be one of the top players in order to meet my expectations.

OBEY YOU, MY GOD. Those values and ideals which pertain to other parts of my life need to be obvious in my relation to you, my child, and your sports participation.

REJECT RETALIATION OR REVENGE. I will be tempted to forget this pledge when others treat me or my child poorly. However, I will stay out of my child's competition, no matter what an inconsiderate parent, coach, official or competitor may say or do to my child. Unacceptable behavior by others *never* justifies my interference.

TRY TO EMPHASIZE EFFORT. Trying to do your best is far more important than winning. I appreciate your effort, even when you perform poorly and lose. By emphasizing effort, I reduce the pressure on you, my child. You can be successful every time you play.

SUPPORT YOU, MY CHILD. I will not criticize your athletic performance, even when it appears you are not trying. I will not offer coaching advice, unless it is requested by you. Instead, I will keep notes while you compete, summarizing the things which you do well. I will share those observations with you. Also, I will ignore your mistakes.

MAKE NO EXCUSES. They detract from your opponent's accomplishments. Therefore, I will expect no explanations from you after a loss or poor performance. Also, I will focus on the strengths of you and your opponents when later discussing the contest with others.

AVOID ALL UNSPORTSMANLIKE ACTS. I will control my temper and avoid profanity as I watch you, my child, participate in sports. By my example, I will show that patience, tolerance of mistakes, gracious losing, and polite winning are important to me.

NEGATE NEGATIVISM. Every situation has both positive and negative elements. I wish to develop a strong positive mental attitude (PMA) by emphasizing the positive aspects in what I do and say. Frequent criticisms of my child, the coach, or the athletic program bring down the spirits of everyone.

(continued)

PARENT'S PLEDGE (*continued*)

SUPPORT YOU, THE OFFICIALS. In athletics you represent authority. I pledge my support of you and your authority, even when you are wrong and I disagree completely with your decision. I promise not to criticize you in public and blame losses on your actions. I degrade myself and set a poor example for my child when I criticize you.

HELP OTHERS. My child, I am ready to help you get the most from this sports season. I will assist you with your studies, your travel and equipment needs, and your practice schedule. My child's coach, I am ready to help you and the sports program. Please ask my assistance at any time.

INTEGRATE ATHLETICS WITH THE REST OF MY LIFE. I view your athletic competition as being very important. I will take time from my schedule to watch you play, unless you prefer that I do not. Also, I will balance the attention I give to you with the needs of my other children.

PROMISE TO POST THIS PLEDGE. I will read it frequently and try my best to follow it faithfully. I know that I must put sportsmanship before winning in order to be successful. I welcome the support and constructive criticisms of you, my child, and you, my child's coach, as I try to be a supportive parent.

---

compared with the goals which you set for the week. You evaluate your progress daily and again at the end of the week. After the weekly evaluation, you then set goals for the following week. With the help of overall principles and a numerical score, progress can be measured and evaluated. This is very important for maintaining motivation.

This program takes sportsmanship a step further than the average approach. Many coaches believe their players should adhere to a certain minimal, socially accepted standard. The thought that players, who are already regarded as good sports, should be working on their sportsmanship skills, is a difficult concept for some coaches to grasp. Some of them advise their good sports to be less charitable and to call those lines a little bit closer. This program, when adoped by more teams, should increase the sportsmanship level of everyone.

COACH'S PLEDGE

I, _____, will do the following things during the (year) season in (sport) at (school).

SUPPORT YOU, MY PLAYER. My respect and support does not depend on your athletic ability. I am grateful to have you on the team. I want to help you reach your potential as a person and as an athlete.

PROMISE TO TREAT MY PLAYERS EQUALLY. I recognize the importance of equal participation by everyone on the team. I will divide my coaching efforts equally between all of you, my players.

OBEY YOU, MY GOD. Those values and ideals which pertain to other parts of my life need to be obvious in my coaching. Accordingly, I will never risk the health of you, my player, if you are sick or injured, by encouraging or pressuring you to play.

REJECT RETALIATION OR REVENGE. I will be tempted to forget this pledge when others treat me or you, my players, poorly. However, unacceptable behavior by others *never* justifies unsportsmanlike conduct by me and you. Any purposeful attempt to injure an opponent cannot be tolerated.

TRY TO EMPHASIZE EFFORT. Trying to do your best is far more important than winning. With this as my standard, all of you, my players, can be successful each time you play, regardless of your ability. I will praise your efforts, even if you play poorly and lose.

SUPPORT FAIR AND OPEN POLICIES. Rules and penalties apply equally to all of you, both the most skilled and least skilled players on the team. Whenever possible, you should know in advance the consequences of your actions.

MAKE NO EXCUSES. They detract from my opponent's accomplishments. Even after the most embarrassing losses, I will refrain from discussing publicly reasons which mention our team's shortcomings. Instead, I wish to give full credit to my opponents by complimenting their strengths.

AVOID ALL UNSPORTSMANLIKE ACTS. I will control my temper and avoid profanity. I will speak positively to myself and my team at *all* times, even when we fall far short of my expectations. I will show by my example that honesty, sportsmanship, and fair play are more important than winning.

NEGATE NEGATIVISM. Every situation has both positive and negative elements. I wish to develop a strong positive mental attitude (PMA) by emphasizing the positive aspects in what I do and say. I reject humiliation and ridicule as a tool to motivate you, my players. Instead, I will use both private and public praise to mold your behavior.

(continued)

COACH'S PLEDGE (*continued*)

SUPPORT YOU, THE OFFICIALS. In athletics you represent authority. I pledge my support of your authority, even when you are wrong and I disagree completely with your decision. I promise to avoid criticizing you in public and blaming losses on your actions. I degrade myself and detract from my opponent's accomplishments when I criticize you.

*H*ELP BUILD TEAMWORK. Optimum motivation occurs when individual and team goals are united. I will encourage you, my players, to put the team first. Individual bragging will be discouraged. I will center much of my praise on teamwork.

*I*NTEGRATE ATHLETICS. During the school year academics need to be the top priority of you, my players. The time I require of you to spend on practice, travel, and athletic contests needs to be limited accordingly. I need to state clearly in advance the hours my sport will occupy, and then not violate that limit.

PROMISE TO POST THIS PLEDGE. I will read it frequently and try my best to follow it faithfully. I know that I must put sportsmanship before winning in order to be successful. I welcome the support and constructive criticisms of you, my players, and your parents as I try to improve my sportsmanship.

ARE YOU READY TO WORK ON SPORTSMANSHIP?

United States Tennis Association (USTA) officials certainly hope that you are. Tennis is a family, lifetime sport which emphasizes self honesty, politeness, and giving others the benefit of the doubt. This perspective is clearly described in the USTA Code. In the last couple of years USTA officials have mounted a campaign to make this emphasis more clear to the public. At the top Davis Cup level, players have been asked to sign court behavior cards if they are to represent the United States. At the grass roots level, the USTA Sportstar Program is now having an impact. Children are learning sportsmanship as they practice other basic tennis skills.

The Intercollegiate Tennis Coaches Association (ITCA) shares the USTA goal for sportsmanship. The emphasis is clear in the ITCA

PLAYER'S PLEDGE

I, _____, will do the following things during the (Year) season in (Sport) at (School).

SUPPORT YOU, MY COACH. I appreciate your willingness to coach me and to take a personal interest in my development. I will support you, even when I disagree with your decisions.

PROMISE TO LOVE YOU, MY PARENT(S). I am grateful for your guidance and support. Through your love, I am becoming a complete person.

OBEY YOU, MY GOD. Those values and ideals which pertain to other parts of my life need to be obvious in my sports competition.

REJECT RETALIATION OR REVENGE. I will be tempted to forget this pledge when others treat me poorly. However, unacceptable behavior by others *never* justifies unsportsmanlike conduct by me.

TRY TO DO MY BEST. Full effort toward team and personal goals is very important. I will continue to try, even when I am playing poorly, and victory seems impossible. Trying to do my best is far more important than winning.

SUPPORT YOU, MY TEAMMATES. I will try to put the welfare of you and the team above my own. I wish to be known as a team player. I can best reach my own potential when I blend my personal goals with team goals. I will not brag about personal accomplishments.

MAKE NO EXCUSES. They detract from my opponent's accomplishments. Even after the most embarrassing losses, I wish to refrain from giving reasons which mention the shortcomings of me and my teammates. Instead, I wish to give full credit to my opponents by complimenting their strengths.

AVOID ALL UNSPORTSMANLIKE ACTS. I will control my temper, avoid profanity, and refrain from equipment abuse. I will speak positively to myself and my teammates at *all* times, even when we fall far short of my expectations.

NEGATE NEGATIVISM. Every situation has both positive and negative elements. I wish to develop a strong positive mental attitude (PMA) by emphasizing the positive aspects in what I do and say. Frequent criticisms of myself, others, my present situation, or even the weather will bring down the spirits of me, my teammates, and coach.

SUPPORT YOU, THE OFFICIALS. In athletics you represent authority. I pledge my support of you and your authority, even when you are wrong and I disagree completely with your decision. I promise to avoid criticizing you in public and blaming losses on your actions. I degrade myself and detract from my opponent's accomplishments when I criticize you.

(continued)

PLAYER'S PLEDGE (*continued*)

HELP OTHERS. My parents, I will not use athletics to avoid my duties at home. My coach, I accept both the privileges and duties of being on this team. I will do what you ask, with no excuses. Also, I will look for ways to help without being asked. My teammates, I will offer assistance and respond to your requests whenever possible.

INTEGRATE ATHLETICS WITH THE REST OF MY LIFE. During the school year, academics need to be my top priority. The time I spend on athletics and traveling to athletic contests needs to be limited accordingly. I reject an emphasis on winning that might cause me to allocate my time improperly or not concentrate when I do study. I renounce the use of all drugs in order to deal with the pressures of athletic competition.

PROMISE TO POST THIS PLEDGE. I will read it frequently and try my best to follow it faithfully. I know that I must put sportsmanship before winning in order to be successful. I welcome the support and constructive criticisms of you, my parents, my coach and my teammates, as I try to improve my sportsmanship.

---

rulebook, distributed to and used by all intercollegiate coaches. Perhaps this training program will enhance their efforts.

Second, the tennis game itself is more fun when both you and your opponent put sportsmanship before winning. So many talented youngsters "burn out" on tennis before they reach adulthood, because winning has been stressed too much. Also, adults have quit playing and have gone to something "less competitive," when unsportsmanlike behavior by opponents has taken the fun and joy out of the game. People who stress only winning often do unpleasant things, which ruins tennis for both the winner and the loser.

Ironically, people who stress sportsmanship over winning may actually win more. One of the biggest deterents to winning is the pressure you put on yourself. Winning does not lie within your control. Therefore, your anxiety level may rise above your efficient range when you think too much about winning in big, pressure packed matches. Indeed, you might win more by focusing on sportsmanship and other noncompetitive goals, that do lie within your control. You should be able to remain more relaxed, and therefore, play better.

_____'s Training Program*

SPORTSMANSHIP TRAINING PROGRAM

Date								
1. Avoided questioning my opponent on any double bounce, let, or line call.								
2. Called my own balls out on the other side of the net when I clearly saw them out.								
3. Complimented others for good shots and acknowledged with a "thank you" compliments given to me.								
4. Called "let" and "out" immediately. Otherwise the ball was good.								
5. Called the score at the beginning of each point.								
6. Avoided all excuse making why I lost, played poorly, could not motivate myself, or could not do what my coach asked me to do.								
7. Avoided swearing.								
8. Avoided all equipment abuse—including hitting balls out of play and racket "dropping."								
9. Avoided bragging—I told about my own accomplishments only when asked.								
10. Offered help to my coach or practice partner.								
TOTAL SPORTSMANSHIP TRAINING SCORE:								

* Directions: Enter a date above each vertical column (e.g., 10/1 for October 1). Opposite each point record a number 4 to 0. (4 means I was truly outstanding. 3 means I did it most of the time. 2 designates average success. 1 means I accomplished it occasionally. 0 indicates an extremely poor day with virtually no success in this category.) Finally, add the points recorded to discover your total score. Next enter your analysis on the back side.

Finally, you will be remembered with deeper appreciation and gratitude for your sportsmanship than your winning. Consider the testimony of Jesse Owens. His illustrious career included four gold medals at the 1936 Olympics in Berlin and a number of other world titles. There was one act of sportsmanship which far overshadowed everything else.

The story, now made famous in a movie about Jesse Owens, centers on the broad jump competition in the 1936 Olympics. Jesse had failed to qualify for the finals. Now he stood one jump away from elimination. His chief German competitor, Lutz Long, approached Jesse and suggested that he put down a towel two inches from the place where he had to begin his jump. Then he could jump, without having to worry about scratching. At first, Jesse was suspicious. Why would a competitor offer a suggestion to help? Jesse trusted, however, that he was sincere. He tried it. Sure enough, Jesse jumped well, and qualified for the finals.

This set the stage for a dual between Jesse and Lutz. Lutz jumped farther than ever before, and set the world's record. But, on the last jump, Jesse jumped farther and won the gold medal.

Imagine your reaction at that moment, if you had been Lutz. How crestfallen might you have been, realizing that your suggestion may have cost you the gold medal? To Lutz's credit, he responded like a true sportsman. He embraced Jesse, raised his arm, and led the Germans in the cheering of Jesse's name. When the crowd was stilled, Jesse raised Lutz's arm and led them in a cheer of Lutz's name.

Jesse looked back at this incident, forty years later, in an article which he wrote for *Rotarian*. "This," he said, "was the most outstanding thing which has happened to me in competitive athletics."

The answer is clear for Eliot Teltscher, Mark Kruger, Tim Corwin, Jesse Owens, and many other champions. Sportsmanship and other people are far more important than winning. Focus on sportsmanship training while developing the other areas of your game.

CHAPTER·10

Dennis Ralston

Dennis Ralston
Men's Tennis Coach
Southern Methodist University

An international champion, both as a player and a coach, Dennis Ralston became SMU's men's tennis coach in July of 1980. Since then Ralston has directed SMU to top 20 national finishes each year and in 1983 was named the Division I Men's ITCA/Wilson Coach of the Year.

As a player, Ralston won 27 national championships including the NCAA singles and doubles titles in 1963 and 1964 and the U.S. Open doubles championship three times. He has ranked among the world's top five twice and in 1966 was the singles runner-up at Wimbledon. Representing the United States Davis Cup play, Ralston won 14 of 20 singles matches and 11 of 14 doubles contests.

A native of Bakersfield, California, born July 27, 1942, Ralston won his first national tennis championship (the 1955 USTA Boys 15 Hard Court doubles) at age 13. He played college tennis at USC, leading the Trojans to the NCAA team title in 1963 and 1964. Ralston was ranked No. 1 in the U.S. in singles in 1964, 1965, and 1966 and No. 2 in 1963. He stood 4th in the World rankings in 1963, 5th in 1965 and 6th in 1964. Today, Ralston still plays. He reached the semi-finals of the 1983 U.S. Open Men's 35 singles.

As a coach, Ralston guided the United States to five consecutive Davis Cup challenge round victories in 1968–72, captained the team four of the nine years he coached the Davis Cup squad and has tutored such prominent pro stars as Chris Evert, Dick Stockton and Roscoe Tanner.

In 1983, Ralston directed SMU to its highest national tennis finish ever as the Mustangs were NCAA runners-up. SMU ranked No. 1 most of the 1983 season, compiling a 23-3 dual match record and winning the ITCA National Team Championships in Los Angeles in February. Following the 1983 season, Ralston was named the ITCA/Wilson Division I Men's Tennis Coach of the Year.

During his first four seasons at SMU,

Ralston's Ponies compiled a 123-27 dual match win-loss record and won three Southwest Conference championships (in 1982, 1983, and 1985). His teams have finished 11th (1981), 3d (1982), 2d (1983), 6th (1984) and 4th (1985) in the annual NCAA playoffs.

Besides coaching at SMU, Ralston also serves as a member of the corporate staff of the T-Bar-M Racquet Club. He is a past recipient of the William M. Johnston Award presented for character, sportsmanship and contribution to tennis. For the past two years he has served on the ITCA Board of Directors.

Ralston and his wife Linda, have three children—Angela, a student at SMU, Laura, and Michael.

COACHING COLLEGE PLAYERS VS. TOP PRO PLAYERS

Dennis Ralston, Men's Tennis Coach, Southern Methodist University

By the early 1970s I had channeled almost all of my competitive tennis instincts into coaching, rather than playing, due to my age and injuries, though perhaps not in that order.

As a player I had always been very analytical and this helped me as I began working as a coach with some of the best players, including Roscoe Tanner, Dick Stockton, Brian Gottfried, Harold Solomon, Stan Smith, Bob Lutz and Chris Evert. In addition to coaching on the tour pretty extensively, I was also the Director of Tennis at Mission Hills in Palm Springs, California.

Coaching college tennis at SMU has really been a learning experience, and it still is. Coaching is dealing with people, trying to get them to play better and I want to work with the best players, the ones that want to go on to the pros, even though realistically speaking, very few are going to be able to do that, or do it well.

This was a big difference for me personally, because I had been used to working with guys who were further along and already established— big names on the tour like Smith and Lutz, Tanner, or Gottfried. The best pros, such as Chris Evert, are dedicated to tennis all the time; but to do this is very tough for college kids who have to concentrate on academics as well as tennis. Freshmen have freshmen problems, sophomores have sophomore problems, juniors have junior problems, and seniors have senior problems.

Take John Ross, who graduated two years ago from SMU. All of a sudden, John realized he was a senior, and wasn't sure what he was going to do after college. He started to play terribly as he faced the reality of having to go out on the tour soon. We needed to spend a lot of time discussing this before he began to feel more positive about it. John came in to college tennis as a good athlete and good competitor but even as a senior, John was just now learning how to hit the ball. You can't bluff in the pro game. You've got to know how to hit the shots hard past your opponent. In the juniors, John never had to do that. He had to learn how to hit through his forehand and to hit more decisive volleys. Also, John had to learn to lob better. Last year he made a lot of progress and has a decent chance to do well in the pros. He made the jump mentally in learning how to take the pressure off of himself and play. He knows he can't be a Jimmy Connors and play at the same intensity all day long. That ability is unusual, and can take you down if you don't know when to rest. You watch Edberg, Wilander, Lendl— they're calmer, and just hitting the shots. I'd much rather have my players emulate that kind of emotional attitude on the court than the clenched fist kind of thing which over the long haul will wear a player out.

So each college class presents a different set of problems, at least for me, and I am still learning how to cope with this as a coach. Also, it is sometimes hard to get recognition or a response from your college players, unlike the pros. After all, the pros are paying you for your time, and they would not have you coach them if they didn't think you could help them. In many ways the professional tennis player is really more responsive than the typical college kid, and this is even more true compared to a high school player.

High school and college kids are torn by the different environments they are facing and all the different things that are going on. They are still growing up. One thing I'm learning, slowly, perhaps, but surely, is to have more patience. I was used to having the pros do things automatically, pick up the right shots quickly, know how to practice and work hard. High school and college kids as a rule don't do these things as easily.

I've had a lot of high school coaches ask me what I do as a college coach. Do I make them all do the same thing, treat everybody the same way? I don't. I take each player as an individual. I have a general practice plan, but I find it necessary to be sensitive to individuals and not run my practice like an army training camp. I know some other coaches who do and that may be fine for them, but I want to have fun with the kids, get to know them and see them get better. The overall thing I try to keep in mind is that the kids are there first for a college education; tennis should not be the only thing that they are at school to accomplish.

When I first began as a player myself at USC, my primary goal was to excel in tennis. But my parents said, "Hey, if you break an arm or something you had better be prepared to do something else." So I worked hard academically in college and I would have finished my degree had I not turned pro and been lucky enough to be successful on the tour. The main difference between college players and professionals is the intensity of the pros—tennis is their livelihood. In high school and college the kids are working at tennis usually two, three or four hours a day, and otherwise are involved in many other activities. Of course, if your team is competing for a national championship, then there is a lot more pressure during this time in preparing for the event.

For example, the ITCA National Indoor Team Championship is like a Wimbledon for us. A month before the 1986 event I told our team that winning this tournament has got to be one of our major goals. I told them that as a player I used to know exactly how many days until Wimbledon and would count down day by day. This helped motivate me for the championship. High school and college players do not, as a rule, look far enough ahead. They just seem to live day to day. As a coach, one of my concerns is to try to have my players change this nearsighted approach and plan ahead.

I keep reminding my players that we need to set goals, personally and as a team, and that way we can all work toward something. But as a coach I am still learning through my own experiences and by observing those who have been coaching college tennis for over twenty years, like Glenn Bassett at UCLA, Dick Gould at Stanford, and Dan Magill at the University of Georgia.

TAKING THE PRESSURE OFF HIGH SCHOOL AND COLLEGE PLAYERS

One danger, I feel, is the temptation of placing too much pressure on the kids to win. One of the most difficult things for a coach is the lack of feedback from your players. It is vital to know if you are doing the right thing, and as a coach you must be sensitive to all of the little signals your players give off. Are they positive and eager during a practice or quiet and moody? Of course, a team is comprised of a variety of individuals, all of whom may respond in different ways to the same situation. This is what makes coaching interesting, but also very difficult. Psychologically, there are so many shades of difference to consider and cope with, particularly with teenagers.

In terms of tennis ability, college kids are about two levels below the guys on the Satellite circuit. Of course, there are college kids who are capable of going out and playing in a major Grand Prix tournament, but this is because there is no pressure on them now. Obviously they are talented, but it's easy to play well when there is no pressure. It really is a question of maturity as a player.

McEnroe and Connors were rarities in their ability to jump straight from the NCAA Championships as freshmen to top positions on the tour. Technically, college players need to learn how to play smart tennis and to win when they are not playing well. Everyone thinks they should play well and win all the time, but this just does not happen. I tell my team these things run in cycles. You play well for a while and then you may play poorly for a stretch. The down cycle is the key to how good you are. If you can win when you are not playing well, then this is a really good indication of how solid a player you are, because this means you are able to compete well mentally.

MENTAL TOUGHNESS AND DEDICATION

Mental toughness is an area where high school and college kids are not nearly as good as the pros. This is natural because they are relatively immature or inexperienced, still learning that you can't get mad and play well. Many college players don't think, they just hit the ball.

Here is an example of the difference in how hard the pros are willing to work compared to college players. Recently, Chrissie came to Dallas for five days. She went to the weight room with the team and worked twice as hard as any of the guys! She was precise and professional about what she was doing, she didn't fool around or waste time. She knew she was there for a purpose. Most guys lift a weight and then talk a little unless you are standing right there holding a whip. But this is why Chrissie has been so good for so long. Obviously, not everybody has her kind of commitment and dedication. But if you want to get the best out of your game, you have to work very, very hard.

I like to tell players about Marty Reissen, one of my contemporaries. Marty wasn't a great tennis talent, but he was a very good natural athlete, who made it because he worked harder than anybody else. He would hang in there. As a coach, you have to bang these kids on the head sometimes, and say look, watch, look, watch. We were talking about a match Lendl and Connors played recently. We watched the first set, and I said, "Lendl's going to win, because Connors has slowed down." Lendl wasn't hanging his head when he lost the first set, 6–1, or moaning or complaining. I hope that watching things like that will rub off on my players.

TIPS FOR HIGH SCHOOL COACHES

High school players are slightly less developed than the college players. Yet for high school coaches I would still suggest the same thing as for college coaches—treat each player individually. I realize that some high school coaches are not trained tennis coaches and are not sure what kind of drills to use or how to treat each kid, but even so, you must avoid the temptation of always doing the same thing with everyone. The successful high school coaches are the ones who are able to work with each player one on one as well as the team as a whole and structure practices this way. Coaches have to recognize that on the high school or college level, players will be distracted by tests, social problems, or family difficulties. On the pro tour, it doesn't matter if you have those problems or not, nobody cares. You have to go out and play well, regardless, if you want to survive as a tennis professional.

In working with the touring pros, I try to structure our practice somewhat differently than those with my college players. For example, when I worked with Roscoe Tanner, I felt that he didn't have a really solid backhand. He couldn't hit over the ball at all, so I worked hours on teaching him how to roll the backhand, put topspin on the backhand. We would practice twice a day. He also had a tendency not to be in such great shape. He needed somebody to push him, so we did a lot of two on ones, a lot of conditioning drills. The great thing about Roscoe was that he did what he was told to do. He worked hard and he was strong, real strong. He looked to someone to tell him when to stop because then he could leave and not feel guilty that he hadn't done enough. He developed confidence that I would work him hard enough. If we practiced one hour, and I said, "That's enough, Roscoe," he accepted this and wouldn't get nervous that he hadn't hit enough. If I said, "Let's practice five hours," he'd be out there working the whole time. He used to call himself brick hands because he had no control on the volley. He learned how to take some pace off the volley by drilling a lot on this aspect of his game.

I didn't have the chance to work with Rodney Harmon for as long a time as with Roscoe, but Rodney worked hard while he was at SMU, and he didn't slough off. I taught Rodney how to hit a one-handed backhand (he grew up with a two-handed shot) and how to approach on the backhand side.

Rodney's backhand didn't have anything on it, though, not enough penetration, just a lot of top, whereas Richy Reneberg, our number one player in 1987 (and the ITCA College Player of the Year) and a finalist in the 1986 NCAA Singles Championships, can really drill the ball off the two-handed side, as can Chrissie, of course. That's the advantage of the two-handed shot—you really can hit it hard and you can disguise a lob off of it. I don't see a trend, but young kids tend to emulate the top few players, and McEnroe, Lendl and Becker hit one-handed backhands. A lot of teachers are still teaching the two-handed backhand. If it's a natural smooth looking shot, then it's fine, I think. Rodney's wasn't and he couldn't approach, which is why I had him switch. We worked on his volley, and he was in better shape from our drills and all the matches we played.

Rodney was a good athlete and played very well in college. He had one good U.S. Open (reaching the quarter finals), but after college he went back to hitting a two-handed backhand and changed his service motion. I really expected Rodney to do better than he did on the tour, but he was plagued by injuries and maybe he thrived more in the environment of the college team, where everybody was working hard together.

I know this was true for Eric Korita. Eric had a weight problem when he came to SMU. He was 250 lbs. When he left SMU, he weighed 198. He needed to get into good shape and learn mobility and quickness. Eric never worked very hard. He had a lot of talent and a huge serve, but was a lazy player. Eric had good hands for a big guy, but was stubborn in that he wouldn't learn how to hit a slice backhand and had days where he would hit everything over the fence. Korita found it difficult to listen or make a commitment to learn how to listen. There is no telling how good he could have been if he had had the right attitude toward hard work.

Rodney Harmon's personality as a college player was very different from Roscoe Tanner's as a pro. Roscoe really wanted to be the best in the world. He had a great weapon in his big serve, but he wanted to do more than just use this serve. We worked twice a day, and each session was very intense, no matter how long. All this culminated in the Wimbledon Finals in 1979 in that great match with Borg, which he was within a whisker of winning. Later that summer he beat Borg in the quarters under lights at the U.S. Open. Often Roscoe would look to me for guidance on where to serve to Borg. We discussed Borg's game and that night Roscoe did everything perfectly.

Roscoe really listened. A lot of the kids today don't really listen, and that's not to imply that as coaches we know all the answers. We make mistakes too. But we try to take some of the pressure off the players by helping them make decisions about practicing and match tactics. Sometimes I have to tell my players that the body needs rest. You can't go out and play five straight hours all the time and expect to come into a big tournament and play well. Structuring your workouts thoughtfully is just as important as a hard workout—you have to learn to pace yourself.

My ideas about coaching actually remain fairly similar whether I am working with high school and college players or with the touring pros, and I use the same type of drills with both groups.

Strangely enough, even though I did very well in doubles, I have never coached a professional doubles team, nor do I know anyone else who has on the pro scene. In college tennis doubles is very important, and I am always trying to improve my ability to coach in this area. But I am not sure if you can always make a good singles player into a good doubles player. Part of doubles is instinct. As a coach you can help him, but I haven't really hit on any real secret here. My own record in doubles was pretty good, and nobody ever taught me anything about doubles. I just picked it up and I played a lot, which helped. At SMU we work a lot on doubles, but this still remains a source of frustration to me, because I see a lot of guys who don't know how to play good doubles, and it is very difficult to teach this skill.

Once again, I think the important thing to realize is that the pro players are making their living from tennis. They are very intense and willing to do anything you suggest and work on it hard enough so that they accomplish the skill. In college I work with my players only from 2:00 to about 5:00, and even then they aren't thinking about tennis all the time. But this is probably the way it should be. There will be plenty of time for those who want to go on the circuit to work hard constantly on their games after college. Meanwhile, as coaches we work on improving their games, but we shouldn't expect to turn out a finished professional right away. Some college players will make quantum leaps, some smaller jumps. Some will take four years to develop, some may need only two years to be good enough to compete with the pros.

I advise the players on my team that if they are out there doing well on the pro circuit over the summer and getting to the quarters of Grand Prix events on a regular basis, then maybe they should seriously think about turning pro. But if all you've done is win a few matches on the tour, you would be nuts to turn pro. You need to realize that as a pro you will not have any free practice time, and nobody will really care about you. You won't have time to improve the areas you need to work on, such as the bad volleys, the weak backhands, etc. And finally, you won't be making much money, if any. So it really makes sense to spend time in school and get your degree. This is what I think coaches should emphasize to help the kids become better players, but also become better educated and prepared for alternative careers to tennis.

Naturally, I like to win—all coaches do. I would love SMU to win the NCAA's, but the most important thing for a coach is the opportunity to teach. At times I have to struggle with my competitive nature and tell myself winning is not what I am in it for. Kids, too, have other interests, and we have to keep everything in balance and perspective. College should be fun. My own college days were great. There was little pressure on me and tennis was really fun. My coach at USC, George Toley, made our practices fun. I also improved a lot, but I didn't approach tennis then as a profession. I have to keep remembering this with my own players now.

Another difference, from a coaching perspective, between the pros and college tennis is that we are permitted by ITCA and NCAA rules to coach on the court during a college match, unlike junior and professional tennis. I think coaching during matches helps us teach our players more effectively. As a coach, I'm aware of situations in a match and can help my players concentrate and at the same time, point out different strategies. When you are out there on your own, you can't always see what is happening.

I hope that my college players will remember these things once they are on their own. I'll tell someone like Chrissie the same advice when I see her opponent doing something, but I have to wait until the end of the match. I think it is a plus to be able to talk to players on the court during the match. In watching a match, you have to think of the strengths and weaknesses of your kids—what is or isn't working for them. I'm in every point but not as if I were playing the match myself. You need to stay objective and keep some distance. Also, I have to guard against looking at the match as if I am playing myself, particularly since I didn't play like most of my kids. But this is true for all coaches, whether or not they were outstanding players in their earlier years. As a coach, all I can do is advise and encourage, and afterwards, congratulate or console, and always, explain.

CHAPTER · 11

Emilie B Foster

Emilie Foster
Women's Tennis Coach
Trinity University

As a player, Emilie Burrer helped bring the Trinity women's tennis team to national championship stature. At the rate she's going, Emilie Burrer Foster may do the same as coach.

As a Trinity tennis player, the then Emilie Burrer ran up an incredible record. She is the only Trinity tennis player, in both men's and women's competition, to win four national championships. In 1968 and 1969 she won the USTA Collegiate Women's singles and doubles championships. Her doubles partner was Becky Vest.

After graduating from Trinity, Foster turned pro. In 1970, she was the fourth ranked doubles player in the country and the thirteenth ranked singles player. She reached the singles quarterfinals at the 1969 U.S. Open and played for the Houston E-Z Riders of World Team Tennis in 1974.

Since taking over the women's tennis program in 1979, Foster's teams have finished 10th, 3rd, 2nd, 3rd, 2nd, 5th, and 4th nationally. The excellent showing has resulted in a 213–41 dual-match record in that seven-year period, good for a .84 winning percentage.

After coaching at Arizona State and Texas Tech, Foster returned to Trinity as head coach of the women's tennis team in 1979. In her eight years at TU, Foster has coached 11 All-Americans (Carrie Fleming, Kim Steinmetz, Mary Lou Piatek, Louise Allen, Felicia Raschiatore, Karen Denman, Gretchen Rush, Lisa Sassano, Elvyn Barrabel, Jana Klepac and Ann Hulbert).

Foster was named 1983 Division I Women's Wilson Coach of the Year by the Intercollegiate Tennis Coaches Association (ITCA).

CHAPTER · 11

TENNIS CAREER—COLLEGE OR PROFESSIONAL?

Emilie Foster, Women's Tennis Coach, Trinity
University (TX)

During recent years much has been written about the pros and cons of junior players turning professional in their teens instead of going on to compete in collegiate tennis while earning an undergraduate degree.

The United States is unique in the way it structures amateur and professional athletics, with a variety of different athletic governing bodies in different sports, each with its own set of rules that define eligibility for competition in its sport. We may be the only country that still differentiates between the amateur and professional. In most other countries olympic (amateur) competitors receive subsidies from athletic corporations, soft drink companies, automobile manufacturers, and even their own governments to enable the athletes to sustain their training and, hopefully, mount a serious challenge for an Olympic medal. Only recently, in the sport of track and field, has the United States Olympic Committee (USOC) loosened its restrictions and allowed its athletes to receive endorsements and expense money for competition. These monies, however, must be put into a trust fund for the athlete and may not be used until the athlete has completed olympic competition. The USOC will also allow an athlete to become a professional and then, by meeting a set of criteria, allow them to regain their amateur status and resume olympic competition.

Tennis became an Olympic sport in the 1988 Olympics in Seoul, South Korea, having been a demonstration sport in the 1984 Olympics in Los Angeles. The competitors in tennis who choose to compete in Olympic games must meet the criteria for eligibility of two governing bodies, the USOC and the United States Tennis Association (USTA). If the competitor is a collegiate player, he or she must not exceed the limits of the rules for amateur athletes as set forth by the National Collegiate Athletic Association (NCAA). In the eyes of the NCAA the USOC's interpretation of eligibility is no longer acceptable, since tennis in the Olympics is open to professionals. The NCAA will not permit an athlete to endorse a product with or without compensation. The amateur may not retain an agent or receive compensation in any manner that is a direct result of his or her performance in a sport. A tennis player who is eligible to compete as an amateur in the Olympic games might not be eligible to compete in the NCAA Championships.

DEFINING AMATEURISM AND PROFESSIONALISM

The confusion between amateurism and professionalism has resulted in many debates among the governing bodies for the various sports. There are as many definitions for these two terms as there are groups that argue over them. Webster's Concise Dictionary defines the word, profession, as a *learned occupation*, while amateur is defined as *nonprofessional*. The New Century Dictionary defines amateur as *one who cultivates any . . . pursuit for the love or enjoyment of it, instead of professionally or for gain*. Professionalism is defined as *following an occupation as a means of livelihood* or *following as a business an occupation ordinarily engaged in as a pasttime*.

But the key distinction between professional and amateur is based upon financial gain, i.e. the professional athlete wins money through competition while the amateur enjoys the satisfaction of competition but does not benefit financially. Many times the tennis community views the professional player simply in terms of the money or endorsements received. But there is more to playing as a professional than simply money. The professional athlete is one who possesses the physical and mental skills and utilizes them to the best of his ability in a competitive situation.

The rules of the professional world are based on the manner in which earning power can be increased, or at least sustained. Sometimes this occurs with little regard for others, and often the playing rules are stretched to the point where specific interpretations must be made regarding these rules. An example of this is the person who hits a two-handed backhand. If the player holds two balls when serving and the return of serve comes to his or her backhand, the player must throw the second ball down before hitting the backhand. Observing this, a professional decided that there could be an advantage if, after the serve, the player took the second ball and threw it in such a manner and position on the court that it would distract the opponent, thus giving himself a better chance to win the point. This situation was not specifically addressed in the USTA rules, so an interpretation had to be made that if a player threw the ball down anywhere, the opponent could claim a distraction and be awarded the point.

Some professional players also use psychological ploys to disrupt the concentration or momentum of their opponents. Rude, derogatory comments to the opponent on the change over, arguing over judgment calls on the part of the officials, even feigning injuries, all have been used to try to gain an edge in a tennis match. In the professional tennis world, the rewards are often measured in terms of wins, regardless of how the wins occur. The process of the win is rarely scrutinized because winning itself is of maximum importance.

The amateur player is not rewarded monetarily for his success, and therefore the process of winning and losing takes priority over the results. The attitude of fair play and regard for the opponent become more significant than just winning. Obviously, this may not be true for all amateurs, but it still is the prevailing attitude among amateur tennis players. Winning is not considered the sole means of judging the person, but instead, it is the process the player went through to achieve the win which is given most importance. The amateur is still growing as a player and has much to learn about the game and about his response to situations that are a direct result of the game.

Naturally, there are some amateur tennis players who are intensely competitive and view their success only in terms of wins and losses. Most amateurs, however, derive their satisfaction from the actual competition rather than the end result. The amateur places him- or herself in a competitive situation but the order of finish does not have an impact on other areas of his or her life. For example—If I win this match, I can then pay my hotel bill. In this sense, the amateur world has a degree of stability since winning or losing does not directly alter the lifestyle or career of the competitor. Perhaps because of this, the amateur usually is more willing to understand a loss as the result of an opponent's superiority rather than his own inferiority; he is willing to give credit to the better player. The amateur will look to the competition with anticipation and excitement, whereas the professional often approaches it with fear and apprehension, given the stakes involved.

SOME DISADVANTAGES OF TURNING PRO

College tennis and amateur tennis are often equated, but this is not entirely correct. Many collegiate players today compete for an athletic scholarship that is awarded based on the player's tennis ability, and in some ways, the game for the collegiate player becomes his livelihood.

Nevertheless, in general and by definition, the collegiate player is still an amateur, and is considered as such by the USTA and the NCAA.

The question of whether a young player should go to college or turn professional has been asked for the past two decades, ever since the advent of open tennis. There are certain characteristics of both amateurs or professionals that we can identify. These traits are not always apparent in all young players, but sometimes can help predict whether or not they will be suited to collegiate life or the professional tour.

The college player is usually an achiever, energetic, educationally oriented and happiest when working toward a goal. Collegians perceive their world as purposeful and exciting. Many will take a situation which occurs on the tennis courts and transpose it to another, nontennis situation. They are eager to accept new challenges and use these challenges to set realistic goals. The satisfaction of performing a task well often is more important than the result itself. Collegiate players are constantly reassessing their goals in terms of their capabilities. Long range planning tends also to be a personality trait of the person who chooses to go to college. Collegians see more than immediate needs to be met and are very concerned about their careers. They tend to be conservative in planning for the future and keep open a number of future possibilities. As collegiate players matriculate through college they become more aware of their capabilities and limitations and make their plans based on these experiences.

Family background and attitudes toward education and choice of a profession play an important role in the decision making process of the college player. Players who choose to go to college usually come from families who stress the importance of maintaining a balance between education and athletics. This attitude is usually one of perceiving the two in a symbiotic relationship.

The development and enrichment of social skills is also a viable part of the decision to go to college or turn professional. Young people tend to want to congregate with persons close to their own age to share mutual experiences. They see college as a secure way to be involved with this type of person and to be placed in situations where social skills can be developed and improved. If a 16-year old is constantly surrounded by people who are much older, he or she will take on the mannerisms and mores of this group in order to be accepted by them. This can become a problem when a young person turns professional as contact with their own age group will become very limited and this then creates a conflict when trying to resolve which social values to follow. The person who chooses to go to college has to make numerous decisions regarding day to day activities, as well as tennis related decisions. The collegiate player is not afraid of the consequences of a decision that has been made, but will channel energy into making the decision a good one. The luxury of being a collegiate player is that there is always the opportunity to make the wrong decision without suffering the consequences too long afterward, a luxury which the professional player does not enjoy.

A college player has a variety of choices regarding a profession—the opportunity to become a touring professional after college or to obtain training in myriad careers. The decision as to which of these to pursue does not have to be made upon graduation from high school. There will be many opportunities to experiment. In contrast, the professional player who makes a career choice before having a chance to experiment with other options or fully assess his or her tennis ability might well end up spending years trying to pursue a profession for which he or she was not sufficiently prepared or talented.

The college player has the opportunity to set realistic goals based upon both capabilities and experience in an environment where one can constantly reassess one's capabilities. The collegiate lifestyle is also far more stable than the professional's. The college player enjoys the constant surroundings, practicing with the same players daily, living in the same quarters, and having consistent companionship. On the other hand, the professional player must be always ready to move on after one tournament to the next. Sometimes, after a loss, this is perceived by the player as getting away from the scene of the crime and moving to a new place where no one knows him. In contrast, the college player is glad to return to his or her campus environment, even after losing a match, because the team and other students will understand what has transpired and provide support and sympathy.

The college player strikes for a balance in life, without unduly emphasizing one area. The professional player, because of his or her commitment, must place tennis above social life, recreation and sometimes even family. But if this job does not go well, it is difficult to shift focus to something else. For the college player, there are other facets to college life besides tennis. There is the challenge of the classroom, the excitement of college social life, and the fun of sharing these with a variety of other people. If the tennis element of his or her life is not going well, the college player can shift focus to another part that is more positive. Maybe a player has lost some matches, but is doing very well academically. This balance in college allows one to emphasize the positive and reduce the negative. For professional players, this balance is more difficult to obtain, particularly for a young tennis professional, and often the effort to achieve a sense of perspective becomes confused with a form of rationalization.

There are many other considerations that should be a part of the decision to turn professional or to pursue the college career. Obviously, one's financial situation will have an effect on the decision. Some players feel compelled to earn as much money as they can as soon as possible, while others are able to sacrifice the money early in the career to obtain an education. Financial circumstances of the family often are paramount in the decision making process. Once the decision is made to turn professional, an agent is usually retained to negotiate contracts and to plan for the player financially. But a player must then be successful enough to generate the money which will justify this financial planning. The player who goes to college has only one decision to make, which university to attend. The pressure for financial security for the college player does not occur until the player has completed four years of eligibility or decides that he will play as a professional before his collegiate eligibility expires.

The professional player often hires a coach to work out with and/or travel with. The college player has a coach for four years during which time the player can develop his game. It is difficult for the professional player to experiment because he must rely upon those skills and strategies that are most certain to achieve a win. The college player may experiment during match play without fear of a financial loss. Another advantage for the college player is that good quality competition is available free or at minimal cost to the player, but the professional must pay for expenses from the prize money earned.

Injuries play a key role in any athletic competition. Learning to prevent injuries, and how to deal with them can be gained at both the professional and amateur levels. The college player has access to a trainer and physician during the school year. The role of the trainer is to set training programs for the athletes and to assist, and in the case of injuries, to rehabilitate. The professional athlete has this on the tournament site, but then must seek his own rehabilitation facility and personnel when there is no tournament in progress. There are also tremendous psychological ramifications for the athlete that must be handled by a competent professional during the rehabilitation period.

There are many considerations for the young player trying to decide which choice, turning pro or attending college, is the better one. Often, it is helpful to make a checklist of the items needed for optimal development as a person and as a tennis player. Discussion with players who have chosen both routes will be of great assistance to the young player. There are young people who need to go to college for the tennis experience, while there are also those who are capable of dealing with life on the professional tour. The more feedback from those who have experienced both, the more rational the decision.

Early in the adolescent's development (between the ages of 12 and 18) a player may realize that he or she would like to have a tennis career. Most attitudes toward a professional or college career are developed at this time. If the young player is exposed to the many opportunities of college tennis, often he or she will choose this route. But if he or she already is playing in some professional tournaments and enjoys the glamour of the pro tour, then turning pro may be very tempting. Family discussions which center around professional tennis also tend to focus interest on the professional career option, and professional coaches striving for their own recognition may also exert pressure on the young player to turn professional. Sometimes realistic goals are ignored by the player because of the influence of the family and coach. Unfortunately, a vicarious existence by the parents and/or coach through the young player will often leave scars that last a lifetime. Once a player becomes a professional, tennis is a one way street. There is no competitive tennis for this player except the professional one. The player must constantly strive to improve a ranking and increase earning potential. A collegiate player always has the option to continue with his or her college career and later turn pro, thereby enjoying the best of both worlds.

The choice of a tennis career is certainly not an easy one. The direction that a player may take is not predicated on any one factor, but rather a multitude of goals and values that must be sorted through. College or professional, the choice greatly affects the development of the person and the tennis player. Enlightenment of the family, coach, and player regarding each possibility will make the decision making process more pleasant, and will afford a young player the maximum opportunity to grow and develop.

VIEWS FROM TWO FORMER TRINITY TENNIS STARS ON COLLEGE TENNIS VS. THE PRO TOUR

At this point I would like to go from the general to the specific, with brief interviews I had with two former Trinity tennis stars, Bobby McKinley, Class of '76 (who later coached the men's varsity team) and Gretchen Rush, who graduated a decade later and was one of my own players these past four years. Each was asked to discuss their own decisions and views on college tennis vs. the pro tour.

Bob McKinley:

I had always planned to go to college and had a clear game plan in mind in terms of what I wanted from a school. I wanted two things: a school that I thought would give me a good education and had the reputation for providing a good, sound education, as well as a school that would give me a top flight tennis program. When both of those criteria were in place, then it was a question of deciding which school I liked best after visiting them and seeing what the overall atmosphere was. Interestingly enough, I had just about made up my mind to go to Rice University because they had a little better academic standing than Trinity did at that time and the same level tennis team. But when I visited Trinity, I just liked it so much more, that this turned the tables and I went here.

I really made up my own mind about college, although my brother, Chuck, was always a very influential person in my life, as he had been down the same road I was travelling. He was very careful not to persuade me one way or another. He felt that as long as a school met the two criteria, that I really couldn't go wrong. He never pushed me toward Trinity, which was his school, but certainly didn't discourage me either.

In general, I think this is a time when young people are becoming adults and have to learn to take responsibility for their actions. The decision should be primarily theirs, with gentle guidance from parents. I don't feel parents should push their kids to make a decision at this time. Kids have to live with the decisions and they are old enough to do this, with parents serving as guides who point out things but don't force a decision. Parents should make sure that their children have considered all the options, and weighed all the plusses and minuses of the different situations that they're looking into.

The major difference between college and the pro tour is that you are totally on your own out on the pro tour. In college you're part of a team and you have moral support from teammates, as well as a coach who is looking after you and telling you what to do and not do. Coaches didn't travel with pros in my day as they do now. There were some similarities, too. You often played many of the individuals that you had competed against in college, and so while the level of competition was a little tougher, it wasn't totally different, not as it is today. Then, the level of college competition was very close to professional calibre because all of the American guys stayed in college then. You had the same intense competition and you needed to work just as hard, if not harder, than in college. The real difference was that you were suddenly doing it all on your own.

For a person to make it on the Pro Tour, he or she has to be an extremely self-motivated person, very disciplined. I think that in college you can help to develop some of these qualities. I don't think that these things are necessarily inherent in a person. But if they don't have those qualities or can't learn them in college, they'll never make it on the Pro Tour, in my mind. A lot of junior players, when I coached them in college didn't have those qualities when they started, and some of them by the time they left had acquired or developed them; some didn't. The ones who were extremely successful in college tennis were the ones who had self-motivation and discipline when they came in.

I feel that the kind of preparation a player must do is the same for either college or the pro tour. I don't think you have to do anything differently in high school to prepare for the Pro Tour that you would do if you planned to go to college. I have a very definite opinion about turning professional before college—Don't, unless you have achieved a measure of success that would allow you to get into professional tournaments without going through the qualifying route. That's extremely difficult to do. Krickstein and Arias have done it. It has to be given that if you're not at that point in your tennis development and career as a junior, it probably won't work out. The qualifying route is just unbelievably tough. You can be a very good player and never get out of the pack.

The emotional traits that identify a successful professional player consist primarily of an ability to control his or her emotional state out on the court. This is essential as far as I'm concerned and college tennis can help a player reach an emotional maturity. Players are exposed to a lot of emotional situations in dual matches: 2,000 people in the stands, the match is at 4–all, the win is hinging on the final No Ad point, for example. It's hard to find a more pressure-filled situation than that. Handling this helps you gain the experience and control of your emotions which you must have to compete as a professional successfully. The ability to keep from getting too high or too low is an emotional state that the good pro is able to do, and this can be nurtured very successfully in college.

I don't think there's a better training ground for you to do this. Time management is critical both in college and out on the tour, out in the world in general. To learn to structure and prepare, etc., all is essential in managing a collegiate career. In addition, if as an outstanding college tennis player you decide not to go out on the tour, you have a variety of options, whether it is as a professional at a club, management of players or a host of other tennis related occupations. But I think it goes beyond that. The traits that are developed by the collegiate tennis player are going to be very valuable to someone hiring from an IBM or any major corporation because of the skills you have developed and the successes you have achieved in college. You are disciplined and self-motivated and used to working hard toward a desired goal.

It's hard to realize it at the time but as you get more distance you can acknowledge just how much you've gained from playing college tennis. I still draw on experiences from my days as a college tennis player in handling situations that come up in my current job as a tennis teaching professional.

Gretchen Rush:

Education was always an important part of my background. My father is a dentist and had a good deal of schooling for that profession and my mother went to college as well, so college and the benefits of a college education were a big part of our family life. Tennis was a way for me to consider going to school outside of Pennsylvania. It expanded my options. I was looking for a tennis scholarship to help me get through school.

Sometimes I thought about leaving school and turning pro, but it was more a yearning to go do something else when you're not enjoying studying or taking tests at a certain point. At the time I wasn't playing that well and I thought that maybe leaving school and devoting my time to playing tennis would make my life less complicated. But in the summer when I was playing all the time, I'd say: Gosh, I can't wait 'til school starts! At school I often wanted to have more free time, time to read, etc., but it was just a question of the grass looking greener.

Just before I began my freshman year at Trinity, I had a good a week at the Open, reaching the quarterfinals, but there wasn't anything in particular to push me into the Pro ranks. The week prior at the 18 and Under Nationals, I had lost to a girl I had never lost to before, and yet, here at the Open I beat her 6–0, 6–1. So, right there I thought, This is just a good week, but I'll have more weeks like the one I had at the

Nationals than I will reaching the quarterfinals of major national events. I had a pretty realistic view of my capabilities and knew how good the people were against whom I was competing. The matches I won were always 7–5 or 6–4 in the third set. So, while I knew I had the ability to play with these pros, I also knew I could just as easily lose a tough three-setter in the first round. Sometimes everything goes your way, your biorhythms are up and you achieve great success. However, that is not the norm, and you have to understand that you will have many more down weeks than up ones. I wasn't mature enough, I needed to learn more about myself, and college was the logical choice at that period in time.

College was always what I wanted to do. My high school coach encouraged me to play and was very supportive of whatever decision I made. He thought it was great that I had the opportunity to go to Trinity where tennis was such a big sport. In fact, after my first year at Trinity, I went back to my high school and told my coach that I wanted to be a high school teacher and it wasn't until after my second year that I changed my mind. I decided in 11th grade where I wanted to go. I wanted a strong academic and strong tennis program. I had seen three schools out of the four or so who were actively recruiting me. I felt it was very important to see the schools, not to rely soley on what the coaches told me about their programs, but to watch the team work out, look closely at how well the girls got along with each other because, obviously, we'd be spending a lot of time together so I wanted to make sure that I could fit in. Trinity was the only school where I really felt at home, where I wouldn't have to change my personality to be successful and get along; I felt that at the other schools I would have to change. Also, I knew a smaller school was important, because I didn't want to be just a number at the larger schools I looked at.

Now that I've been on the tour for half a year, I would advise anyone in college who is considering the professional circuit to practice harder because it is not easy out here. There are many players as good or better than you are. You may reach a certain ability level where you're comfortable and content, or you may develop a nonchalant attitude and remain on a plateau. I would have practiced a lot harder, taken more advantage of the good coaching available to me, and appreciated more the opportunities to travel in college than I did. I would prepare for tournaments better. But of course, you learn to do these things as you get older. Once I became a senior I could appreciate how valuable the collegiate experience had been for me.

If you're not very mature and don't have a good understanding of how the world works, how people work (all of which a college experience helps you deal with) then a young person is going to have a rough time, although most very young players have people on the tour to take care of them. It's very beneficial to have a college education so that you can take control of your own life. For example, you can understand better what an agent or manager is advising you concerning your earnings and career choices. College stretches you and you learn to deal with a lot of different pressures. College is an excellent training ground for the demands of the world in that you get to know yourself and how to deal with things better in a pretty safe, secure, and known environment.

The protective aspect of college tennis was positive for me. I only wish I had been more observant of what was being done for me. I remember being stuck in a line at the airport in England for an hour and panicking because I had to get to Paris to play in a tournament. Since I hadn't had to worry about this for four years, I felt helpless. I don't even know how to order a case of tennis balls because this was done for me! But I think it was good with so many other things you have to think about in college to have someone making your life easier in this respect.

The one thing which should not be a factor for young players concerning the college or Pro decision is financial pressure from parents. It makes me sick to see young kids pushed onto the Pro circuit before they're emotionally or sometimes physically ready to handle it just because they're a potential gold mine for the family. I see so much of this and it's depressing! But if kids have the skills and a burning desire to do nothing but commit themselves to tennis, if their hearts tell them this is right, they should do it. But if they are a little uncertain and have the intellectual capacity to go to college, I think they should go to college.

After my college years, I wasn't sure I wanted to play professionally. I thought it might be better to do other things that I'd wanted to do that might be just as rewarding. But I began to enjoy playing tennis more and more. It got to be fun again. And I also felt I hadn't filled my potential in tennis yet and I was curious to see how I'd do. I feel that I have plenty of time to do the other things and that right now I have the freedom and the energy to travel around, etc.

College is or should be a maturing process, so that when you begin on the tour you have travelled, you have experienced the pressure of matches, you can change hats, because you have done this on a smaller scale in college. I thought that school was a perfect training ground because it does take experience playing out there and dealing with all the emotional ups and downs.

The most important thing, though, is to keep tennis in perspective. Tennis is a wonderful thing and offers a lot of opportunity, but it's not the only sport in the world, the only thing in the world. It's not the end of the world if you lose, even though it sometimes may feel like it. I feel that what you learn about yourself playing tennis and the college experience in particular should be the main goal. To find out your strengths and limitations, to have the opportunity to travel and meet all sorts of people, is just invaluable.

CHAPTER·12

Dan Magill

Dan Magill
Men's Tennis Coach
University of Georgia

Dan Magill, who has been working for Georgia ever since he was bat boy for the baseball team as a youngster in the early 1930s, experienced his greatest thrill as a Bulldog in May, 1985, when his tennis team won the NCAA team and singles crowns and also ranked No. 1 in the final ITCA doubles rankings.

Magill, on the verge of finishing his 32nd year as the Bulldog mentor, is the nation's all-time most winning collegiate tennis coach with a record of 665–172. A 1942 graduate of Georgia, Magill competed on both the tennis and swimming teams.

As well as building the Georgia tennis program to its lofty heights, Magill's efforts for collegiate tennis have been immense. The ITCA College Hall of Fame, located adjacent to Henry Field Stadium in Athens, is largely the result of his efforts.

In addition to his duties as Director of Tennis, Magill also serves as the assistant athletic director for public relations and the Georgia Bulldog Clubs. The Dan Magill Award, created in 1985, is given to a Bulldog Club member showing the most spirit towards the Bulldog athletic teams.

A native of Athens, Magill was voted National Coach of the Year by the USPTA in 1979 and was the ITCA/Wilson Coach of the Year in 1980. He has had seven teams in the NCAA Team Tournament since it was inaugurated in 1977, and four of the last five seasons his teams have made it to the final four of the national tournament.

He was president of the ITCA from 1973–75 and chairman of the NCAA tennis committee from 1975–80 and is currently serving as Chairman of the Collegiate Tennis Hall of Fame committee. He is a member of the Georgia State Hall of Fame, the Southern Tennis Hall of Fame and the Georgia State Tennis Hall of Fame.

Magill has coached three national champions, 1983 doubles champions Allen Miller and Ola Malmqvist and two-time NCAA singles champion (and 1986 French Open finalist) Mikael Pernfors. His team not only won the NCAA team title in 1985 but repeated this feat in 1987.

He is married to the former Rosemary Reynaud of New Orleans and they have three children, Dr. Ham Magill, a tennis player at Princeton and now an Athens physician, Mrs. William Brown of Atlanta and Mrs. Stephen Sloan of Rye, New York.

HOW TO ORGANIZE, PROMOTE, AND RUN A TENNIS TOURNAMENT

Dan Magill, Men's Tennis Coach, University of Georgia

Fifty years' experience in running off tennis tournaments has taught me much about the art of directing these events so important to our sport.

It's much like running a big department store. Now I don't have any experience in running a department store, but in running a tennis event you have to have the philosophy that the customer is always right and you do everything for the customer.

You have to have a great facility and fine tennis courts. A player has to feel like playing tennis when he gets out on the court. You want him to think, Now this is a nice court. This is a solid court. And for a high school or collegiate championship tournament, you should have championship-quality facilities. For the NCAA's at the University of Georgia, we resurface our courts every twenty-four months. Probably no other tennis site in the country resurfaces its courts that often, except perhaps for Flushing Meadow in New York, but we've found out that if you wait three years, the courts are a little worn. It costs us well over $20,000 annually to maintain their high quality, but we feel this is critical.

ASSURING A SUCCESSFUL TOURNAMENT

There are many things the director must do to assure the successful conduct of his or her tournament. First and foremost, the facilities must be ship shape in every respect, especially the tennis courts themselves. There is nothing worse for players than having to play on courts that are cracked and in need of resurfacing. The courts must be kept clean. Hard-surfaced courts must be hosed down with a power nozzle. College play is almost exclusively on hard-surfaced courts now, but if the courts are clay or rubico, etc., they will require much more work to get them in good shape for all day tournament play.

The nets and center straps must be in good shape. Patch up the holes in the net or, preferably, get new nets. Check the center straps to see if they are slipping. Old ones tend to do this rather frequently.

Singles sticks must be used for singles matches and taken down, of course, for doubles. It would be wise to put a mark on the court designating the spot where the singles sticks should be placed (36 inches from the singles alley).

Chairs should be placed on the courts for the players to use during the rest time at the court switch over. It is helpful to have additional chairs for the coaches to use if they wish to coach their players during the switch over.

It is most important that there be scoreboards on each court. Scoreboards are essential in order to get and keep fan interest. The best scoreboards are the type originally designed by Coach Stan Drobac of Michigan State and now produced by a number of companies. These scoreboards have large numerals and room for three sets. They also can be read from both sides, which is a great feature. There is also a place for the name of each of the competing schools.

There must be comfortable umpire chairs, preferably high enough to have a commanding view of the full court. And it goes without saying that you need to have good umpires who can call the score out loud and clear and who understand the No Ad system which we use in college matches.

Dark curtains or screens should be at both ends of the playing court. Players must have a dark background in order to keep the ball in focus.

The grandstand or bleachers must be in good order and kept clean at all times. It is necessary to have an attendant or several helpers to keep the courts and tournament area clean. There should be a small trash can on each court and larger ones at appropriate places throughout the tournament area.

The tournament headquarters should be a structure or room easily accessible to the players and officials and clearly marked. Ideally, it should be equipped with at least one telephone and a public address system. There should be telephones at another site for the public's use and even the players' use.

There should be several bulletin boards for draw sheets and other announcements pertaining to the tournament. One attractive feature is having all the newspaper clippings from past events here mounted along the wall along the arcade under the grandstand. Spectators can look at these during a lull. At Athens, Georgia, our ITCA Collegiate Tennis Hall of Fame building is a great addition to the NCAA's because people can see attractive pictures and mementoes of the past collegiate champions.

For a major tournament, like the NCAA Division I Men's Championships which we have conducted in Athens, Georgia, in recent years, we have a chair umpire or monitor for every match—singles and doubles. Beginning in the quarterfinal round, we use several linesmen and ball boys/girls. These officials, of course, are under the direction of the tournament referee. In the NCAAs, we have several deputy referees who oversee the action throughout the area. For example, there is a deputy referee in charge of play for three or four courts. It is ideal to employ walkie-talkie radios for use by the deputy referees in their contact with tournament headquarters.

It is ideal to have dressing room facilities, shower rooms and toilets for the players and officials, and toilet facilities for the fans. If permanent toilet facilities are not at the tournament site, portable toilets should be installed.

There should be a trainer or trainers on duty at all times. The trainers are responsible for attending to injured or sick players, sometimes even fans. Trainers are also responsible for supplying the players with towels, ice and drinks.

Too much emphasis cannot be placed on having the very best facilities and officials possible. The players are certainly more at ease and appreciative when they realize that everything has been done to create a complete championship atmosphere.

If there is a shortage of experienced umpires, linesmen and ball boys/girls, it is the responsibility of the tournament sponsor or tournament director to train a crew. The local tennis clubs should have many members interested in learning to officiate at tournaments.

Even if you have the finest facilities and the best officials and a cast of outstanding players, your tournament will not be a complete success unless it is well attended by fans. All athletes like to perform before large, appreciative and enthusiastic crowds. They perform better when inspired by cheering fans. Although fan interest in college tennis is ever increasing throughout the country, there are some areas where it is difficult to get good attendance at matches.

ATTRACTING FANS

The first ingredient necessary to attract fans is to have outstanding players in the field. For the NCAAs and other big collegiate tournaments, this first requirement is easily met. For a dual match, it is vital that the home team be a winner. It is a fact of life that fans will rarely follow a loser. But there are also some winning teams that do not attract good crowds. I believe it must be because of three reasons: (1) inadequate publicity; (2) inadequate support of local tennis clubs, whose support must then be organized; (3) inadequate viewing facilities.

It takes a lot of work by the coach and the sports information director to get the news media to publicize a tournament in advance and then to cover it on a daily basis. Many times the coach or an assistant must do practically all the work himself. That is telephone the news outlets in advance and then telephone the results in afterward. The proper personnel in the various media must be cultivated and be made aware that there are numerous tennis fans in the community.

You have to have good publicity, so we get our sports information department here in Georgia heavily involved. I spend a lot of time myself talking to key media people around the state, giving them feature stories which they can play up. The Athens papers are wonderful in this respect, and the Atlanta papers are also great. I can't stress enough the absolute necessity of having good publicity. Tennis has been built up so that it is a major sport at the University of Georgia and in Athens. Folks know about it and take pride in having the tournament here.

Fortunately, we now have all the necessary ingredients to put on a successful NCAA Championship at the University of Georgia in Athens. But that was not the case in the beginning. It took years and much hard work by many people for us to reach our present level.

The first thing we had to do was to develop a winning team. When I began coaching at Georgia in the mid-fifties, our mediocre teams attracted only a handful of fans (mostly relatives). In the late 1960s and early 1970s we were strong enough to contend for the conference championship and we began winning most of our matches. We put together a home court winning streak of 76 straight from 1968 to 1972 and it was then that fans began coming out in large numbers. They were anxious to see the winning streak continue, and they found out that tennis was really a great, competitive sport, as entertaining as the so called major sports. The students also found out that they could get a good suntan at the same time. Our tennis matches gradually became a social event—a happening.

After we had drawn several crowds of between 2,000 and 3,000 (mostly college students, but quite a few townfolk) for big dual matches, our athletic director, Joel Eaves, rewarded us by building a $125,000 grandstand (3,500 aluminum seats) in 1977. Heretofore, most of the fans had sat on the grassy hillside overlooking the courts, with only a few bleachers available.

Our enthusiastic crowds had caused Dale Lewis, Miami's coach and then chairman of the NCAA Tennis Committee, to award us the NCAAs in 1972, the first year we hosted it. Since then, we have built four indoor courts, made possible by a generous contribution from a wealthy Georgia alumnus, the late Lindsey Hopkins, Jr., father of one of our captains. We are continually improving our facilities and striving to improve every phase of the NCAA Championships in Athens.

YOUR COMMITTEES

Ticket sales committees are essential to promote season ticket sales. We have women from the Athens Country Club and the Athens Tennis Association who promote ticket sales. We have a university ticket sales group. We have committees to sell tickets in other towns near Athens. The Atlanta Tennis League has something like 50,000 tennis players, and so we try to promote a lot of sales with them and have been successful.

We have a very important grounds crew that keeps the place clean. It's like cleaning up after the circus, but we need to have everything look good, and we have a night watchman who makes sure no one steals anything from the grounds.

We have a Program Committee, a Hospitality Committee, Host Family Committee, Transportation Committee. We have good officials who come from all over the country. We are budgeted for $14,000 but spend over $20,000 (we being the University and the Athens Tennis Association, who are our co-sponsors). The Athens Tennis Association is responsible for meeting the guarantee to the NCAA for this tournament. The Georgia Athletic Association, which provides the facilities for the event, gets around 15 percent of the net. We turn in a net of between $60,000 and $70,000, of which $9,000 or $10,000 goes back to the Athletic Association. We usually spend most of these monies as part of our Operating Budget. In ten years we have never had a surplus.

I cite a few of our own examples because I believe any other school can do the same by tapping its great natural resources—wealthy and interested alumni, as well as tennis fans in the community.

Another important ingredient necessary to the success of a tournament is making the draw. Of course, there is the official way listed in the USTA Guidebook. But modifications should be made for various tournaments. In our college tournaments, we frequently place players from the same school in different quarters, which is fair and logical. There's no point for a player to face his teammate in the first round. In the NCAAs we go a step further. Players from the same geographic region are not permitted to meet each other in the first round.

In college tennis, we have made our own rules for the draw, and these modifications have helped us improve our tournaments. Naturally, in USTA championships the tournament director must follow the USTA guidelines.

Perhaps it might be helpful to illustrate the differences between a major college event such as the NCAA Division I Championships and a high school or junior tournament by describing our annual local Crackerland Tournament here in Athens.

The Crackerland event started in the early days of my tennis career. When I was growing up I had a job in the summer assisting the head caretaker maintaining the six clay courts at the University of Georgia. In my senior year of high school, I was put in charge of the courts from June to August. We had to put on two tournaments—the city tournament, and the Northeast Georgia Championships. I had to learn how to run these tournaments as one of my responsibilities. I had an older friend who knew how to run tournaments and he helped me make up draws according to the USTA Rulebook. I learned one step at a time, but after doing it one year, I thought it would be good to have a bigger tournament here. My father, who was editor of the *Athens Banner Herald*, gave us a nickname for the Northeast Georgia tournament because that name was too confining for an event that we wanted to make bigger. He came up with Crackerland, and that's where the tournament got its name (the natives of Georgia are often called crackers).

The year 1939 was our first tournament and I held it from '39 to '41. Then for eight years I wasn't involved with Athens tennis because I was in the Marine Corps and then working in Atlanta. I came back in '49 as the University of Georgia Sports Information Director. I resumed tennis in the summer of 1950 with General Jones, who was the tennis coach then and a good friend of mine, and we started the Crackerland tournament again. I've run it since I became head tennis coach here in 1955.

Our tournament has grown tremendously over the years. From a draw of sixteen to thirty-two in men's and women's singles, now in some of our junior events in the 14's and 16's we have a draw of 128 or more and we have to use every court in town—some thirty courts all over the city. We have juniors one week and the adults the next week. We have 700–800 competing when you add it all up! All different age divisions participate. We're trying to limit the draw in some divisions now to sixty-four because 128 is almost impossible to schedule when it rains. No Ad scoring has been the savior for us. It prevents matches from going on forever.

Because of Crackerland's large size now, we can't set up hospitality committees and the like as we used to do. At one point we had so many officials we couldn't keep track of them all—maintaining tournament logistics, seeing that matches were started on time, that warm up periods were adhered to because there were so many matches going on every day. We couldn't have an umpire in every chair. Now what we've done is set up deputy referees for every three matches. I think this has worked extremely well. Local people do the officiating for the Crackerland. We have a particularly good person in charge of umpires; members of the faculty serve as officials.

Once the tournament begins, I go over my checklist. I have two troubleshooters who are always at the clubhouse and they do things for me if I see something wrong. The groundskeeper is always around to assist me from that point of view. In addition, we have someone in charge of ballboys and ballgirls for these tournaments. We set up stringing facilities, with one good stringer always available, as well.

There is nothing quite like a tournament to create excitement for the players, officials and fans. It takes much hard work by a lot of people to promote and manage a successful tournament, but everyone is well pleased when he or she has played a part in the successful conduct of a tournament.

Jerry Noyce

Jerry Noyce
Men's Tennis Coach
University of Minnesota

From 1974 to 1988, Jerry Noyce was the architect of Minnesota's outstanding tennis program. Among the accomplishments of the Gopher tennis teams under Noyce's direction are: three Big Ten titles; thirteen Individual Big Ten singles titles; four Individual Big Ten doubles titles; twenty-four All Big Ten players; three All American players; a U.S. team ranking of thirteenth (in 1984); qualification for the NCAA Championships three times (in 1974, 1975 and 1984); and twelve Williams Scholars.

A University of Minnesota graduate and former three-time Gopher tennis MVP, Noyce retired after fifteen seasons as head coach of the Gopher tennis team to pursue other tennis interests. At Minnesota he compiled an excellent 265–137 dual match record. His record is among the top college coaches in NCAA tennis and year in and year out, Minnesota has one of the most attractive and challenging schedules in collegiate tennis. In 1986 Noyce was honored as the ITCA Men's Wilson Coach of the Year.

Noyce is a native of Evanston, Illinois, where he won a state high school doubles championship as a prep before enrolling at Minnesota. During his college career at Minnesota, he continued his outstanding play as the number one singles and doubles player and an All Big Ten selection. He graduated in 1967 with a business degree.

Currently, Noyce is the Director of Tennis for the Normandale Tennis Clubs. Since graduating from Minnesota, Noyce has won singles titles in state competition in Minnesota, Illinois, Iowa and Indiana and was the top-ranked player in the Northwest Tennis Association. He has also been a top-ranked player in the Men's 35 and over division in the same association.

Jerry and his wife Jane, also a University of Minnesota graduate, have two children, Jennifer and David.

TEAM PROMOTION: BOOSTER CLUBS AND FUNDRAISING

Jerry Noyce, Men's Tennis Coach, University of
Minnesota

Next to great players who are motivated, committed, and have a great work ethic to succeed, possibly the most important ingredient to a program's success today is proper and constant team promotion.

Many aspects of a tennis program must function properly for success to be achieved:

> Recruiting
> Scheduling
> Effective team workouts
> Facilities
> Coaching

And team promotion, through booster clubs and fundraising, can provide the glue to bring it all together.

HOW THREE TENNIS POWERS USE BOOSTER CLUBS AND FUNDRAISING

Let's look at some of the most successful men's college tennis programs in America and see how fundraising and booster clubs have played an integral part in their success.

Stanford University

Coach Dick Gould and his Stanford teams have been the most successful school in America, winning eight national titles, along with numerous Pac Ten championships. Stanford has boasted some of the great names in tennis on its squads. McEnroe, Tim Mayotte, Dan Goldie, Scott Davis, Jim Grabb, Peter Rennart, and many more.

When asked how important fundraising has been to the Stanford program, Coach Gould will say it has been critical. We will look at the Stanford Program in more detail later.

University of Georgia

No one in college tennis today can equal what Coach Dan McGill at Georgia has accomplished through his fundraising efforts.

The University of Georgia team, fifteen years ago a good program, but not a dominating one, is today one of the premier programs in the land. What has made the difference? Many things have to come together to achieve greatness as Georgia has done. But, one of the keys has been the creation of a home for one of the most successful NCAA championships annually. With the hosting of the tournament has come tremendous financial and fan support from the community, state, and region.

This has helped foster some fabulous performances by Georgia players in front of a highly partisan and supportive home crowd, which has further encouraged more great performances by the players and better recruiting, and finally an NCAA team title in 1985—the first NCAA team title by a non-California team since 1972. All from the creation of home town support for the NCAA Tournament and its resulting energy transmitted to the home town program.

With these very successful efforts, the sport of college tennis has benefitted from the great crowds, great excitement and the creation of the college tennis Hall of Fame at Athens, Georgia.

Trinity University

Traditionally one of the finest programs in America, Trinity University in San Antonio, Texas has fielded some of the best squads in history. The 1972 NCAA championship team, featuring Brian Goetfried, Dick Stockton, Paul Gerkin, Pancho Walthall, and later coach Bobby McKinley, is considered by many the best college team of all time.

One early Trinity team, for example, was anchored by two of the top ten players in the world at that time, Chuck McKinley and Frank Froehling.

One of the key elements to the continuation of that great tradition has been a special fundraising event Trinity holds each Fall. This is a special Pro Am weekend which features the return of many Trinity team alumni combining with present team members to play with area amateurs—all to raise $30,000 or more for the program.

Other cases of coaches using their talents and energy to create or increase support of their teams are becoming more numerous. All of which indicates how critical this aspect of the program has become.

The subject of Fundraising and Booster Clubs is much like the question of which came first, the chicken or the egg?

The question is often raised, "Should I first work to establish a fundraising network, or a booster club?"

The answer varies for every situation and every tennis program. All programs can use more fan support and enthusiasm. But, for some teams, program improvement (or in some cases, its very existence) may be in focusing efforts in the fundraising effort first.

As a coach who has gone through struggling with these issues, and whose program has tremendously benefitted from the efforts in the areas of fundraising and booster clubs creation, let me share some thoughts on this subject.

SIX PROVEN PROMOTION IDEAS

Whether it is fundraising or booster clubs creation that is your goal, it is important to:

1. *Establish a list of needs for your program.* Number them in order of priority of need. Have them handy. Make them public. Then, when someone may ask what help you need for the team, you are ready to respond.
   It is critical that people know that, number one, you have needs which others can help you achieve, and two, that meeting these needs will improve your team.
2. *List the needs in order of priority so the easiest to accomplish can be attacked first.* Every coach would like to have a 4,000 seat tennis stadium, overflow crowds for home matches, and a generous travel budget.

These or other needs/wants may be on your wish list for the program. To begin achieving these needs, list every want you have for the team. Put them in order, not by importance, but by ease of accomplishment.

Consistent with the theory of showing how your program is progressing, this list of needs can be a powerful tool to enlist support. People will help you work to fill needs that they perceive as being achievable. Then as needs are filled, they will be ready to move to the next, and more difficult, need on the list.

3. *Develop goals for your program.*
   Obviously, we all have a goal of being as competitive as possible with
   the resources available. This goal, however, may not move others to
   get on the bandwagon, and help you in your efforts. Your goals for the
   team must encompass more than being competitive.
      For example, at Minnesota, I established these goals for our
   program when I began going to the community for support:

   A. *Competitive*
      · to be the best in the Big Ten
      · to be the best team in the Northern United States
      · to be in the top 20 teams in the United States
      · to qualify annually for the NCAA's
   B. *Sportsmanship*
      · to be a positive influence on tennis at all levels as role models
        of fair play on the court
   C. *Scholarship*
      · to achieve the best possible results in the classroom as well as
        on the court
      · to graduate from the University of Minnesota with a quality
        education

Developing goals in several key areas does several things for you.
First, it gives people who are your potential supporters a variety of
goals, one or more of which could well be important to their concept of
how college athletics and, specifically, college tennis should be directed. I found that some of our boosters or contributors may not be
terribly interested in whether our squad finishes in the top twenty in
the United States. But, mention being role models in tennis for younger
players as a team goal, and those same boosters are very interested in
supporting our efforts.

Second, multiplicity of goals allows you the opportunity to show
progress. The more goals, the better your chances to meet or exceed at
least one of them.

Third, people are motivated by achieving goals. Many of your
supporters, hopefully, will be successful business people. These people
unlock many doors for you—financial support, promotional expertise,
organizational ability, etc. Business people understand the goal setting
and goal achieving process. They are comfortable with it and are more
moved by striving to meet specific goals than by more esoteric aspects
to the sport (i.e., the right to participate, being a part of a total sports
program).

Fourth, the team has formal, public goals to meet. This process of goal setting helps crystalize one's philosophy for his or her program.

4. *Enlist Support*

You have now established your needs, and formulated a series of athletic and academic goals for the program.

Now, to make them become a reality, recruiting supporters becomes the key.

A. One way that I have found of recruiting such support is what I call the Give to Get theory.

Simply stated, you invest your time in someone else's projects to receive reciprocal support from others. For example, in our area, we have a series of Sunday afternoon Pro-Ams at various tennis clubs. Now, Sunday is not my favorite day to work, but I made sure that I attended every Pro-Am when I began building our program. By giving my time, I met influential tennis people. They learned of my needs and philosophy, and commitment. Then, they began to ask the most important question, How can I help?

Later, other projects have arisen in the tennis community. I have tried to make myself available to help in any way possible to make these projects work.

It is only through this attitude of giving first, that we have received help.

B. Send newsletters to your alumni and tennis friends. These people are certain to be interested in what is happening with the team. Let them know what the team needs now to help it improve.

C. *Find someone in the community to spearhead the fundraising or booster club effort.* It is a much easier task to create interest and support for your team when there is someone who helps open doors for you. Hopefully, this sponsor will be a respected business leader, a person involved in community tennis with a fine reputation. Or, possibly, a leading school team alumnus. This person will bring others to your aid, informing them of your needs, selling them on your goals. In general, this person will help get your team exposed to the community.

D. *Have a meeting—invite prospects.* Usually a tennis oriented meeting with tennis followed by a short program works quite well. It makes people feel comfortable, and you'll know they like tennis.

Take this opportunity to lay out your program goals and needs. Follow up with thank you notes the next day. And, invite them in your letter to join your booster club or fundraising effort.

5. *Organize the Support*

   This is critical. Bring your staunchest supporters together and form your Board of Directors to manage your booster club. Have an open election system to the Board, so that all those interested in being very involved can get on the Board.

   Finally, turn over your Board of Officers on a regular basis (every two to three years) so that new blood can be constantly infused in the club.

6. *Report Your Progress*

   Again, a newsletter on a monthly to quarterly basis will keep everyone informed of the progress.

Now let's look at the successful Stanford program, and how team promotion has helped it rise to the top.

Stanford University Men's Tennis

Dick Gould has a very purposeful philosophy—raise enough financial support to make the program self-sufficient. This takes the form of goals to:

1. fully endow all scholarships
2. cover operational expenses

The successful Stanford Model for fundraising is outlined below:

STANFORD MODEL

Philosophy: must be as self-sufficient as possible
  —endow scholarships
  —cover operational expenses
  (secretary, computer, facility maintenance)

1. *Scholarship Endowment Program*
   A. Have begun 5 endowed scholarships
     · requires $300–$350 thousand per scholarship to fully endow
   B. Method of fundraising:
      1. *Former Players Endowment*—2 major exhibitors plus players' donations
      2. *Group Endowment*—San Diego Endowed Scholarship
      3. *Individuals Endowment*

- contribute $20,000/up for 5 years
- "Living Scholarships"—only pledges of $10,000/year for duration of player's time in school

Total Endowment Program at $400,000

2. *Operational Expenses*
    A. Name a budget of $40,000 per year to cover these items
    B. Methods:
        1. Team member/guest day
            - $100 to play with team and lunch (raises $4,000)
        2. Tennis Club—Stanford Day
            - area club hosts team for play and lunch ($50 fee)
            - raises $1,000
            - other benefits include no organizing time ("clean deal") and other contributions (computer)
        3. Solicitation
            Key item: built a strong mailing list
            - 2,000 names on list from:
                —season ticket holders
                —clinics and summer camp
                —people in tennis business (pros, club owners)
            - send press guide and solicitation letter to list
            - sells ads in pressguide to cover its cost
            - sells ad space on scoreboard for $3,000/year
            - no booster club now—next step and tie in with season ticket package
        4. Clinic
            - for people in community
            - travel with team to Puerto Rico, Hawaii, Bahamas
            - pay enough for clinic to cover team airfare
            - get to know players
        5. Summer Camp
            - 2 week day camp on campus
            - raises $20,000 for team
            - $135/week (5 days–3 hours)
            - 6 : 1 on court × 12 courts
            - 3 sessions/week
        6. Home Matches
            - grosses $25,000/year on home match gate sales
    Philosophy: Emphasize a couple events to get a great gate
            - UCLA/USC match and mixed match with Cal.
            - sell tickets at $6 and $3
            - averages 5,000 people/match
            - matches start out and conclude indoors at night

3. *Results*
   · average receipts of $200,000–$300,000/year
   · high of $500,000 in '83
4. *Gould's Advice*
   "Coaches who think their schools owe them their programs are sadly mistaken."
   "We must become self-sufficient."

In summary, successful teams often develop or require financial support to complete the program. All that is required is the opportunity, granted by your Athletic Director to pursue the options of booster clubs and fundraising.

A result of your hard efforts will be fans and players who are more committed because on one hand they know their help makes a success possible, and on the other hand, the team feels more supported.

Best wishes in your efforts.

CHAPTER·14

Stanley J. Clark

Chair, Department of Kinesiology and Physical Education California State University, Hayward

Before taking on his current responsibility as Chair of the Department of Kinesiology at California State University, Hayward, Clark was its very successful men's tennis coach from 1976 through 1982, leading his teams to seven consecutive Northern Caliornia Athletic Conference championships. For this achievement, he was named Coach of the Year all seven years.

During his tenure as men's tennis coach, Clark compiled a seven year dual match record of 107 wins and 26 losses for a winning percentage of .80. Competing at the NCAA Division II level, Hayward lost only one dual match to another Division II institution in seven years. Cal State, Hayward finished among the top ten teams in the country each of Clark's years as coach, compiling 56 consecutive conference wins without a loss.

In 1983, Clark was named the ITCA/ Wilson Coach of the Year for Division II men's tennis. Clark served as chair of the Division II Men's Tennis Committee from 1980–86, as a member of the NCAA Men's National Tennis Committee during that same period, and as chair of the NCAA Men's National Tennis Committee in 1985–86. A long-time member of the ITCA Board of Directors, Clark also serves in the important role of ITCA liaison to the NCAA on collegiate tennis issues.

CHAPTER·14

THE WORLD OF SMALL COLLEGE TENNIS

Stanley J. Clark, California State University, Hayward

Small college tennis refers to men's collegiate tennis programs and organizations that are not classified within Division I of the National Collegiate Athletic Association—the NCAA. These organizations include Divisions II and III of the NCAA,[1] the National Association of Intercollegiate Athletics (NAIA), the National Junior College Athletics Association (NJCAA), and the California Association of Community Colleges (CACC).

In this chapter, a very brief synopsis of the historical evolution of the NCAA, NAIA, NJCAA, and the CACC will be given. The philosophies of these organizations and a chronology of the champions they produced will also be presented.

It is beyond the scope of this chapter to provide a detailed history of the National Collegiate Athletic Association. Suffice it to say that the NCAA was founded in 1906. Some of its primary purposes are to organize and control intercollegiate athletics among member institutions in the United States. All member institutions must abide by the rules and regulations of the NCAA, which are detailed in the NCAA manual. Coaches and players should familiarize themselves with the rules and regulations of the Association in order to answer questions about student eligibility, regulations for accepting prize money, entrance requirements to colleges and universities, and to impart other important information.

Because of differences in philosophies, levels of financial support, and other factors, the NCAA developed divisional structures. There are three divisions in the NCAA. For example, Stanford University is in Division I, Cal State Hayward in Division II, and Gustavus Adolphus

---

[1] Maps depicting the regional alignments for Divisions II and III are located in this chapter.

College in Division III. The vital statistics of Division I colleges and universities are not included in this report, because Division I institutions are not a part of the world of small college tennis.

DIVISION II TENNIS

There are four regions in Division II, as depicted in the map below. Currently, 152 Division II institutions sponsor men's intercollegiate tennis. Division II held its first NCAA championship tournament in 1963. Beginning in 1983, eight teams have been selected each year to compete in dual match play for the NCAA Division II men's Tennis Championship. The top team from each region is guaranteed entrance into the team competition, and four other teams are selected at-large. The team competition is followed by an individual tournament comprised of 64 singles players and 32 doubles teams. The singles and doubles champions and finalists gain automatic entry into the NCAA Division I Men's National Tennis Championships.

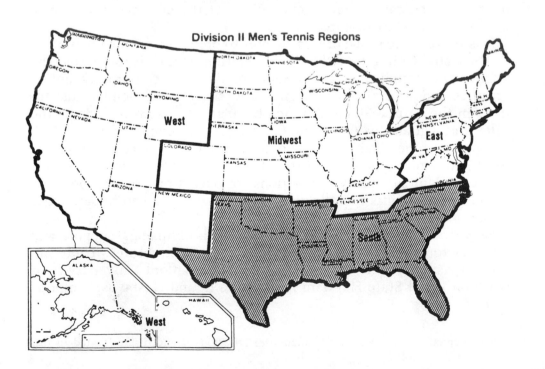

Division II Men's Tennis Regions

Similar in policy to Division I, most Division II institutions offer athletic grants-in-aid (athletic scholarships) to student athletes, albeit on a more modest basis than that permitted in Division I. The only Division II conference in the United States which expressly prohibits athletic grants-in-aid for student athletes is the Northern California Athletic Conference. Member institutions of the Northern California Athletic conference who currently sponsor men's tennis include California State University, Hayward, San Francisco State University, Stanislaus State University, Sonoma State University, and the University of California, Davis. Insofar as geographic location and conference scheduling patterns permit, a Division II institution attempts to schedule a majority of its competition with other Division II institutions.

During the 1960s Los Angeles State College was a dominant force in Division II men's tennis, winning three national championships and finishing second twice. Gil Rodriguez and Gary Johnson of Los Angeles State were two of the dominant players of this decade. The 1967 singles champion, Sherwood Stewart of Lamar College, became a highly successful player on the professional circuit.

Kent DeMars

Juan Farrow with Chuck McKinley

Myron McNamara's teams at the University of California, Irvine set the standard for excellence in the early and mid-nineteen seventies, winning six national championships and finishing second twice.

Division II was dominated in the late 1970s through the mid-1980s by Southern Illinois University, Edwardsville. Coach Kent DeMars led his teams to a phenomenal seven consecutive national championships, from 1978 through 1984. Juan Farrow of Southern Illinois University, Edwardsville was the first Division II player to win three national singles championships and two doubles championships, from 1977 through 1980. Not to be outdone, Ken Flach of SIUE established a standard of excellence that may never be equalled. He won three consecutive national singles championships and two consecutive national doubles championships, from 1981 through 1983. His doubles partner in 1983 was Robert Seguso. Flach and Seguso are currently the number one rated doubles team in the world, and represent the United States in Davis Cup competition.

Ken Flach

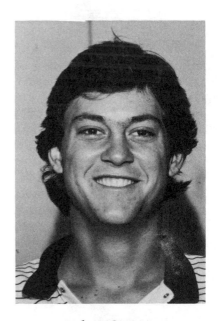

Robert Seguso

DIVISION III TENNIS

Division III NCAA

The National Collegiate Athletic Association created a third divisional structure in men's tennis in the mid-1970s. A significant number of institutions in the United States not only differed in size, but also philosophically and financially, from those in both Division I and Division II. Division III evolved as a result of these differences, and held its first separate championships in 1976.

Division III institutions place special importance on the impact of athletics on the participants, rather than spectators. These institutions construct their programs to meet the needs of their internal constituencies—students, alumni, and special friends—rather than focusing on the general public and its entertainment needs. Division III institutions are not allowed to offer athletic grants-in-aid or tennis scholarships to student athletes.

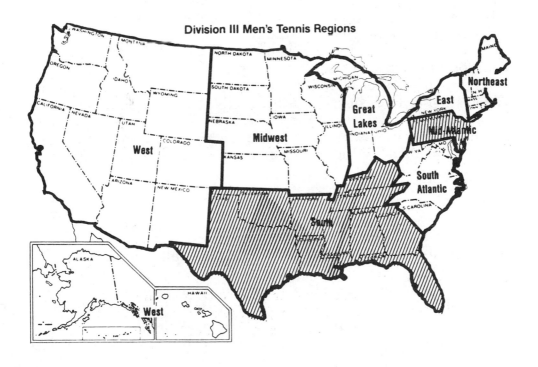

Division III Men's Tennis Regions

Division III currently has 263 institutions which sponsor men's tennis. There are eight regions in Division III, as depicted below.

Since 1983 eight teams in Division III have received invitations to compete in dual match play for the national tennis championship. Unlike Division II, none of the eight regions are guaranteed a team entry into the tournament, as all teams are selected on an at-large basis. Following the team competition an individual tournament is held, with a draw of 64 singles players and 32 doubles teams, to determine the national champions in each category. The champions in singles and doubles in Division III qualify for entrance into the Division I NCAA Men's National Tennis Championship Tournament.

During the ten year team championship history of Division III, the University of Redlands won three team titles under coach Jim Verdieck. Coach Steve Wilkinson has led Gustavus Adolphus College to two national championships, and George Acker of Kalamazoo College accomplished the same feat.

No Division III player has won more than one national singles championship. Shaun Miller of Gustavus Adolphus College is the only Division III player to win two national doubles titles, in 1981 and 1982. Perhaps the most recognizable name from Division III is John Mattke, who played at Gustavus Adolphus College. A Division III national doubles champion in 1980, Mattke is currently a touring professional. In 1984, Mattke defeated well known professional Andres Gomez, of Ecuador, in the Japan Open.

As does the National Collegiate Athletic Association, the National Association of Intercollegiate Athletics (NAIA) administers programs of intercollegiate athletics. The NAIA is an autonomous association, having no affiliation with the NCAA. The NAIA has a membership of over five-hundred fully accredited colleges and universities of moderate enrollment.

The NAIA

The NAIA is organized into thirty-one geographical districts spread over fifty States and part of Canada. Eligibility rules within the NAIA govern all play, not just post-season competition. All eligibility guidelines must be met by member institutions, including those holding dual affiliation with other associations. It is possible for a member institution to belong to the NAIA and the NCAA.

The first NAIA team championships in men's tennis were held in

1952. Since 1960, the national championships have been held every year in Kansas City, Missouri. Each of the thirty-two districts conducts a tournament to determine team and individual qualifiers to the NAIA national tournament. The team champion, the singles champion, and the doubles champions from each district automatically qualify for entrance into the national tournament.

During the 1950s, Lamar Tech of Texas dominated the NAIA national championships. From 1961 through 1965, Pan American of Texas captured five consecutive national titles. From 1966 through 1975, the University of Redlands established a phenomenal record, winning nine of the ten national championships. The early years of the NAIA reflect dominant teams who established their superiority for numerous years. Since 1976, however, only one team has won consecutive national championships—Southwest Texas State. This trend is similar to other sports where athletic parity seems to have become characteristic of the entire intercollegiate athletic scene.

James Schmidt of Lamar Tech distinguished himself by winning consecutive national singles championships in 1955 and 1956, an impressive accomplishment which has been surpassed only by Doug Verdieck from the University of Redlands. From 1967 through 1970, Verdieck won four consecutive national singles championships!

Although NAIA players have won consecutive doubles championships, the accomplishments of two individuals are noteworthy. Between 1959 and 1962, Don Russell of Pan American won four consecutive national doubles championships. Doug Verdieck of Redlands won three consecutive doubles championships between 1968 and 1970. Considering his accomplishments in singles, Verdieck set a standard of excellence in collegiate tennis that may never be repeated.

While the world of Small College Tennis consists of the National Collegiate Athletic Association's Divisions II and III and the National Intercollegiate Athletic Association, a majority of the two-year colleges for freshmen and sophomores are members of the National Junior College Athletic Association (NJCAA). The idea for the NJCAA was conceived in 1937 in Fresno, California, and in 1938 it became a functioning organization.

There are 224 NJCAA member institutions which currently sponsor men's tennis. These institutions are located in twenty-four geographical regions throughout the United States. (See Appendix.)

Details about the specific institutions which sponsor men's tennis in each of the twenty four regions can be obtained from the National

Junior College Athletic Associations' executive offices, which are located in Hutchinson, Kansas.

The top two teams in each of the regions qualify for entrance into the national team competition. Additionally, the individual winner in number one singles and the number one doubles team from each region qualify for entrance into the national tournament.

The history of the national tournament dates back to 1948. Although no teams became dominant forces within the NJCAA by capturing consecutive national championships over significant periods of time, Odessa College won the championship or tied for it seven times between 1948 and 1985.

Because of the two-year maximum participation limit at the junior college level, it is impossible for players to establish records in national play that can compare to the consecutive national honors won by individuals mentioned earlier in this chapter, such as Ken Flach, Juan Farrow, or Doug Verdieck. As noted below, a number of players achieved maximum honors by winning the national doubles title two times. However, no singles player has won the national championship in consecutive years since the NJCAA began recording champions in

Doug Verdieck (University of Redlands) won four consecutive singles titles and three consecutive doubles championships.

Doug Verdieck

Mikael Pernfors

1959. Perhaps the most recognized name among the singles and doubles champions is that of Mikael Pernfors, who won the NJCAA singles and doubles championships in 1983. Pernfors matriculated to the University of Georgia, where he won consecutive NCAA Division I national singles championships in 1984 and 1985 and also won the national doubles championship in 1984. He is currently a highly successful touring professional.

Although listed within Region I of the National Junior College Athletic Association, the State of California has an entirely separate Association. There are currently sixty-eight community colleges in California which sponsor men's tennis. They are all members of the California Association of Community Colleges. These institutions do not participate in NJCAA national championship competition, but conduct their own regional and State playoffs.

By authority of the California legislature and the State Education Code, the California Association of Community Colleges has been given the authority to establish rules and regulations which govern the athletic program for the over 22,000 men and women student athletes within the state. After World War II, the California community colleges became the largest nontuition postsecondary education system in the world.

There are two regions in the State of California, designated as the Northern and Southern regions. Currently, there are thirty-six community colleges in the south which sponsor men's tennis and thirty-two in the north. The community colleges are further separated into twelve different conferences.

The first statewide championship tournament was held in 1960. As is the policy of the NJCAA, individuals who participate in California Community College programs are limited to a maximum of two years eligibility. Therefore, they cannot possibly match the consecutive championship records established by participants at four year institutions.

Two separate team champions are recognized by the California Association of Community Colleges. The dual team championship was established in 1974 and is comprised of matches of six singles players and three doubles teams. The tournament champions have been recognized since the inception of the championships in 1960, and are determined by points earned by players competing in the individual singles and doubles competition.

The dual team championship has been dominated by Northern

institutions. Canada Community College in Redwood City won five of the twelve State championships. Foothill Community College in Los Altos captured four State championships, giving the Northern schools nine of the twelve State dual team championship titles.

The history of the California State Community College Tournament Champions, determined by points earned in the individual competition, is similar to the dual team history. Of the twenty-six championships, the Northern schools have won twenty. Foothill Community College captured ten titles under coach Tom Chevington, and Canada Community College won six titles under former coach Rich Anderson.

Some of the names of the individual singles and doubles champions from the California Community Colleges are easily recognized by tennis aficionados. Larry Hall, the 1966 singles and doubles champion, is currently the coach at Brigham Young University. Larry Stefanki, the 1976 singles and doubles champion is currently playing on the professional tennis tournament circuit. Chip Hooper, the 1977 doubles champion, is also active on the professional circuit. But perhaps the best known name is that of Brad Gilbert, who won the State singles title

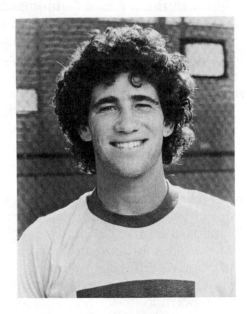

Brad Gilbert

in 1981. Presently, Gilbert is a touring professional who is rated among the top ten singles players in the entire world by the Association of Tennis Professionals.

The world of small college tennis, as is evident, is rich in tradition. It has produced the world's number one ranked doubles team and the U.S. Davis Cup Team representatives, one of the top ten singles players in the world, and numerous touring professional players. There is nothing small about the accomplishments of these players, nor of the institutions which produced them.

CHAPTER · 15

Candy Royer
Women's Tennis Coach
MIT

Candy Royer has served as the women's tennis coach and assistant professor of physical education at MIT since 1981. In 1985 Royer led MIT to a 14–2 record, which was the team's best mark in eleven years of varsity competition. That same year she was cited by the ITCA as the Division III Wilson Women's Coach of the Year in honor of her team's superior achievement.

A native of Sunbury, Pennsylvania, Royer is a 1971 graduate of Penn State, where she coached the Lady Lion's women's tennis squad for four years before joining MIT.

Royer is a USTA professional who has served as secretary and regional vice president of the Middle States Division. She is currently the Massachusetts State Chairman for Tennis, and a member of both the Eastern College Athletic Association (ECAC) and National Collegiate Athletic Association (NCAA) Division III Selection and Seeding tennis committees.

For the past several years Royer has served on the Board of Directors of the ITCA, as well as chair of its Division III women's rankings and awards committees.

CHAPTER · 15

SMALL COLLEGE TENNIS—
IN MICROCOSM

Candy Royer, Women's Tennis Coach—MIT

Stan Clark, in his chapter on The World of Small College Tennis, presents an outline and brief history of the organization and structure of Division II, III, NAIA and NJCAA. The purpose of my chapter is to expand on this by describing in greater detail a variety of aspects of importance within this world, including: educational opportunities; athletic scholarships; schedule of competition; dual match formats; and special awards.

EDUCATIONAL OPPORTUNITIES

The number of colleges with active tennis programs which are considered part of the small college tennis world exceeds 500 and are a widely diversified body of schools which encompass every type of institution from liberal arts and junior colleges to world-renowned technical institutes. Their philosophies and offerings are as diverse as the numbers of students searching for the right college. All major courses of study are available at small colleges—from Tyler junior college, which offers a major leading to a degree in professional tennis management and teaching, to MIT, which offers highly specific degrees in various fields of engineering, to a multitude of institutions capable of satisfying virtually any academic appetite.

The prospective student-athlete should consult one of the professionally prepared guides to colleges and universities in preparing to make an initial college application list. These guides are carefully designed to answer questions regarding admissions requirements, course offerings, size of the institutions, and estimated tuition and boarding costs. A student-athlete would be wise to consider the philosophy of an institution's education system. Compatability of the school and student will greatly enhance athletic performance and personal happiness.

ATHLETIC SCHOLARSHIPS/GRANTS-IN-AID

Under the current divisional structure, athletic aid is unavailable to Division III athletes. Division II, NAIA, and NJCAA schools all permit athletic aid to some degree. The typical aid-awarding institution might have 50–75 percent of its team on some percentage of financial assistance awarded on an athletic-talent basis. How aid is awarded, how much aid is given, and the criteria a student-athlete might be required to meet to receive aid is as varied as schools awarding aid.

There are a few source booklets available that will list the institutions, their division, and a contact person for information. One such guide is published by the USTA Center for Education and Recreational Tennis, 729 Alexander Road, Princeton, NJ 08540.

Another method of determining availability of aid based on tennis talent would be to call or write the colleges directly requesting such information from the Admissions office (be sure to mention you are an athlete and in what sport you have expertise). College admission offices generally have a good working relationship with all departments, and the athletic department is certainly no exception. Establishing early contact with the college coach is often a benefit in making initial admissions contact, as usually the Admissions office will refer athlete inquiries to the appropriate coach. The college coach is the resource when trying to determine whether aid is available and whether one's talents are appropriate for consideration of that school.

Athletic grants vary greatly from school to school but usually include room and board, tuition, books and fees. Not every student-athlete can expect to receive a full grant-in-aid, but might expect to receive a portion of aid commensurate with his or her expertise or financial need. For example, tuition costs at many state supported schools vary with the residency of the student (in-state/out-of-state). An institution might elect to award the in-state portion of tuition grants only. If the student-athlete is not from the institution's state, the out-of-state portion of costs would have to be assumed by the student-athlete. How aid is apportioned in each case is dependent on the coach's/institution's resources, philosophy and need of specific talent. The details of athletic grants are generally worked out by some combination of the financial aid officer, coach, parents/legal guardian, and the student-athlete.

SCHEDULE OF COMPETITION

It is important to note that while there are NCAA Rules and Regulations which dictate the total number of events permissible in an academic year (only, of course, for NCAA member schools) and these numbers vary by division, the individual institution is not required to play the maximum number of events allowed. A close look at an institution's history of event scheduling is important in assessing the seriousness of the program and the amount of competition to be expected.

Small college programs vary widely in the realm of event scheduling. Among the possibilities are institutions that compete during the fall, winter, and spring and also practice nine months of the year, to programs offering only one season of competition (usually fall or spring in tennis) with just a short pre-season practice schedule. Between these two extremes are the majority of Small College programs. Most Small Colleges play a minimum of ten to a maximum of thirty dual meet team matches per year. In addition, three to six individual tournaments per academic year might round out the competitive schedule. However, it should not always be assumed that more is necessarily better! The order and quality of match play frequently determines the successful programs which eventually qualify for national competition. It should also be remembered that not all institutions hold qualification for the national championships as a primary objective of their programs. For reasons of academic philosophy, coaching philosophy, or budgetary restraints, they may aspire only to league, conference or regional championship levels.

The institutions that frequently qualify for national events are generally those with two seasons of competition or a long pre-season (beginning in January) and a spring schedule of competition. Since all NCAA National Tennis Championships are held in May and June, it is vital to a team with national ambitions to have competition during the March through May period.

An institution is free to construct a match play schedule that includes teams that are located within close proximity or permits the team to travel inter-regionally. The prospective college student would be well advised to examine the travel-time dictates of a particular college's schedule of competition.

DUAL MATCH AND CHAMPIONSHIP FORMATS

The dual match format at the Small College level is six singles and three doubles with the option to have singles players repeat in doubles combinations. A college coach is responsible for ranking singles players 1–6 with the number one player being the best, number two being second best, and so forth. Any singles players may be combined as a doubles team, but the doubles teams must also be arranged in order of ability. It is customary to play the singles matches prior to the doubles, but if both coaches agree, doubles may be played first. There is usually a ten minute rest period following singles matches before the start of doubles.

Dual matches are presently scored with the modified No Ad system —a sudden death point at 3 points-all decides the winner of each game. Sets that reach a tie at 6 games-all are decided by a 12-point tie-breaker. A team match is won by the team who wins at least five of the nine matches. Although it is possible that a match may be decided by singles play, it is customary to complete all matches. Upon the agreement of both coaches, however, a match may be shortened or suspended after one team has won the five matches necessary for a team victory.

Team conduct at dual matches is monitored by both coaches and usually a certified referee. Team members are permitted to encourage and cheer for each other as long as such activity is not distracting to the opponent.

CHAMPIONSHIP FORMATS

The NCAA National Championships are held in May for Divisions II, III, the NAIA and NJCAA, and the sites vary for each of these groups. The Championship format for Men's Small Colleges has been presented earlier by Stan Clark, but the structure for the Women's Small College Championships is somewhat different:

NCAA Division II and III Women's Tennis is divided into four regions of the country. An invitation to compete is extended to the top team in each of these regions. The remaining four teams are selected to the championship at large from all other institutions that apply. For the individual section of the championships, one singles player and one doubles team is automatically admitted to the 32 singles and 16 doubles teams draw. All other players are selected at large. The Division II singles and doubles finalists qualify for the Division I Championships. In Division III, only the singles and doubles champions are admitted to the Division I Championships.

The NAIA is divided into 32 districts nationally. The district team champion, as well as the district singles and doubles individual champions, advance to the national tournament. The draw is a full 256 draw for singles (the largest in the world) and 128 draw for doubles. Both draws are not flighted, but are open, and all players #1–6 from a team are put into the open draw. If the draw is not full after the district team and individual winners are in, then the second place team from the district that won the championship in the previous year is given an

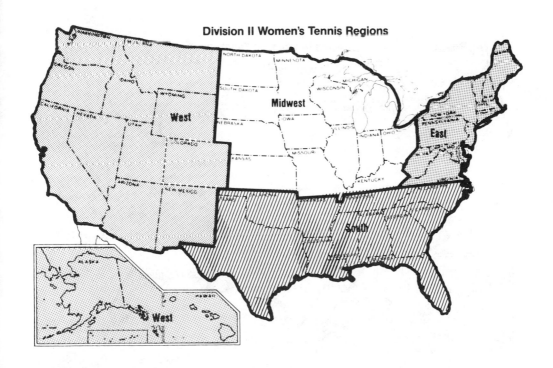

Division II Women's Tennis Regions

at-large berth. This process continues down the line, along with individual at-large berths to top-ranked NAIA-ITCA individuals.

Qualifications to the National Junior College Tennis Championships may occur in one of two ways: The top two teams of each region throughout the country may send their teams in full to the NJCAA National Tournament. The only other way to attend the tournament is to win a No. 1 position in singles or doubles. Only the individuals in the No. 1 position who are not a part of the two top teams may advance.

Only complete teams may be eligible to win the national title. Each team must have six singles players and three doubles teams. There are six flighted tournaments (#1–6) and three doubles flights (#1–3). Each team is awarded one point for each match one of its players wins. If a player has a bye in the first round, then he/she can only receive points after winning the first match. The team that accumulates the most points in both singles and doubles positions is declared the National Champion.

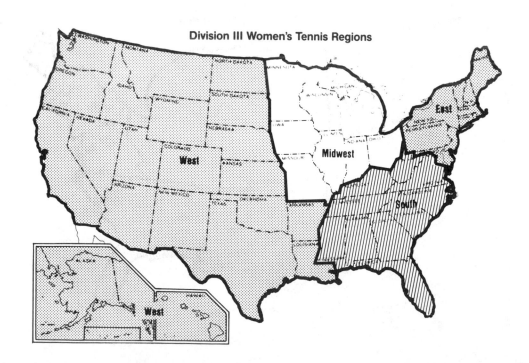

Division III Women's Tennis Regions

AWARDS

The Intercollegiate Tennis Coaches Association, in conjunction with both tennis industry companies and corporations, such as Rolex and Volvo, presents a variety of awards each year to players and coaches for both playing achievements, sportsmanship and scholarship. Selection procedures vary slightly among divisions. However, all players are eligible for nomination by their coaches or an opposing coach as long as the coach is a member of the ITCA.

The NCAA as an organization presents championship competition awards only. These go to the first eight finishers in Men's Division I, II, and III individual championships and the first three finishers in team competition. In Women's Division I competition, awards are presented to the first eight finishers in the team championship. In individual competition Divisions II and III present awards to the top four singles and doubles teams and the top three finishers in team competition. There are no other official awards presented by the NCAA to intercollegiate tennis players.

The ITCA has assumed an important leadership role in establishing its array of awards. ITCA awards embrace all divisions and are an indication of the importance of and commitment to all tennis players regardless of divisional status. Those of us involved in the world of small college tennis today are very proud of offering the same quality of recognition formerly reserved for only large college players.

It is our hope that the information presented here gives the reader an inside view of small college tennis. We believe there is excitement, quality competition, and student-athlete reward available to the small college participant that is not surpassed by the large college environment. The world of small college tennis is an experience restricted only by the imaginations of those who decide to make it their world.

CONCLUSION

College tennis is an exciting and challenging world, one which offers outstanding young players the special opportunity to improve their tennis skills in a carefully structured environment and at the same time experience all of the social and educational benefits of a college education.

It is no accident that most of the best American tennis players over the past one hundred years—Richard Sears and Dwight Davis at the turn of the century, Big Bill Tilden in the 20s, Ted Schroeder in the 30s, Pancho Segura and Tut Bartzen in the 40s, Tony Trabert and Vic Seixas in the 50s, Chuck McKinley, Arthur Ashe, Dennis Ralston and Stan Smith in the 60s, Jimmy Connors and John McEnroe in the 70s, and most recently Tim Mayotte, Paul Annacone and Mikael Pernfors—all of these superb tennis players competed in collegiate tennis.

We are very proud of the dedication and expertise of our collegiate coaches and believe that much of the success of our players is due to the important help which we have provided our student-athletes, both as tennis players and as people. There is an extraordinary variety of skills necessary to coaching tennis well—recruiter, psychologist, tactician, promoter, fundraiser, diplomat, cheerleader, confidante—all of these and more are vital roles played by the college coach. The need for creativity and resourcefulness never ends. Neither does the need for patience, and more patience, and even more patience, in dealing with a sport which is often a study in frustration.

And then there is the additional challenge of coaching collegiate athletes who are often as committed to their studies as they are to their world of sports. Yet, this same commitment to academics—in a recent ITCA poll the grade point average of the varsity college tennis players was 2.85, and over 90 percent received their college degrees—is ultimately the strength of our system. Not only the intrinsic value and importance of the college education, but also the severe test which it provides of the mental toughness and emotional stamina of our college athletes. Those players who can excel on the college level, and at the same time complete their undergraduate degrees, have survived a baptism by fire which will serve them well once and if they jump into the rigors of the pro-tour, besides offering an invaluable safety valve for those who don't make it as playing professionals. Similarly, the experience of competing in intercollegiate tennis provides a unique, transcendent training ground for the thousands of college tennis players who will be going on to leadership roles in such careers as law, medicine, teaching, business, and government. Once you have learned to handle the pressures of a tiebreaker with the team match outcome in the balance, few pressures later in life will seem unmanageable.

If one vital mandate of the ITCA as a service organization has been to improve the quality of our coaching, another equally important goal has been to enhance the level of competition for our collegiate players through national and interregional tournaments, as well as increasing the visibility and recognition of our tennis athletes through a multi-faceted system of rankings and awards.

Just ten years ago, the only national championships on the college tennis scene were the NCAA Championships at the end of the year, and collegiate tennis rankings didn't exist. Yet now, with the generous help of the tennis industry and such major corporate sponsors as Rolex Watch USA and Volvo Tennis and the steadfast support of our college tennis scene by the United States Tennis Association, we have been able to create a comprehensive structure of national ITCA championships for men and women (the Volvo Tennis/Collegiate Championships, the ITCA Women's All American Championships, the DuPont Clay Court Championships, Rolex National Small College and Rolex National Indoor Intercollegiate Singles and Doubles Championships, the USTA/ITCA Men's and Women's National Indoor Team Championships, and over sixty ITCA interregional events). These events take place throughout the academic year and are all part of our Volvo Tennis/Collegiate Series. As such, they will receive additional promotional exposure and increased credibility through our partnership with Volvo Tennis. Volvo Tennis will also be supporting on all levels— NCAA Divisions I, II, III; the National Association of Intercollegiate Athletics (NAIA); and junior and community colleges—our ITCA Volvo Tennis/Collegiate Rankings for teams, singles, and doubles.

And yet, despite all of the exciting progress made over the past decade by the ITCA and collegiate tennis in general, we still have much to accomplish on many fronts. It is our hope that this book will be a positive step in our march toward these sometimes elusive, but nevertheless reachable, goals.

ITCA RULES AND REGULATIONS

INTRODUCTION

The purpose of the official ITCA Rulebook is to unify for college players, coaches and officials all of the rules and regulations which are unique to college tennis and also to highlight those USTA rules which most often apply to college tennis.

The rules set forth in our booklet govern all collegiate play except in the few cases where a specific conference rule or NCAA tournament rule differs from the ITCA rule. In this case the conference rule or NCAA rule takes precedence over the ITCA rule. Otherwise, all ITCA coaches are expected to follow the ITCA rules as closely as possible. Failure to do so should be reported immediately to the ITCA Ethics and Infractions Committee and/or the ITCA National Ranking Committee.

We shall be providing copies of our revised ITCA Rulebook to all college tennis coaches, as well as to many college players and officials. In doing so we hope to make it easier for all participants in collegiate tennis events to enjoy college tennis at the highest level of sportsmanship and intercollegiate competition.

I. GENERAL RULES AND GUIDELINES

A. The Code

All college match play will follow "The Code."

B. Calls

1. In all matches without an umpire and linesman, or with only a solo chair umpire, each player must make all calls on his/her side of the court, and whenever there is any doubt, must make the call in favor of his/her opponent.

2. If a player is not sure of a call, it must be played as good. Balls should be called "out" only when there is a space visible between the ball and the line. There are no "unsighted" calls. A player should never seek aid from a solo chair umpire, spectator, teammate or coach in making a line call.

3. "Out" calls must be made immediately as the ball bounces, or

simultaneously with hitting the ball. If no audible or visible call is made immediately, the ball must be considered good. A player may reverse an erroneous "out" call after an inspection of a mark; in this case the player reversing the call will lose the point.

4.   An "out" call must be reversed if the player making the call realizes he/she has made a mistake or is uncertain of the call. The point goes to the opponent. It never is played over. There are never any lets in such circumstances.

5.   In a solo chair umpired match without linespersons, should a player make an erroneous call which is overruled by the umpire (following a verbal appeal made by the opponent), the player making the erroneous call shall lose the point.

6.   A player is obligated to call against himself/herself (with the exception of a first service) any ball that he/she clearly sees out on the opponent's side of the net.

7.   Any call by one's opponent should be challenged only by the query: "Are you sure of your call?" No further discussion or delay is permitted. If the player having made the call is uncertain, he/she loses the point. It is never played over.

8.   A doubles partner is obligated to disagree with his/her partner if an erroneous "out" call is made. When doubles partners disagree on a line call, the point goes to the opposing team. The point is never replayed.

9.   No player is allowed to cross his/her side of the net in order to point out a mark or discuss a problem while the match is in play. A player doing so is subject to the ITCA Point Penalty System.

10.   Calls involving a ball touching a player, a player touching the net, a player touching his or her opponent's court, hitting an opponent's return before it has passed the net and a double bounce must be called by the player committing the infraction. If there is a solo chair umpire, he or she also has the right to make these calls.

11.   There are no lets in college tennis except for a let cord, an interruption by an official or a spectator, or if play is interfered with by an outside object. Let calls must be made by either opponent at the instant that the let occurs. Requests for lets may not be made after a point is ended. The solo chair umpire will call a let if, in his or her judgment, the player is unaware of an invading object and is endangered by it.

12.   A player may request a linesperson(s), who will be provided if

and when available, but play must continue within five minutes even if attempts are still being made to obtain a linesperson.

13. A player or coach may request a footfault judge. A player may request that an opponent avoid footfaults, but he/she cannot call a footfault on an opponent. All footfaults must be called by an umpire or roving footfault judge, who need not be stationed on the baseline in order to call footfaults as long as his position give him/her a clear view of the fault.

14. The server should call the score before each point. If a disagreement occurs, the disputed point or game must be replayed (except if in reference to a question of fact). Otherwise, the match is resumed at the point where both players can agree.

15. In a solo chair umpired match, if a player has been overruled twice on his/her own calls, each and any subsequent overrule by the chair will be penalized through the ITCA Point Penalty System. Please note that the failure to have an appeal upheld is not considered an overrule.

16. During a solo chair umpired match, the umpire cannot overrule a call unless it is challenged verbally at that moment (not at the end of the point) by the opposing player. The umpire cannot give assistance on unsighted balls. The umpire will caution any player making excessive appeals for the apparent sake of disrupting play; this will be followed by the application of the ITCA Point Penalty System, if the umpire's judgment determines this necessary.

C. Service and Service Returns

1. During each game, the server and receiver must both be ready to begin the next point within a thirty-second interval, but each has the right to the full thirty seconds to prepare for the next play.

2. The receiver should make no effort to return a serve when not ready, if wishing to maintain a valid right to a let.

3. Faults played as good must be questioned before the service return is played by the server. All challenges must be made verbally. If the receiver returns the ball in a solo chair umpired match and the server believes the serve is long, the server is allowed to make a first volley or half-volley before appealing to the chair umpire for an overrule. But if he/she remains in the back court, an appeal must be made before playing the ball. If the overrule is granted, the server gets

two serves if the overrule is on the first serve and one serve if the overrule is on a second serve. If the overrule is not granted, then the point goes to the receiver.

4.   A player is entitled to feint with his/her body. He/she may change position on the court at any time including while the server is tossing the ball to serve. In doubles the partner of the server or the receiver may do the same. A player may not wave a racquet, or arms, nor may he/she talk or make noise in an attempt to create a distraction.

5.   Returning a service that is obviously out (accompanied by an "out" call) is a form of rudeness, and when the receiver knows that in making these returns it bothers the server, it is gamesmanship. However, a fast serve that just misses the line will frequently be returned as a matter of self-protection, even though an "out" call is made. The speed of deliveries is such that if the receiver waited for a call before starting to make a return, he/she would be overpowered.

6.   If the receiver returns a ball and simultaneously calls it "out" but then overrules the first call because he/she realizes that the serve was good, the receiver loses the point because of interference of play, even if the return is good.

7.   In doubles, if the receiver has indicated that he/she is ready and the server serves an ace, the receiver's partner cannot claim a let because he/she (the partner of the receiver) was not ready. The receiver's indication of being ready is tantamount to indicating that their team is ready.

8.   In returning service, it is preferable that the partner of the receiver should call the service line, with the receiver calling the center line and the side line.

D. ITCA Scoring Systems

1.   In small college tennis (NCAA Divisions II, III; the NAIA and junior and community colleges) the Van Alen Simplified Scoring System (No Ad Scoring) will be used in all ITCA tennis matches, both team and individual, except for the Rolex National Small College Intercollegiate Championships.

2.   In all Division I men's and women's ITCA national singles and doubles events, regular scoring will be used.

3.   In Division I men's tennis, regular scoring may be used in dual meet matches if both coaches agree in advance to use it and its use does not conflict with conference rules. Unless both coaches agree to use regular scoring, no ad scoring will be used.

4. In Division I women's tennis, regular scoring will be used in all dual meet competition unless both coaches agree otherwise, or conference rules dictate otherwise.

5. The USTA 12-point tiebreaker will be used whenever a set reaches 6-6. All sets, including the final set, will use the tiebreaker system.

E. ITCA Point Penalty System

1. The referee should always issue a general explanation to players and coaches prior to the match about the ITCA Point Penalty System and define appropriate court behavior and enumerate specific types of conduct violations (such as racquet abuse, ball abuse, abuse of officials, delay of game, inappropriate language, or physical contact), and in general, unsportsmanlike conduct.

The "Warning" is no longer part of the ITCA Point Penalty System, which now consists of the following:

(a) Point Penalty
(b) Game Penalty
(c) Disqualification *
  * The referee has sole power to disqualify players during dual meet matches and sanctioned tournaments. During ITCA national and sanctioned events, the referee has the power to disqualify upon consultation with the tournament committee; the referee is always a member of the tournament committee in ITCA national and sanctioned events.

2. Ethical and sportsmanlike conduct of players shall be observed at all times. Use of profanity, obscene gestures or unsportsmanlike behavior shall subject the offending player to the ITCA Point Penalty System.

3. The ITCA Carry Over Rule will be in use during ITCA national and sanctioned tournaments (singles, doubles and team) and dual match competition, as follows:

(a) In a team match, the ITCA Point Penalty System is cumulative throughout any individual singles match but is also self-contained. Assessed penalties do not carry over to doubles; doubles starts clean. If a player is defaulted in singles, he/she can still play doubles, except in extraordinary and extreme circumstances determined by the referee. In doubles, two players are penalized as a team and not as individual players.

(b) In team matches where doubles are played first, the assessed penalties to a doubles team are also self-contained and not carried over to singles. If a doubles team is defaulted during its match, the players can still play singles, again except in extraordinary circumstances, as determined by the referee.

(c) In a dual meet match in which singles are played first, if a player commits a code violation after his or her match is over, regardless of whether he or she had been assessed penalty points during the match, a point penalty will be assessed to his or her doubles match. If he or she is not playing doubles, the point penalty will be assessed to the No. 1 doubles team, or the highest other doubles match still in progress.

(d) In a dual meet match, if a doubles team finishes its match and at the end of the match one or both of the doubles players acts in a manner which violates the behavior code, a point penalty will be assessed to the highest other doubles match still in progress.

(e) In a dual meet match where doubles are played first, if a player commits a code violation after the doubles match is over, regardless of whether he or she had been assessed during the match, a point penalty will be assessed to his or her singles match. If he or she is not playing singles, the point penalty will be assessed to the highest singles match about to start or already in progress.

4. All physical contact between players during a team match is prohibited. Any such contact will result in an immediate default to the player who initiates this contact. If the offense takes place in the singles match and the offending player is playing doubles, he or she will be defaulted from doubles and another player may be substituted in his or her place. In the case of a dual match where doubles are played first, the offending player will be prohibited from playing in the singles match; all other players will move up a position and a player will be substituted at the bottom of the line-up.

5. In team matches, it is only the referee or chair umpire who may implement the ITCA Point Penalty System, unless both coaches agree otherwise.

F. Playing Court Restrictions

1. No players or spectators will be allowed on the playing court or an adjacent court other than the participants, except to attend to an ill or injured player, or in the case where both coaches agree otherwise. Under no circumstances may a player suffering from natural loss of condition be attended to.

2. In no case may the team players harrass the opposing players; the ITCA Point Penalty System will be applied in this situation upon the match in progress of the offending team.

G. Warm-up

1. Players will have a maximum of five minutes for warm-up prior to a match: but if the teams are not able to take their thirty minute warm-up before the start of the team match, then a ten minute warm-up is permitted. The chair umpire or tournament referee is the timekeeper; otherwise, the coaches must oversee the warm-up period.

2. All warm-up serves must be taken prior to the start of play. If the match is umpired, the umpire should give a warning when two minutes are left in the warm-up.

H. Injury Time-Outs

1. One injury time-out is permitted, per injury per match, for a maximum of three minutes once the trainer begins treating the player. A player may suffer more than one injury per match and have a stoppage for each injury. Each injury may be further treated at the changeover. (A trainer should always be available at the playing site to render assistance to the player.)

2. Cramps are considered loss of condition and do not qualify as an injury time-out. If a player cannot continue to play due to cramps, the ITCA Point Penalty System will go into effect.

3. A blister is also a loss of condition, but a blood blister qualifies as an injury time-out.

4. Loss of a contact lens is considered an equipment time-out; a player will be given three minutes to take care of the problem.

I. Rest Periods.

1. There shall be no rest period between the second and third sets.

2. When changing sides, a maximum rest period of 90 seconds may be taken by the players. Umpires, if any, should call "Time, Gentlemen" at the end of 1 minute to get the players back on the court if they haven't already left their chairs.

3. Following a two-set match a maximum of a 45-minute rest period will be permitted in a singles or doubles tournament before the next

match. After a three-set match, players will be permitted a maximum one-hour rest period prior to playing the next match. The tournament committee has the right to modify this if considered necessary.

J. Coaching

1.   Coaching of the players is permitted to be continuous throughout the match as long as it does not interfere with play. It is understood that the purpose of such coaching is solely to offer advice to the player and not in any way to distract or annoy the opposing player.

2.   In men's tennis, coaching is allowed by the head coach and either the assistant coach or a designated player who is not competing at that moment; a maximum of two coaches is permitted to coach at any one time during the match. In women's tennis, coaching is permitted by both the coaches and the players, but only one person may coach on a court at one time.

3.   During match play a coach is only permitted to sit at the center side of the court and can only move from one court to another during changeovers. No coaching is permitted within the playing area by coaches standing at the side or corners of the court; coaching is permitted by coaches standing anywhere outside the fence surrounding the court, as long as this does not distract the other player during a point.

4.   At no time is a coach permitted to initiate a conversation with the opposing player or in any way get involved with an on-court problem, except at the request of the solo chair umpire, tournament referee or the player or the coach of the player involved. At no time should a player initiate a conversation with an opposing coach.

5.   Should it become necessary for a coach to be consulted due to a problem on the court, it is preferable that the opposing coach also be present.

K. Coaches' Code of Conduct

1.   It is understood that the conduct of coaches throughout the dual meet match—before, during and after—must be exemplary in terms of sportsmanship and behavior. Any deviation from such behavior will result in: first, a direct warning from the referee in charge of the match; subsequently, the barring of the coach from continuing to coach for the rest of the team match. If the coach refuses to obey the referee,

the referee will have the right to declare the team match a default. Subsequent to either of the latter two incidents, the referee must make a written report to the Athletic Director of the coach in question, also copying the Ethics and Infractions Committee of the ITCA.

L. Equipment and Attire

1. Tennis Balls

(a) A minimum of three new yellow tennis balls, USTA-approved, must be provided for each match, unless both coaches agree otherwise. The balls must be changed at the end of the second set unless both coaches agree otherwise.

(b) The official tennis ball of the ITCA is the Wilson ball, which must be used in all ITCA national and regional championships, and all ITCA sanctioned events.

(c) Whenever possible, ITCA coaches should use the Wilson tennis ball in all dual meet matches.

(d) In a solo chair umpired match, it is the judgment of the umpire whether and when to replace a lost or damaged ball. In any other situation, the referee should make this decision. If a referee is not available, then both coaches must agree on this decision. In all cases, replacement with a new ball may only occur within two games of when the new balls were first introduced. Otherwise, replacements should be made with balls of comparable quality to those lost.

2. Tennis Attire

(a) Whenever possible, all ITCA competitors should wear exclusively the official uniform of their institutions in competition, warm-up for competition and during the awards ceremonies. In the event official uniforms are not available, wearing apparel with institutional emblems or initials and/or name may be worn and are recommended as alternative uniforms.

(b) The use by college players of all athletic equipment and clothing from a manufacturer or commercial enterprise must adhere strictly to NCAA rules.

M. Seeding

Under ITCA rules, it is permissible to seed players in a ratio of one seed per four players. It is also permissible to place additional players under a similar ratio of one to four.

N. Draws

In all national ITCA events, both singles, doubles and team, it is obligatory (unless impossible) to separate players (and teams) by geographical regions in all first-round matches, and also to separate players from the same team in opposite halves, quarters, etc.

II. TEAM AND TOURNAMENT COMPETITION

A. Dual Meet Matches

1.   Conference rules will supersede ITCA rules when matches are played between two teams within the conference. If a dual meet match is played between teams from different conferences, then the ITCA rules must be followed without exception.

2.   Competing schools should employ written contracts for dual matches. These contracts should be initiated by the home team and should include all specified agreements or arrangements, such as practice times and courts, starting time of match, use of indoor facilities, scoring system, match format, balls, etc. Failure of a team to honor the contract will result in a default unless the nonparticipating team is released in writing from this obligation by the other coach.

3.   Each team should be accompanied by a bona fide institutional representative at all matches.

4.   It is the obligation of the home coach to provide a neutral qualified referee for every team match; if at all possible, a USTA certified referee. It is obligatory for any Division I team wishing to be ranked by the ITCA to do so. Failure to do so should be reported immediately to the ITCA Rankings Committee.

5.   It is the obligation of the referee to make sure that the start of the team match conforms to the time agreed upon by both coaches in their contract. The home coach should make this decision only if there is no referee.

6.   Umpires or scorekeepers for each match should be provided whenever possible.

7.   It is the obligation of the home coach to make sure that the behavior of the spectators remains fair and unabusive. Under no circumstances may alcoholic beverages be permitted at the site of a

collegiate tennis match. Failure of the coach to insure proper behavior shall result in the application of the ITCA Point Penalty System against the home team and in extreme cases, forfeiture of the match.

8. In small college tennis, a collegiate team match must consist of six singles and three doubles to be considered for team ranking purposes.

9. In Division I tennis, in a collegiate team match any format other than six singles/three doubles may be used as long as six individual players per team are involved, both coaches agree on the format, and the format used is not in conflict with conference rules.

10. The order of play if three courts are used is: 1,2,3 singles followed by 4,5,6 singles unless both coaches agree otherwise. Match No. 4 will follow Match No. 1; 5 will follow Match No. 2; and 6 will follow Match No. 3.

11. All matches shall be best of three sets.

12. Unfinished individual matches shall not count in any way as team scores.

13. The winner of a dual match shall be determined when a majority of individual matches have been won (i.e. five of nine).

a) In women's tennis and all men's tennis except Division I, unless there are extenuating circumstances, all other matches should be played to completion. An unfinished match will be treated as a default by the withdrawing team, unless the decision not to finish is mutually made by both coaches.

b) In men's Division I tennis, the team match will be stopped immediately once the singles matches have been completed and one team has won five team points, unless both coaches agree otherwise or conference rules so dictate.

14. In the event of inclement weather, a team match must be played and/or continued indoors if tennis facilities are available and of intercollegiate varsity quality, as determined either by the conference or ITCA regional committee. The decision to move indoors should be made before the start of the match except in the case of rain or darkness. Inclement weather is defined as follows: If one hour before the start of the match: (a) The temperature is less than 50 degrees; (b) Rain; (c) Wind at 20 miles per hour or greater. If the match is moved indoors due to inclement weather or darkness, it must stay indoors until the completion of the match, unless both coaches agree otherwise.

15.   Procedure to follow in the event of darkness or inclement weather or lack of acceptable indoor facilities should be reached between coaches prior to the start of a match, preferably in the original match contract. If a postponed match can be scheduled within a 48 hour period, the match should resume at the point of interruption. Otherwise, the match is not replayed or continued at a later date unless both coaches agree to do so or unless conference rules dictate otherwise.

B. Facilities and Equipment

The host school shall provide for each match:
(1)   Center net straps
(2)   Singles sticks and net measuring sticks
(Note: Singles sticks shall be used in all matches where singles will be played on a doubles court.)
(3)   Scoreboards to display the running score for each court.
(4)   Team scoreboards and scorekeepers, when possible*
(5)   USTA approved championship tennis balls
(6)   Water, first aid supplies and trainer services, when possible
(7)   Dressing facilities, if requested by the visiting team (The visiting team is usually responsible for its own towels.)

*Such scorekeepers must act in an impartial and nonpartisan manner.

C. Practice Courts

1.   A minimum of three practice courts (the same courts as will be used in the match itself) must be made available to the visiting team for a minimum of two hours in the afternoon before the scheduled match (if requested by the visiting coach); and one hour on the morning of the match with the visiting coach requesting these arrangements in writing a minimum of one week before arrival. The only exception to this rule will be made if extenuating circumstances governing varsity court usage renders this impossible, and this must be confirmed in writing by the Director of Athletics of the host institution.

2.   The visiting team must be permitted to hit on three of the match courts for a minimum of 30 minutes directly before the start of the team match.

D. Umpire, Footfault Judge and Linespersons

It is the home coach's responsibility to have available qualified volunteers, if such a request is made, and to make such an assignment immediately, in consultation with the neutral referee. Play may be suspended for a maximum of five minutes while an official is sought. If no one else is available, the neutral referee may be asked to become the solo chair umpire, while still also serving as neutral referee to the best of his/her ability.

E. Trainer

It is the obligation of the host institution to provide the services of a qualified trainer, preferably at courtside or at a training facility close (within a five-minute walk) to the match site. The referee must use his/her discretion in determining the time allotted to locate a trainer if one cannot be found or is not available with five minutes of the injury.

F. Starting Time

All matches should begin promptly at the specified starting time. Individual matches may be delayed a predetermined period of time to accommodate a player late for a legitimate reason, by mutual agreement of both coaches.

G. Warm-up

The length of the warm-up shall not exceed five minutes, except if the visiting team has not had a minimum of 30 minutes warm-up directly before the start of the team match.

H. Team Line-ups

1. Coaches shall exchange their complete singles and doubles line-ups simultaneously, no later than 30 minutes prior to the start of the team match. At the same time each coach must also exchange his or her ITCA Scorebook, with all team results throughout the year up to that day. Players must be physically able to play a match in order to be kept in the line-up of the team match.

2.   In singles, players must compete in order of ability, the best player on the team playing at the No. 1 position, the second best at No. 2, and so on through all positions. In case of injury or sickness, all players must move up. This rule shall also apply to doubles play, with the strongest doubles team at No. 1, etc. The team appearing with an insufficient number of players shall default matches at the bottom of the line-up (i.e. the six-man team appearing with five players must default at the No. 6 singles position and in doubles, at the No. 3 position).

(a)   If the No. 1 player is not available to compete, all players must move up one position. The No. 1 singles match cannot be forfeited.

(b)   If either coach feels that the line-up as presented is not fair, an appeal may be made to the referee, who must then decide as to what the corrent line-up should be. If such an appeal cannot be made before the start of the match, a coach should notify the opposing coach that a protest will be filed with the ITCA Ranking Committee following the match. If the ITCA Ranking Committee should decide this line-up was not fair, it has the right to consider the entire team match forfeited and this forfeit to be counted as such for ITCA ranking purposes and also be recommended for similar consideration to the NCAA Selection Committee.

3.   Once a dual meet match has begun, an individual singles or doubles match has begun, the match must remain on the same court until its conclusion, unless both coaches agree to move it to another court. In an ITCA national or sanctioned event, the referee has the authority to move matches, as necessary.

4.   In singles prior to the start of each individual team match (the point when both players begin their warm-ups on the court together), any player may be withdrawn from the line-up; in this case, all players move up a spot. If individual matches have begun, which prohibits players from moving up, then the withdrawn player forfeits that match.

5.   Each player shall be ready to start doubles competition with 15 minutes of his/her singles match. Once all four players are available to begin one of the doubles matches, it is understood that it shall be played on whatever court may be available unless both coaches agree that they prefer to wait until the end of the remaining singles matches.

6.   In men's tennis, once the team match has officially begun, only a direct line substitution may be made for any of the three submitted

doubles teams and a maximum of one player may be substituted for any of the doubles teams. If both players in a doubles team are incapacitated, then that doubles match must be forfeited.

7.   In women's tennis, if two players are incapacitated the other two doubles teams must move up and a new doubles team submitted at the third spot. However, if the doubles matches have already begun, the new team must be directly substituted for the incapacitated team.

8.   In men's and women's tennis, if the team match has been won in singles, teams may be substituted in doubles without restriction, but the teams must still be kept in order of ability.

9.   In back-to-back dual meet matches, the team line-up may be changed. In women's tennis, a player may move up or down two positions when matches are scheduled on consecutive days. In men's tennis, a player may move up or down one position in this situation.

10.   If a player is injured or ill and cannot play for a week or longer, the coach should use his/her discretion in determining where to place the player in the team line-up. If the player has played the majority of his/her matches at one position, he or she must be placed within two positions up or down to be within a "range."

I. Post Match Considerations

1.   After the completion of a dual meet match, players have five minutes to gather their equipment from the court and leave the playing area.

2.   It is the obligation of the home coach to report the scores of the team match to the local media.

3.   In all ITCA national championship events, it is mandatory that the players make themselves available upon request for media interviews within ten minutes immediately following the completion of their matches. Failure to do so may result in disqualification from the tournament or disqualification from the next ITCA rankings, such decision to be made by the Men's and Women's ITCA National Tournament Committees.

4.   If a coach feels that a decision by the neutral referee was incorrect and affected the result of the team match, he or she should make an official protest in writing to the ITCA Ranking Committee, also copying his/her athletic director and, when appropriate, the conference

commissioner, and the referee and the USTA office if the referee is USTA certified. The decision made about this situation by the ITCA Ranking Committee will be binding concerning ITCA rankings and will also be communicated to the athletic directors, conference commissioners and NCAA Chairs for their consideration.

J. Sanctioned Team Tournaments

1. In a sanctioned team tournament, any team withdrawing from the event once a written commitment has been made may only do so because of injuries or academic probation affecting a minimum of three of the starting eight players. The injuries and probation must be attested to by the team doctor and athletic director in writing. Otherwise, the team withdrawing will be penalized with three defaults for ranking purposes.

2. In a men's ITCA sanctioned or national team event, all team line-ups must be submitted to the tournament committee the day prior to the start of the tournament. Once these team line-ups have been submitted and approved, no changes may be made in the order of the singles or doubles line-up throughout the duration of the entire team tournament.

3. Failure to follow the ITCA rules as outlined in the ITCA Rulebook in any ITCA sanctioned team tournament will cause the forfeit of the ITCA sanction, and the results from such an event will not be considered for ITCA ranking purposes.

III. SELECTION CRITERIA FOR ITCA NATIONAL AND ITCA REGIONAL CHAMPIONSHIPS

(ITCA national or regional championships are by definition only those tournaments exclusively organized and administered by the National and Regional ITCA Tournament Committees.)

A. *Women's All American Championships; Men's Volvo Tennis/Collegiate Championships*

1. Regional Selection Criteria

(a) Regional results have major priority over national results.

(b) Last year's results as reflected in the final ITCA Volvo Tennis/Regional Rankings have first priority.

(c) Summer results should be used only in the extreme case of every criteria being equal.

(d) A region may decide to use a regional tournament as a qualifier for the national event.

2. National At-Large Selection Criteria

(a) ITCA Volvo Tennis/Preseason Rankings have first priority.

(b) Early Fall college results, when available

(c) Significant summer results

(d) National Tournament Committee reserves right of making final decisions which are binding.

Note: Freshmen are eligible only as Wild Cards or as earned berths in the main draw through the qualifying tournament.

3. Wild Cards are determined by sponsors and tournament directors.

4. Procedure:

(a) All players' complete entry information must be sent by the coach to the National Tournament Committee and Regional Tournament Committee by published deadlines.

(b) Regional entries will be notified by Regional Chairs; national at-large selections notified by ITCA office.

(c) Complete seeding information must be sent to National Tournament Chairs by coaches of all participants.

B. *DuPont National Clay Court Championships*

1. Regional Selection Criteria

(a) Regional results have priority over national results.

(b) National results should be used only if everything else appears even.

(c) A region may decide to use a regional tournament as a qualifier for the national event.

2. National At-Large Selection Criteria

   (a) ITCA Volvo Tennis/Preseason Rankings have first priority.
   (b) Early fall college results, when available.
   (c) National Tournament Committee reserves right of making final decisions which are binding.

3. Wild Cards are determined by sponsors and tournament directors.
4. Procedure:

   (a) All players' complete entry information must be sent to the National Tournament Committee and Regional Tournament Committee by published deadlines.
   (b) Regional entries will be notified by Regional Chairs; national at-large selections notified by ITCA office.
   (c) Complete seeding information must be sent to National Tournament Chairs by coaches of all participants.

C. *Rolex National Indoor Intercollegiate Singles and Doubles Championships (Small College and Division I)*

   1. Regional Selection Criteria

      (a) Selection is based exclusively on the ITCA Rolex Regional Qualifying Championships
      (b) Participation is not mandatory in the regional tournament to be considered for at-large selection to the national championship; however, players who do compete in the regional event will be given special consideration.
      (c) If a player is not attending school or is considered ineligible for collegiate competition by the school or its governing body during the time-frame of the regional championship, he/she will not be allowed to participate in these events but still will have the right to be considered by the National Tournament Committee for at-large or wild card selection for the National Tournament Championship.

   2. National At-Large Selection Criteria—Division I
      (a) Fall college results

(b) ITCA Volvo Tennis/Fall Rankings

(c) The following players will automatically be selected as at-large participants in the ITCA National Indoor Championships and they are not permitted to participate in the Regional Qualifying Tournaments:

- Winners, Women's All American Championships—singles and doubles
- Winners, Men's Volvo Tennis/Collegiate Championships—singles and doubles
- Winners, DuPont National Clay Court Championships
- Top 5 Returning Singles Players
- Top 2 Returning Doubles Teams
- Last year's ITCA National Indoor Champions

(e) If a player withdraws up to two weeks prior to the tournament, and as a result one region is lacking two representatives, then the Regional Committee may select a replacement. After this point, the replacement will be made from the alternate at-large list.

(f) If the winner of the regional doubles tournament is unable to play in the national event, and that region does not have another doubles team in the tournament, the finalist of the regional tournament will be invited.

(g) Once a player (or doubles team) has formally accepted its invitation to the national championship, he/she may not withdraw except for documented medical reasons. Failure to comply with this rule will count as two losses for ITCA ranking purposes.

3. Rolex National Small College Doubles Championships

Each small college division will select by Tournament Committee its best doubles team to participate in this event for men and women.

D. USTA/ITCA National Indoor Team Championships

1. Regional Selection Criteria

(a) Fall team regional results

(b) Last year's results, if a minimum of 50 percent of starting players are back.

(c) Recruits

(d) Fall Volvo Tennis/Collegiate Regional Rankings

(e) Regional championship results, if a region chooses to have a qualifier for the National Indoor Team Championship.

2. National At-Large Selection Criteria

(a) Fall Volvo Tennis/Collegiate Rankings

(b) National Tournament Committee judgment

3. Selection Process

The ITCA Tournament Committee will first make the at-large selections first, Number 1-20 (men) and Number 1-16 (women). After these at-large selections, any region which does not yet have a team representing it will then be asked to submit its No. 1 team, which will take the place of the last team selected at-large, in descending order. The ITCA Tournament Committee also has the right to make a wild card team selection if it should so wish.

4. Varsity Team Size

In the ITCA National Indoor Team Championships, a maximum of eight players on any one team will be permitted to compete throughout the event.

5. The team which wins the ITCA National Indoor Team Championship will automatically be ranked No. 1 in the next Volvo Tennis/Collegiate Rankings. Any team invited to participate in this championship which refuses to do so, unless three or more team members have documented medical excuses, will not be ranked among the top ten teams in the next three Volvo Tennis/Collegiate Rankings.

6. Consolation Tournaments

Participation in the consolation events of all national championships is mandatory. Failure to do so will result in two losses against the player's ranking record.

IV. GENERAL INFORMATION

A. *Composition of ITCA Men's and Women's National Tournament Committees*

1. Chairs selected by the ITCA Executive Director
2. Committee members appointed by the Chairs of the National Tournament Committees
3. The National Tournament Committees should be comprised of no less than five coaches, taking geographical representation into consideration.

B. *Selection of ITCA Regional Chair and Composition of Regional Tournament Committees*

1. Chairs are appointed annually by Chairs of Men's and Women's Operating Committees.
2. Regional Committee should be comprised of no less than five coaches, appointed annually by each Regional Chair.
3. Regional Committee consists of representation from all major conferences and independents.
4. Regional Committee Chairs and members should be rotated every few years, whenever possible.

C. *Player Records*

It is the absolute obligation of all coaches to send complete player records to the appropriate ITCA Regional Committee and the ITCA National Tournament Committee at least a full week prior to the selection process if they wish their players to be considered. The complete ITCA national tournament calendar will be circulated in ITCA Newsletters in the Spring before each season and again early in the Fall. A coach's failure to submit complete and accurate player records by each deadline may result in automatic disqualification of the player for this event.

D. *Sanctions*

(See also Section II.J 1-3)
1. A tournament must be sanctioned by the ITCA in order for its results to count for ranking purposes.
2. The Tournament Director is responsible for obtaining the ITCA sanction, paying sanction fees, ensuring that participants' coaches are current ITCA members and filing results with the ITCA office within three days of completion of the tournament.

3. Complete typed results must be filed with the ITCA office, the national ranking coordinator and ITCA chair of the regional in which the sanctioned event took place.

4. The ITCA office will notify all regional chairs of tournaments sanctioned in their designated regions and inform them of any infractions which make the tournament results null and void for rankings purposes.

5. It is the responsibility of the coach to file his or her team's and individual player's results with the appropriate regional and national rankings coordinator within the deadlines for reporting dates in order for the team and players to be eligible for rankings consideration. Results from all sanctioned tournaments should also be recorded in the ITCA/Volvo Tennis Scorebook.

6. Failure to follow the outlined sanctioning procedure will make all results from that tournament ineligible for ITCA ranking procedures.

APPENDIX·II

SMALL COLLEGE TENNIS

DIVISION II TEAM CHAMPIONSHIP RESULTS—MEN

Year	Champion	Coach
1963	Los Angeles State	Scotty Deeds
1964	Los Angeles State	Scotty Deeds
	Southern Illionis	John LeFevre
1965	Los Angeles State	Scotty Deeds
1966	Rollins	Norm Copeland
1967	Long Beach State	Dan Campbell
1968	Fresno State	Richard Murray
1969	Northridge State	Dave Sterle
1970	Cal-Irvine	Myron McNamara
1971	Cal-Irvine	Myron McNamara
1972	Cal-Irvine	Myron McNamara
	Rollins	Norm Copeland
1973	Cal-Irvine	Myron McNamara
1974	San Diego	Hans Wichary
1975	Cal-Irvine	Myron McNamara
	San Diego	Hans Wichary
1976	Hampton	Robert Screen
1977	Cal-Irvine	Myron McNamara
1978	SIU-Edwardsville	Kent DeMars
1979	SIU-Edwardsville	Kent DeMars
1980	SIU-Edwardsville	Kent DeMars
1981	SIU-Edwardsville	Kent DeMars
1982	SIU-Edwardsville	Kent DeMars
1983	SIU-Edwardsville	Kent DeMars
1984	SIU-Edwardsville	Kent DeMars
1985	Chapman College	Mike Edles
1986	Cal Poly, San Luis Obispo	Hugh Bream
1987	Chapman College	Mike Edles
1988	Chapman College	Mike Edles

DIVISION II SINGLES CHAMPIONS—MEN

Year	Champion	Institution
1963	Gil Rodriguez	Los Angeles State
1964	Gary Johnson	Los Angeles State
1965	Gary Johnson	Los Angeles State
1966	George Dickinson	Tenn-Chattanooga
1967	Sherwood Stewart	Lamar
1968	Bob Delgado	Los Angeles State
1969	Steve Messmer	Northridge State
1970	Earl O'Neill	Cal-Irvine
1971	Bob Chappell	Cal-Irvine
1972	Charlie Owens	Samford
1973	Bob Chappell	Cal-Irvine
1974	Andy Rae	San Diego
1975	Andy Rae	San Diego
1976	Tim Monroe	Cal-Davis
1977	Juan Farrow	SIU-Edwardsville
1978	Juan Farrow	SIU-Edwardsville
1979	Arjun Fernando	SIU-Edwardsville
1980	Juan Farrow	SIU-Edwardsville
1981	Ken Flach	SIU-Edwardsville
1982	Ken Flach	SIU-Edwardsville
1983	Ken Flach	SIU-Edwardsville
1984	Steve Riza	Stephen F. Austin
1985	Brian Talgo	Rollins
1986	Neil Smith	Stephen F. Austin
1987	Pat Emmet	Rollins
1988	Miles Walker	Chapman

DIVISION II DOUBLES CHAMPIONS—MEN

1963	Gil Rodriguez-John Lee, Los Angeles State
1964	Don Gaynor-Lee Reid, Cal Santa Barbara
1965	John Yeomans-Bill Schoen, Redlands
1966	Fred Suessmann-Ken Stuart, Long Beach State
1967	Fred Suessmann-Dennis Trout, Long Beach State
1968	Jim Powers-Gary Ogden, Fresno State
1969	Steve Messmer-George Benedict, Northridge State
1970	Gregg Jablonski-Charles Nachand, Cal-Irvine
1971	Ron Lague-John Lowman, Rollins

DIVISION II DOUBLES CHAMPIONS—MEN (Continued)

1972	John Lowman-Mike Strickland, Rollins
1973	Bob Chappell-Glenn Cripe, Cal-Irvine
1974	Andy Rae-Russell Watts, San Diego
1975	Scott Charnahan-Bob Wright, Cal-Irvine
1976	Roger de Santis Guedes-Bruce Foxworth, Hampton
1977	Jeff Williams-Curt Stalder, Cal-Irvine
1978	Par Svensson-Rick Goldberg, San Diego
1979	Juan Farrow-Arjun Fernando, SIU-Edwardsville
1980	Juan Farrow-Hugo Nunez, SIU-Edwardsville
1981	Brian Lusson-Bart Berstein, SW Texas State
1982	Ken Flach-Doug Burke, SIU-Edwardsville
1983	Ken Flach-Robert Seguso, SIU-Edwardsville
1984	Dave Delsini-Johan Sjogren, SIU-Edwardsville
1985	Tom Goles-Chris Langford, Stephen F. Austin
1986	Paul Landry-Bob Zoller, Cal Poly San Luis Obispo
1987	Barry Hancock-Paul Wekesa, Chapman College
1988	Robert Green-Barry Petts, Rollins

DIVISION II TEAM CHAMPIONSHIP RESULTS—WOMEN

Year	Champion	Coach
1982	California State-Northridge	Tony Davilla
1983	Tennessee-Chattanooga	Tommy Bartlett
1984	Tennessee-Chattanooga	Tommy Bartlett
1985	Tennessee-Chattanooga	Tommy Bartlett
1986	SIU-Edwardsville	Bob Meyers
1987	SIU-Edwardsville	Bob Meyers

DIVISION II SINGLES CHAMPIONS—WOMEN

Year	Champion	Institution
1982	Iwona Kuczynska	California State-Bakersfield
1983	Suzanne Kuhlman	Georgetown
1984	Elisabeth Calander	SIU-Edwardsville
1985	Elisabeth Calander	SIU-Edwardsville
1986	Nancy Roe	Northern Colorado
1987	Xenia Anastasiadou	Cal Poly-Pomona

DIVISION II DOUBLES CHAMPIONS—WOMEN

Year	Champions	Institution
1982	Wendy Luhmann-Cindy Woodhouse	California State-Northridge
1983	Sandra Elliott-Mary Gillach	Northern Colorado
1984	Sue McCulloch-Christine Picher	Tennessee-Chattanooga
1985	Sandra Elliott-Nancy Roe	Northern Colorado
1986	Sandra Elliott-Nancy Roe	Northern Colorado
1987	Christina Bokelund-Portia George	SIU-Edwardsville

DIVISION III TEAM CHAMPIONSHIP RESULTS—MEN

Year	Champion	Coach
1976	Kalamazoo	George Acker
1977	Swarthmore	Wm. C. B. Cullen
1978	Kalamazoo	George Acker
1979	Redlands	Jim Verdieck
1980	Gustavus Adolphus	Steve Wilkinson
1981	Claremont Mudd-Scripps	Hank Krieger
	Swarthmore	Michael Mullan
1982	Gustavus Adolphus	Steve Wilkinson
1983	Redlands	Jim Verdieck
1984	Redlands	Jim Verdieck
1985	Swarthmore	Mike Mullan
1986	Kalamazoo	George Acker
1987	Kalamazoo	George Acker
1988	Washington & Lee	Gary Franke

DIVISION III SINGLES CHAMPIONS—MEN

Year	Champion	Institution
1976	John Blomberg	Claremont-Mudd
1977	A. J. Shaka	Claremont-Mudd
1978	Chris Bussert	Kalamazoo
1979	Mark Tappan	Redlands
1980	Chris Burns	Kalamazoo
1981	Donovan Jones	Claremont-Mudd-Scripps
1982	Shaun Miller	Gustavus Adolphus

DIVISION III SINGLES CHAMPIONS—MEN (*Continued*)

Year	Champion	Institution
1983	Erik Michelsen	Redlands
1984	Scott Moore	Redlands
1985	Toby Clark	Principia
1986	Tim Corwin	Kalamazoo
1987	Toby Clark	Principia
1988	Noel Occomy	Brandeis

DIVISION III DOUBLES CHAMPIONS—MEN

Year	Champions & Institution
1976	Larry Davidson and John Irwin, Swarthmore
1977	Ben Johns and Stewart Jackson, Washington & Lee
1978	Chris Bussert and Jim Hosner, Kalamazoo
1979	Mike Capelouto and Ken Whitmer, Redlands
1980	John Mattke and Paul Holbach, Gustavus Adolphus
1981	Jim Hearn and Shaun Miller, Gustavus Adolphus
1982	Shaun Miller and Rich Skanse, Gustavus Adolphus
1983	Alex Gaeta and Bob Swartout, Rochester
1984	Eugene Jones and Dan Beers, U.C. San Diego
1985	Jeff Krieger and Shep Davidson, Swarthmore
1986	Jim Burda and Alex Palladino, Kalamazoo
1987	Jim Burda and Alex Palladino, Kalamazoo
1988	Frank Hinman and Lance Au, Claremont Mudd-Scripps

DIVISION III TEAM CHAMPIONSHIP RESULTS—WOMEN

Year	Champion	Coach
1982	Occidental	Lynn Pacala
1983	Principia	Lynn DeLaney
1984	Davidson	Caroline Brown
1985	UC-San Diego	Elizabeth Dudash
1986	Trenton State	Brenda Campbell
1987	UC-San Diego	Liz LaPlante

DIVISION III SINGLES CHAMPIONS—WOMEN

Year	Champion	Institution
1982	Beckie Donecker	Elizabethtown
1983	Jean Marie Sanders	Occidental
1984	Courtney Allen	Principia
1985	Courtney Allen	Principia
1986	Debbie Daniel	Trenton State
1987	Courtney Allen	Principia

DIVISION III DOUBLES CHAMPIONS—WOMEN

Year	Champions	Institution
1982	Kathleen McFadden-Jean Marie Sanders	Occidental
1983	Kristi Martin-Wendy Clark	Principia
1984	Courtney Allen-Suzy Verheul	Principia
1985	Jessica Vernon-Nadine Akimoto	UC-San Diego
1986	Courtney Allen-Sue Godfrey	Principia
1987	Courtney Allen-Sue Godfrey	Principia

NAIA TEAM CHAMPIONSHIP RESULTS—MEN

1952	Pepperdine CA
1953	Hardin-Simmons TX
1954	Redlands CA
1955	Lamar Tech TX
1956	Lamar Tech TX
1957	Lamar Tech TX
1958	Lamar Tech TX
1959	Lamar Tech TX
1960	Lamar Tech TX
1961	Pan American TX
1962	Pan American TX
1963	Pan American TX
1964	Pan American TX
1965	Pan American TX
1966	Redlands CA
1967	Redlands CA
1968	Redlands CA

NAIA TEAM CHAMPIONSHIP RESULTS—MEN *(Continued)*

1969	Redlands CA
1970	Redlands CA
1971	Redlands CA
1972	East Texas State
1973	Redlands CA
1974	Redlands CA
1975	Redlands CA
1976	Mercyhurst PA
1977	Flagler FL
1978	East Texas State
1979	Atlantic Christian MO
1980	Redlands CA
1981	Southwest Texas
1982	Southwest Texas
1983	Belhaven MS
1984	Atlantic Christian MO
	Southwest Baptist MO
1985	Lander College SC
1986	Flagler FL
1987	Auburn-Montgomery AL
1988	Lander College SC

NAIA SINGLES & DOUBLES CHAMPIONS—MEN

Singles

1952	Butch Krikorian, San Jose State CA
1953	S. L. Shofner, Central State OK
1954	Gene Land, Central State OK
1955	James Schmidt, Lamar Tech TX
1956	James Schmidt, Lamar Tech TX
1957	George Nadlay, Lamar Tech TX
1958	Pedro Bueno, Lamar Tech TX
1959	John Bennett, Lamar Tech TX
1960	Rudy Hernando, Lamar Tech TX
1961	John Sharpe, Pan American TX
1962	Don Russell, Pan American TX
1963	Ken Lang, Pan American TX
1964	Don Kierbow, Corpus Christi TX
1965	George Kon, Pan American TX
1966	John Yeomans, Redlands CA

NAIA SINGLES & DOUBLES CHAMPIONS—MEN (*Continued*)

Singles

1967	Doug Verdieck, Redlands CA
1968	Doug Verdieck, Redlands CA
1969	Doug Verdieck, Redlands CA
1970	Doug Verdieck, Redlands CA
1971	George Amaya, Presbyterian SC
1972	Harry Fritz, East Texas State
1973	Bob Hochstadter, East Texas State
1974	Stan Franker, Texas Southern
1975	Dave Petersen, Gustavus Adolphus MN
1976	Kari Pesonen, Mercyhurst PA
1977	Gordon Jones, Flagler FL
1978	Grancois Synaeghel, Belhaven MS
1979	Garry Seymour, Southwest Texas
1980	John Mattke, Gustavus Adolphus MN
1981	Brian Lusson, Southwest Texas
1982	Chuck Munn, Southwest Texas
1983	Al Jordan, Southwest Baptist MO
1984	Peter Pristach, Lander SC
1985	Martin Dyotte, Belhaven, MS
1986	Tobias Svantesson, Flagler FL
1987	Jeff Skeldon, Auburn-Montgomery AL
1988	Keith Evans, Belhaven MS

Doubles

1952	Harvey Grimshaw-Bill Delay, Pepperdine CA
1953	Carl Nunn-Wayne Miller, Hardin-Simmons TX
1954	Ron Palmer-Jery Loas, Redlands CA
1955	Don Coleman-Rafael Reyes, Lamar Tech TX
1956	Rafael Reyes-Paul Wilkins, Lamar Tech TX
1957	Pedro Bueno-Paul Wilkins, Lamar Tech TX
1958	James Schmidt-Eugene Saller, Lamar Tech TX
1959	John Sharpe-Don Russell, Pan American TX
1960	Co-Champions—Finals Rained Out John Sharpe-Don Russell, Pan American TX & Reginald Bennett-Tim Heckler, Lamar Tech TX
1961	Don Russell-John Sharpe, Pan American TX
1962	Don Russell-Jerry Wortelboer, Pan American TX
1963	John Hunter-Ken Lang, Pan American TX

NAIA SINGLES & DOUBLES CHAMPIONS—MEN (*Continued*)

Doubles

1964	Don Kierbow-Gabino Palafox, Corpus Christi TX
1965	Detlev Nitsche-Sherwood Stewart, Pan American TX
1966	John Yeomans-Bill Schoen, Redlands CA
1967	Eduardo Guell-Vincente Zarazua, Corpus Christi TX
1968	Doug Verdieck-Bruce Nelson, Redlands CA
1969	Co-Champions—Finals Rained Out
	Doug Verdieck-Randy Verdieck, Redlands CA &
	George Amaya-Jim Amaya, Presbyterian SC
1970	Doug Verdieck-Randy Verdieck, Redlands CA
1971	George Amaya-Milan Kofol, Presbyterian SC
1972	Harry Fritz-Bob Hochstadter, East Texas State
1973	Dave Peterson-Tim Butorac, Gustavus Adolphus MI
1974	Bengt Anthin-John Blomberg, California Baptist
1975	Benny Sims-Glenn Moolchan, Texas Southern
1976	Reijo Tuomola-Martin Sturgess, Mercyhurst PA
1977	Gordon Jones-Jim Twigg, Flagler FL
1978	Jeff Gibson-Bruce Gibson, East Texas State
1979	Mike Puc-Dave Kraus, Flagler FL
1980	Tony Mmohe, Bullas Hussaini, St. Augustine's NC
1981	Brian Lusson Bart Bernstein, Southwest Texas
1982	Jeff Bramlett-Russell Angell, Southwest Texas
1983	Stephen Bonneau-Martin Dyotte Belhaven MS
1984	Kevin Kopp-Gregg Yarbrough, Southwest Baptist MO
1985	Tobias Svantesson-Paul Valois, Flagler FL
1986	Tobias Svantesson-Per Asklund, Flagler FL
1987	Matthew Wilson-Eric Girrard, College of Charleston SC
1988	Per Asklund-Michael Malvebo, Flagler FL

NAIA TEAM CHAMPIONSHIP RESULTS—WOMEN

1981	Grand Canyon AZ, Guilford NC (tie)
1982	Westmont CA
1983	Charleston SC
1984	Arkansas-Little Rock
1985	Arkansas-Little Rock
1986	North Florida
1987	Flagler FL

NAIA SINGLES & DOUBLES CHAMPIONS—WOMEN

Singles

1981	Pat Smith, Grand Canyon AZ
1982	Tarja Koho, Guilford NC
1983	Laura Cotter Ingram, Centenary LA
1984	Berit Bjork, Arkansas-Little Rock
1985	Berit Bjork, Arkansas-Little Rock
1986	Berit Bjork, Arkansas-Little Rock
1987	Janine Perkinson, Columbus GA

Doubles

1981	Pat Smith-Karen Regman, Grand Canyon AZ
1982	Pat Smith-Karen Regman, Grand Canyon AZ
1983	Karen Regman-JoAnne Murtro, Grand Canyon AZ
1984	Berit Bjork-Katy Livijn, Arkansas-Little Rock
1985	Berit Bjork-Katy Livijn, Arkansas-Little Rock
1986	Berit Bjork-Katy Livijn, Arkansas-Little Rock
1987	Berit Bjork-Sharon Feighan, Arkansas-Little Rock

GEOGRAPHIC REGIONS OF THE NJCAA

Region I	Arizona, California and Nevada
Region II	Arkansas and Oklahoma
Region III	Upper New York State
Region IV	Upper Illinois
Region V	New Mexico and West Texas
Region VI	Kansas
Region VII	Kentucky and Tennessee
Region VIII	Florida
Region IX	Colorado east of the Continental Divide, Eastern Montana, Nebraska and Wyoming
Region X	North Carolina, South Carolina, Virginia and West Virginia
Region XI	Iowa
Region XII	Indiana, Lower Michigan Peninsula and Ohio
Region XIII	Minnesota, North Dakota, South Dakota, Upper Michigan Peninsula and Wisconsin
Region XIV	Eastern Texas
Region XV	Lower New York

GEOGRAPHIC REGIONS OF THE NJCAA (*Continued*)

Region XVI	Missouri
Region XVII	Georgia
Region XVIII	Alaska, Idaho, Oregon, Washington, Western Montana, Colorado west of the Continental Divide and Utah
Region XIX	Delaware, Eastern Pennsylvania and New Jersey
Region XX	District of Columbia, Maryland and Western Pennsylvania
Region XXI	Connecticut, Maine, Massachusetts, New Hampshire, Rhode Island and Vermont
Region XXII	Alabama
Region XXIII	Mississippi and Louisiana
Region XXIV	Lower Illinois

NJCAA NATIONAL CHAMPIONS—MEN

1948	Long Beach City College, Long Beach, California
1949	Modesto Junior College, Modesto California
1950	Modesto Junior College, Modesto California
1959	Pratt Junior College, Pratt, Kansas
1960	Tie, Lubbock Christian College, Lubbock, Texas Tarleton State College, Stephenville, Texas
1961	Pratt Junior College, Pratt, Kansas
1962	Schreiner Institute, Kerrville, Texas
1963	Tie, Odessa College, Odessa, Texas Central Florida Junior College, Ocala, Florida
1964	Odessa College, Odessa, Texas
1965	Henry Ford Community College, Dearborn, Michigan
1966	Miami-Dade Community College North, Miami, Florida
1967	Miami-Dade Community College North, Miami, Florida
1968	Odessa Junior College, Odessa, Texas
1969	Miami-Dade Community College North, Miami, Florida
1970	Wingate College, Wingate, North Carolina
1971	Wingate College, Wingate, North Carolina
1972	Mesa Community College, Mesa Arizona
1973	Central Texas College, Killeen, Texas
1974	Central Texas College, Killeen, Texas
1975	Odessa College, Odessa, Texas
1976	Odessa College, Odessa, Texas
1977	Central Texas College, Killeen, Texas

NJCAA NATIONAL CHAMPIONS—MEN (*Continued*)

1978   Tie, Odessa College, Odessa, Texas
        Midland College, Midland, Texas
        New Mexico Military Institute, Roswell, New Mexico
1979   Odessa College, Odessa, Texas
1980   Tyler Junior College, Tyler, Texas
1981   Central Florida Community College, Ocala, Florida
1982   Seminole Community College, Sanford, Florida
1983   Seminole Community College, Sanford, Florida
1984   Tie, Abraham Baldwin Ag. College, Tifton, Georgia
        Tyler Junior College, Tyler, Texas
1985   Tyler Junior College, Tyler, Texas
1986   Anderson Junior College, Anderson, South Carolina
1987   Anderson Junior College, Anderson, South Carolina and North Greenville, South Carolina (tie)

NJCAA NATIONAL SINGLES CHAMPIONS—MEN

Year[2]	Name	Institution
1959	Bob Folz	Phoenix College
1960	D. Chrane	Lubbock College
1961	Terry Smith	Pratt Junior College
1962	Roland Ingram	Schreiner Junior College
1963	Tom Shattuck	Central Florida Junior College
1964	Ed Waits	Jackson Junior College, Michigan
1965	Jay Schlosser	Miami Dade CC, North
1966	Richard Gilmore	Miami Dade CC, North
1967	Michael Keighley	Miami Dade CC, North
1968	Steve Siegel	Miami Dade CC, North
1969	Paul Tobin	Mesa College, Colorado
1970	Tony Pospisil	Wingate College, NC
1971	Juan Diaz	Wingate College, NC
1972	Ross Walker	San Jacinto College, Texas

[2] From 1948 through 1958 no official results of singles and doubles champions were recorded.

NJCAA NATIONAL SINGLES CHAMPIONS—MEN (*Continued*)

Year[2]	Name	Institution
1973	Samuel Nunez	Central Texas
1974	Fernando Maynetto	Wingate College
1975	Perfecto Alina	Odessa College
1976	Virgilio Sison	Odessa College
1977	Alex Marshall	Central Texas
1978	Eddie Gayon	South Caroline, Sumpter
1979	Mich Brunnberg	Miami Dade CC, North
1980	Scott Nichol	Tyler Junior College
1981	Renauld Etienne	Miami Dade CC, North
1982	David Goodman	Central Florida CC
1983	Mikael Pernfors	Seminole Community College
1984	Carlos Perez	Abraham Baldwin Ag & Tech
1985	Mike Cooper	Central Florida College
1986	Mark Freyman	Jefferson State
1987	Marco Rincon	North Greenville College

NJCAA NATIONAL DOUBLES CHAMPIONS—MEN

Year	Names	Institution
1959	Larry Rhodes-Tom Brungardt	Pratt Junior College
1960	Ed Stasney-Wayne Kiser	Tarleton
1961	No names reported	Pratt Junior College
1962	Bee Wood-Roland Ingram	Schreiner
1963	Charles Bower-Robert Reed	Odessa Junior College
1964	Charles Bower-Bob Rivers	Odessa Junior College
1965	Ken Germain-Hank Germain	Henry Ford CC, Michigan
1966	Richard Gilmore-Mike Keighley	Miami Dade CC, North
1967	Steve Siegel-Dick Gilmore	Miami Dade CC, North
1968	Leo Estopare-Paul DeMesquita	Odessa Junior College
1969	Leo Estopare-Bruce Banisky	Odessa Junior College
1970	Gewan Maharaj-John Antonas	Miami Dade CC, North
1971	Joe Kelly-Turner Ragsdale	Jefferson State CC, Alabama
1972	Stellan Bjork-Jan Erik Palm	Messa CC, Arizona
1973	Ali Kahn-Asghar Abid	Central Texas
1974	Martin Vasquez-Paul Fineman	Odessa Junior College
1975	Paul Fineman-Firgilio Sison	Odessa Junior College
1976	Virgilio Sison-Perfecto Alina	Odessa Junior College
1977	Reuben Zarate-Sergio Campos	Miami Dade CC, North

NJCAA NATIONAL DOUBLES CHAMPIONS—MEN (*Continued*)

Year	Names	Institution
1978	Alberto Jimenez-Manuel Dropeza	New Mexico Military Institute
1979	K. Richter-Bill Heiser	Odessa Junior College
1980	Scott Nichol-Doug Hall	Tyler Junior College
1981	Wayne Simpson-Dale Houston	Paris Junior College, Texas
1982	Rocardo Acioly-Mark Wilder	Tyler Junior College
1983	Mikael Pernfors-T. Svantesson	Seminole Junior College
1984	L. Castro-Malaga & Steve Medam	Tyler Junior College
1985	Robert Vrij-Sean Strikling	Midland Junior College
1986	Patrik Sundh-Craig Whitteker	McClennan Junior College, Texas
1987	Mats Malmberg-Mikael Stadling	Anderson Junior College

NJCAA NATIONAL CHAMPIONS—WOMEN

1975	Midland College, Midland, Texas
1976	Midland College, Midland, Texas
1977	Odessa College, Odessa, Texas
1978	Odessa College, Odessa, Texas
1979	Odessa College, Odessa, Texas
1980	Palm Beach Junior College, Palm Beach, Florida
1981	Midland Community College, Midland Texas, and Schreiner Junior College, Kerrville, Texas (tie)
1982	Indian River Community College, Fort Pierce, Florida
1983	Tyler Junior College, Tyler, Texas
1984	Tyler Junior College, Tyler, Texas
1985	Palm Beach Junior College, Palm Beach, Florida
1986	Midland College, Midland, Texas
1987	Tyler Junior College, Tyler, Texas

NJCAA NATIONAL SINGLES CHAMPIONS—WOMEN

Year	Name	Institution
1975	Vicky Lancaster	Midland College
1976	Mary Sawyer	Midland College
1977	Sandy Collins	Odessa College
1978	Sandy Collins	Odessa College
1979	Karen Gulley	Schreiner College
1980	Mary Renaud	Navarro College
1981	Mary Renaud	Navarro College
1982	Julie Quanne	Sinclair Community College
1983	Lisa Lovett	Cooke County Community College
1984	Jonrak Sri-eud	Palm Beach Junior College
1985	Jonrak Sri-eud	Palm Beach Junior College
1986	Henriette Knols	McLennan Community College
1987	Amila Fetahagic	Tyler Junior College

NJCAA NATIONAL DOUBLES CHAMPIONS—WOMEN

Year	Names	Institution
1975	Vicky Lancaster–Carol Reger	Midland College
1976	Mary Sawyer–Carol Draper	Midland College
1977	Sandy Collins–Debbie Phillips	Odessa College
1978	Sandy Collins–Debbie Phillips	Odessa College
1979	Jill Patterson–Diane Kobs	Odessa College
1980	Robin Fall–Janet Kniffin	Tyler Junior College
1981	Karen Gibbs–Ulla Hanson	Paris Junior College
1982	Chris Power–Anna Happonen	Indian River Community College
1983	Inge Cooper–Anna Happonen	Indian River Community College
1984	Deanne Laverock–Catherine Massey	McLennan Community College
1985	Jonrak Sri-eud–Sirichan Sri-eud	Palm Beach Junior College
1986	Samantha Gough–Jamie McCaffery	Cooke County College
1987	Lene Holm-Larsen–Cathrine Vigander	Tyler Junior College

CALIFORNIA STATE COMMUNITY COLLEGE DUAL TEAM CHAMPIONS—MEN

Year	Champion
1974	San Diego City College
1975	Foothill Community College
1976	Canada Community College
1977	Canada Community College
1978	Canada Community College
1979	Canada Community College
1980	Foothill Community College
1981	Foothill Community College
1982	Canada Community College
1983	A dual team championship was not held in 1983.
1984	Saddleback Community College
1985	Foothill Community College
1986	Grossmont Community College

CALIFORNIA STATE COMMUNITY COLLEGE TOURNAMENT CHAMPIONS—MEN

Year	Tournament Champion
1960	Santo Monica Community College
1961	Modesto Community College
1962	San Francisco City College
1963	San Francisco City College
1964	Foothill Community College
1965	Foothill Community College
1966	American River Community College
1967	Fullerton Community College
1968	San Diego Mesa Community College
1969	Santa Monica Community College
1970	Foothill Community College
1971	Orange Coast Community College
1972	Foothill Community College
1973	Canada Community College
1974	Canada Community College
1975	Foothill Community College
1976	Foothill Community College
1977	Canada Community College

TOURNAMENT CHAMPIONS—MEN (*Continued*)

Year	Tournament Champion
1978	Canada Community College
1979	Foothill Community College
1980	Foothill Community College
1981	Foothill Community College
1982	Canada Community College
1983	Canada Community College
1984	Saddleback Community College
1985	Foothill Community College
1986	Grossmont Community College
1987	West Valley Community College

CALIFORNIA COMMUNITY COLLEGE MEN'S SINGLES CHAMPIONS

Year	Player	College
1960	Chris Crawford	Menlo Community College
1961	Charles Rombeau	Los Angeles Valley Community College
1962	Reider Getz	Modesto Community College
1963	Horst Ritter	Foothill Community College
1964	Rodney Kop	Foothill Community College
1965	Larry Collins	Pasadena Community College
1966	Larry Hall	American River Community College
1967	Jim Rombeau	Los Angeles Community College
1968	John Penero	Delta Community College
1969	John Fort	Santa Monica Community College
1970	Steve Stefanki	Foothill Community College
1971	Robbie Cunningham	Orange Coast Community College
1972	Rich Andrews	Foothill Community College
1973	John Hursh	Canada Community College
1974	Rocky Maguire	Canada Community College
1975	Andy Lucchesi	Canada Community College

CALIFORNIA COMMUNITY COLLEGE MEN'S
SINGLES CHAMPIONS *(Continued)*

Year	Player	College
1976	Larry Stefanki	Foothill Community College
1977	Matt Wooldridge	Canada Community College
1978	Dick Metz	Canada Community College
1979	John Sevely	Foothill Community College
1980	John Sevely	Foothill Community College
1981	Brad Gilbert	Foothill Community College
1982	Eduardo Esteban	Canada Community College
1983	Chris Green	Foothill Community College
1984	Dave Salmon	Saddleback Community College
1985	Todd Stanley	Shasta Community College
1986	Miles Walker	Marin Community College
1987	Jim Wilbanks	West Valley Community College

CALIFORNIA COMMUNITY COLLEGE MEN'S
DOUBLES CHAMPIONS

Year	Players	College
1960	Chris Crawford-Yoshi Menegishi	Menlo Community College
1961	Reidr Getz-Tom Muench	Modesto Community College
1962	Bob Siska-Ed Jilka	San Francisco City College
1963	Bob Siska-Ed Jilka	San Francisco City College
1964	Rodney Kop-Dale McGowan	Foothill Community College
1965	Raul Contreras-Jeff Kerber	Foothill Community College
1966	Larry Hall-Mike McLean	American River Community College
1967	Eric Joachim-Mike Woodward	Fullerton Community College
1968	Dan McLaughlin-Jim Logan	San Diego Mesa Community College
1969	John Fort-Jerry Van Linge	Santa Monica Community College
1970	Carlos Kirmayr-Charlie Panui	Modesto Community College
1971	Mike Caro-Art Rosetti	Orange Coast Community College

DOUBLES CHAMPIONS (*Continued*)

Year	Players	College
1972	Tom Smith-Ken Malley	Fullerton Community College
1973	Steve Whitehead-Mark Berner	San Diego Community College
1974	David Bacon-Ted Williams	San Diego Community College
1975	Andy Lucchesi-Matt Iwersen	Canada Community College
1976	Larry Stefanki-Chris Andrews	Foothill Community College
1977	Bill Porter-Chip Hooper	Canada Community College
1978	Dick Metz-Herman Bauer	Canada Community College
1979	Graeme Robertson-Beto Bloise	Canada Community College
1980	Eric Quade-Roger Shepard	Fullerton Community College
1981	Jacques Herbet-Mark McNally	Canada Community College
1982	Eduardo Esteban-Hide Fujita	Canada Community College
1983	Eduardo Esteban-Bob Hepner	Canada Community College
1984	David Salmon-Jim Stephens	Saddleback Community College
1985	Marcello Tella-Layne Lyssy	Foothill Community College
1986	Sean Wade-David Calder	Grossmont Community College
1987	Bobby Fenton-Dan Joelson	Foothill Community College

CALIFORNIA STATE COMMUNITY COLLEGE DUAL TEAM CHAMPIONS— WOMEN

Year	Champion
1978	Los Angeles Pierce
1979	Los Angeles Pierce
1980	Golden West
1981	Orange Coast
1982	Los Angeles Pierce
1983	(not held)
1984	Orange Coast
1985	Orange Coast
1986	Palomar
1987	Orange Coast

CALIFORNIA STATE COMMUNITY COLLEGE TOURNAMENT CHAMPIONS— WOMEN

Year	Tournament Champion
1978	Los Angeles Pierce
1979	Los Angeles Pierce
1980	Golden West
1981	Pasadena
1982	Los Angeles Pierce
1983	Cerritos
1984	Orange Coast, Sacramento City (tie)
1985	Orange Coast
1986	Fullerton
1987	Orange Coast

CALIFORNIA COMMUNITY COLLEGE WOMEN'S SINGLES CHAMPIONS

Year	Player	College
1978	Jane Natenstedt	Los Angeles Pierce
1979	Alexandra Ordonez	Los Angeles Pierce
1980	Mary Ellis	Pasadena
1981	Anna Marie Bernstein	Pasadena
1982	Terri Spence	Cerritos
1983	Terri Spence	Cerritos
1984	Becky Barmore	Orange Coast
1985	Michelle Hain	Riverside
1986	Julie Hammon	Cerritos
1987	Nicole Brechtbuhl	Fullerton

CALIFORNIA COMMUNITY COLLEGE WOMEN'S DOUBLES CHAMPIONS

Year	Players	College
1978	Carrie Zarrawondia-Lisa Tolley	Marin
1979	Jill Johnston-Melinda Myers	Orange Coast
1980	Debbie McCormick-Laura Rice	Golden West
1981	Kelly Michaels-Patty Grutz	Santa Monica
1982	Shannon Smith-Debbie Findcisen	Santa Barbara
1983	Ruth McMahon-Jill Burke	American River
1984	Becky Barmore-Noel Gayton	Orange Coast
1985	Becky Barmore-Cindy Lancaster	Orange Coast
1986	Nicole Brechtbuhl-Michelle Ponce	Fullerton
1987	Lisa Newman-Becky Recavarren	Orange Coast

ITCA AND NCAA CHAMPIONS

━━━

PAST ITCA CHAMPIONS—WOMEN*

A. ITCA All-American Champions

> 1983—Lisa Spain, Georgia
> 1984—Gretchen Rush, Trinity
> 1985—Beverly Bowes, Texas
> 1986—Monique Javer, San Diego St. Univ.
> 1987—Anne Grousbeck, Texas

B. Rolex National Intercollegiate Indoor Singles Champions

> 1984—Gretchen Rush, Trinity
> 1985—Beverly Bowes, Texas
> 1986—Caroline Kuhlman, USC
> 1987—Sonia Hahn, Kentucky
> 1988—Halle Ciofi, Florida

C. Rolex National Intercollegiate Indoor Doubles Champions

> 1984—Gretchen Rush and Louise Allen, Trinity
> 1985—Leigh Anne Eldredge and Linda Gates, Stanford
> 1986—Lisa Gregory and Ronnie Reis, Miami
> 1987—Jill Hetherington and Cathy Goodrich, Florida
> 1988—Sue Russo and Betsy Somerville, Arizona

PAST ITCA CHAMPIONS—MEN†

A. Volvo Tennis/All-American Champions

> 1979—Scott McCain, Cal.-Berkeley
> 1980—Scott Davis, Stanford
> 1981—Robbie Venter, UCLA
> 1982—Peter Doohan, Arkansas
> 1983—Fredrick Pahlett, Minnesota
> 1984—Mikael Pernfors, Georgia
> 1985—Steve DeVries, California

* Rolex assumed its title sponsorship role in 1985.

† Volvo Tennis assumed its title sponsorship role in 1984 and Rolex and the USTA in 1985.

1986—Richey Reneberg, SMU
1987—Scott Melville, USC

B. Rolex National Intercollegiate Indoor Singles Champions

1978—Eric Iskersky, Trinity
1979—Eric Iskersky, Trinity
1980—Mel Purcell, Tennessee
1981—Chip Hooper, Tennessee
1982—David Pate, TCU
1983—Ted Farnsworth, Princeton
1984—Paul Annacone, Tennessee
1985—Dan Goldie, Stanford
1986—Joey Blake, Arkansas
1987—Luke Jensen, USC
1988—Andrew Sznajder, Pepperdine

C. Rolex National Intercollegiate Indoor Doubles Champions

1979—Gary Leeds and Matt Doyle, Yale
1980—Tony Giammalva and John Benson, Trinity
1982—Allen Miller and Ola Malmquist, Georgia
1983—Paul Smith and Robert Saad, Wichita State
1984—Tim Pawsat and Rick Leach, So. California
1985—Richard Matuszewski and Brandon Walters, Clemson
1986—Royce Deppe and Charles Beckman, Texas
1987—Rick Leach and Luke Jensen, USC
1988—Scott Melville and Eric Amend, USC

D. USTA/ITCA National Intercollegiate Indoor Team Champions

1973—Stanford
1975—Stanford
1976—Stanford
1977—Trinity
1978—Stanford
1979—SMU
1980—Cal-Berkeley
1982—Cal-Berkeley
1983—SMU
1984—UCLA
1985—Stanford
1986—Pepperdine
1987—USC
1988—USC

COLLEGIATE ITCA TENNIS HALL OF FAME MEMBERS

1983

Wilmer Allison (Texas—P&C)
Arthur Ashe (UCLA—P)
Dr. James Dwight (Harvard—C&Con.)
William A. Larned (Cornell—P)
J. D. Morgan (UCLA—C)
Emmet Pare (Tulane—C)
Dr. Daniel Penick (Texas—C)
Alex Olmedo (USC—P)

Rafael Osuna (USC—P)
Dennis Ralston (Stanford—P)
Ted Schroeder (Stanford—P)
Richard D. Sears (Harvard—P)
George Toley (USC—C)
Tony Trabert (Cincinnati—P)
Malcolm D. Whitman (Harvard—P)

1984

William C. Ackerman (UCLA—C)
Paul Bennett (Northwestern—C)
Dwight Davis (Harvard—P)
Dale Lewis (Indiana, Miami—C)
Robert C. Lutz (USC—P)
Clarence Mabry (Trinity—C)
Gardnar Mulloy (Miami—P)
William Murphy (Michigan—C)

Francisco Segura (Miami—P)
Victor Seixas (North Carolina—P)
Stan Smith (USC—P)
William F. Talbert (Cincinnati—P)
James H. Van Alen (Con.)
John van Ryn (Princeton—P)
Richard N. Williams II (Harvard—P)

1985

Jack Barnaby (Harvard—C)
Bernard Bartzen (William & Mary—P)
M. G. Chace (Brown & Yale—P)
W. J. Clothier (Harvard—P)
John Conroy (Princeton—C
Robert Falkenburg (USC—P)
Bryant M. Grant (North Carolina—P)
Jack Kramer (Con.)

Bill Lufler (Presbyterian, Miami—C)
Gene Mako (USC—P)
Chet Murphy (California—C)
Charles McKinley (Trinity—P)
Don McNeill (Kenyon College—P)
Ham Richardson (Tulane—P)
Holcombe Ward (Harvard—P)

1987

George M. Lott, Jr. (Chicago—P)
Barry MacKay (Michigan—P)
Charles Pasarell (UCLA—P)
William Potter (Florida—P)

1988

Clifford S. Sutter (Tulane—P)
Ernest M. Sutter (Tulane—P)
Jim Verdieck (Redlands—C)

Oliver S. Campbell (Columbia—P)
Clarence C. Chaffee (Williams College—C)
Herbert Flam (UCLA—P)
Harry James (Utah—C)

Fred B. Alexander (Princeton—P)
Tom Fallon (Notre Dame—C)
Allen Fox (UCLA—P&C)
Winthrop C. Lenz (Princeton—Con.)

Key: P—Player; C—Coach; Con.—Contributor

PAST NCAA TEAM CHAMPIONS—MEN

Year	Champion	Coach	Pts	Runner-up	Pts.	Host or Site
1946	Southern Cal	William Moyle	9	William & Mary	6	Northwestern
1947	William & Mary	Shavey G. Umbeck	10	Rice	4	UCLA
1948	William & Mary	Sharvey G. Umbeck	6	San Francisco	5	UCLA
1949	San Francisco	Norman Brooks	7	Rollins, Tulane	4	Texas
1950	UCLA	William Ackerman	11	Washington, California.	5	Texas
1951	Southern Cal	Louis Wheeler	9	Southern Cal.	7	Northwestern
1952	UCLA	J. D. Morgan	11	Cincinnati	5	Northwestern
1953	UCLA	J. D. Morgan	11	California	6	Syracuse
1954	UCLA	J. D. Morgan	15	Southern Cal	10	Washington
1955	Southern Cal	George Toley	12	Texas	7	N. Carolina
1956	UCLA	J. D. Morgan	15	Southern Cal	14	Kalamazoo
1957	Michigan	William Murphy	10	Tulane	9	Utah
1958	Southern Cal	George Toley	13	Stanford	9	Navy
1959	Notre Dame	Thomas Fallon	8			Northwestern
	Tulane	Emmett Pare	8			
1960	UCLA	J. D. Morgan	18	Southern Cal	8	Washington
1961	UCLA	J. D. Morgan	17	Southern Cal	16	Iowa State
1962	Southern Cal	George Toley	22	UCLA	12	Stanford
1963	Southern Cal	George Toley	27	UCLA	19	Princeton
1964	Southern Cal	George Toley	26	UCLA	25	Michigan St.
1965	UCLA	J. D. Morgan	31	Miami (Fla.)	13	UCLA

Year	Champion	Coach	Pts.	Runner-up	Pts.	Site
1966	Southern Cal	George Toley	27	UCLA	23	Miami (Fla.)
1967	Southern Cal	George Toley	28	UCLA	23	Southern Ill.
1968	Southern Cal	George Toley	31	Rice	23	Trinity (Texas)
1969	Southern Cal	George Toley	35	UCLA	23	Princeton
1970	UCLA	Glenn Bassett	26	Trinity Texas, Rice	22	Utah
1971	UCLA	Glenn Bassett	35	Trinity (Texas)	27	Notre Dame
1972	Trinity (Texas)	Clarence Mabry	36	Stanford	30	Georgia
1973	Stanford	Dick Gould	33	Southern Cal	28	Princeton
1974	Stanford	Dick Gould	30	Southern Cal	25	Southern Cal
1975	UCLA	Glenn Bassett	27	Miami (Fla.)	20	Pan American
1976	Southern Cal	George Toley	21	UCLA	21	Pan American
1977	Stanford	Glenn Bassett		Trinity (Texas)		Pan American
1978	Stanford	Dick Gould		UCLA		Georgia
1979	UCLA	Dick Gould		Trinity (Texas)		Georgia
1980	Stanford	Glenn Bassett		California		Georgia
1981	Stanford	Dick Gould		UCLA		Georgia
1982	UCLA	Dick Gould		Pepperdine		Georgia
1983	Stanford	Glenn Bassett		SMU		Georgia
1984	UCLA	Dick Gould		Stanford		Georgia
1985	Georgia	Glenn Bassett		UCLA		Georgia
1986	Stanford	Dan Magill		Pepperdine		Georgia
1987	Georgia	Dick Gould		UCLA		Georgia
1988	Stanford	Dan Magill		LSU		Georgia
		Dick Gould				Georgia

(Note: Prior to 1977, individual wins counted in the team's total points. In 1977, a dual-match single-elimination team championship was initiated, eliminating the point system.)

ITCA COLLEGE PLAYERS OF THE YEAR

Men

1980 Peter Rennert, Stanford University
1981 Tim Mayotte, Stanford University
1982 Marcel Freeman, UCLA
1983 Greg Holmes, University of Utah
1984 Paul Annacone, University of Tennessee
1985 Mikael Pernfors, University of Georgia
1986 Rick Leach, University of Southern California
1987 Richey Reneberg, Southern Methodist University
1988 Robby Weiss, Pepperdine

Women

1982 Vicki Nelson, Rollins College
1983 Beth Herr, University of Southern California
1984 Gretchen Rush, Trinity University (TX)
1985 Gretchen Rush, Trinity University (TX)
1986 Caroline Kuhlman, University of Southern California
1987 Patty Fendick, Stanford University
1988 Halle Cioffi, University of Florida

PAST NCAA SINGLES CHAMPIONS—MEN

Year	Player	School
1883	J. S. Clark (spring)	Harvard
	H. A. Taylor (fall)	Harvard
1884	W. P. Knapp	Yale
1885	W. P. Knapp	Yale
1886	G. M. Brinley	Trinity (Conn.)
1887	P. S. Sears	Harvard
1888	P. S. Sears	Harvard
1889	R. P. Huntington, Jr.	Yale
1890	F. H. Hovey	Harvard
1891	F. H. Hovey	Harvard
1892	W. A. Larned	Cornell
1893	M. G. Chace	Yale
1894	M. G. Chace	Yale
1895	M. G. Chace	Yale
1896	M. D. Whitman	Harvard
1897	S. G. Thompson	Princeton

PAST NCAA SINGLES CHAMPIONS—MEN (*Continued*)

Year	Player	School
1898	L. E. Ware	Harvard
1899	D. F. Davis	Harvard
1900	R. D. Little	Princeton
1901	F. B. Alexander	Princeton
1902	W. J. Clothier	Harvard
1903	E. B. Dewhurst	Pennsylvania
1904	Robert LeRoy	Columbia
1905	E. B. Dewhurst	Pennsylvania
1906	Robert LeRoy	Columbia
1907	G. P. Gardner, Jr.	Harvard
1908	N. W. Niles	Harvard
1909	W. F. Johnson	Pennsylvania
1910	R. A. Holden, Jr.	Yale
1911	E. H. Whitney	Harvard
1912	G. M. Church	Princeton
1913	R. N. Williams, II	Harvard
1914	G. M. Church	Princeton
1915	G. C. Caner	Harvard
1916	C. S. Garland	Yale
1917	No Tournament Held	
1918	No Tournament Held	
1919	L. M. Banks	Yale
1920	Philip Neer	Stanford
1921	Lucien Williams	Yale
1922	Carl Fischer	Philadelphia Osteo.
1923	R. N. Williams II	Harvard
1924	Wallace Scott	Washington
1925	E. G. Chandler	California
1926	E. G. Chandler	California
1927	Wilmer Allison	Texas
1928	Julius Seligson	Lehigh
1929	Berkeley Bell	Texas
1930	Clifford Sutter	Tulane
1931	Keith Gledhill	Stanford
1932	Clifford Sutter	Tulane
1933	Jack Tidball	UCLA
1934	Gene Mako	Southern Cal
1935	Wilbur Hess	Rice
1936	Ernest Sutter	Tulane

PAST NCAA SINGLES CHAMPIONS—MEN (*Continued*)

Year	Player	School
1937	Ernest Sutter	Tulane
1938	Frank Guernsey	Rice
1939	Frank Guernsey	Rice
1940	Donald McNeil	Kenyon
1941	Joseph Hunt	Navy
1942	Fred Schroeder	Stanford
1943	Francisco Segura	Miami (Fla.)
1944	Francisco Segura	Miami (Fla.)
1945	Francisco Segura	Miami (Fla.)
1946	Robert Falkenburg	Southern Cal
1947	Garner Larned	William & Mary
1948	Harry Likas	San Francisco
1949	Jack Tuero	Tulane
1950	Herbert Flam	UCLA
1951	Tony Trabert	Cincinnati
1952	Hugh Stewart	Southern Cal
1953	Hamilton Richardson	Tulane
1954	Hamilton Richardson	Tulane
1955	Jose Aguero	Tulane
1956	Alex Olmedo	Southern Cal
1957	Barry MacKay	Michigan
1958	Alex Olmedo	Southern Cal
1959	Whitney Reed	San Jose State
1960	Larry Nagler	UCLA
1961	Allen Fox	UCLA
1962	Rafael Osuna	Southern Cal
1963	Dennis Ralston	Southern Cal
1964	Dennis Ralston	Southern Cal
1965	Arthur Ashe	UCLA
1966	Charles Pasarell	UCLA
1967	Bob Lutz	Southern Cal
1968	Stan Smith	Southern Cal
1969	Joaquin Loyo-Mayo	Southern Cal
1970	Jeff Borowiak	UCLA
1971	Jim Connors	UCLA
1972	Dick Stockton	Trinity (Texas)
1973	Alex Mayer	Stanford
1974	John Whitlinger	Stanford
1975	Bill Martin	UCLA

PAST NCAA SINGLES CHAMPIONS—MEN (*Continued*)

Year	Player	School
1976	Bill Scanlon	Trinity (Texas)
1977	Matt Mitchell	Stanford
1978	John McEnroe	Stanford
1979	Kevin Curren	Texas
1980	Robert Van't Hof	Southern Cal
1981	Tim Mayotte	Stanford
1982	Mike Leach	Michigan
1983	Greg Holmes	Utah
1984	Mikael Pernfors	Georgia
1985	Mikael Pernfors	Georgia
1986	Dan Goldie	Stanford
1987	Andrew Burrow	Miami
1988	Robby Weiss	Pepperdine

PAST NCAA DOUBLES CHAMPIONS—MEN

Year	Player	School
1883	J. S. Clark—H. A. Taylor	Harvard (Spring)
	H. A. Taylor—P. E. Presbrey	Harvard (Fall)
1884	W. P. Knapp—W. V. S. Thorne	Yale
1885	W. P. Knapp—A. L. Shipman	Yale
1886	W. P. Knapp—W. L. Thatcher	Yale
1887	P. S. Sears—Q. A. Shaw, Jr.	Harvard
1888	V. G. Hall—O. S. Campbell	Columbia
1889	O. S. Campbell—A. E. Wright	Columbia
1890	Q. A. Shaw, Jr.—S. T. Chase	Harvard
1891	F. H. Hovey—R. D. Wrenn	Harvard
1892	R. D. Wrenn—F. B. Winslow	Harvard
1893	M. G. Chace—C. R. Budlong	Yale
1894	M. G. Chace—A. E. Foote	Yale
1895	M. G. Chace—A. E. Foote	Yale
1896	L. E. Ware—W. M. Scudder	Harvard
1897	L. E. Ware—M. D. Whitman	Harvard
1898	L. E. Ware—M. D. Whitman	Harvard
1899	Holcombe Ward—D. F. Davis	Harvard
1900	F. B. Alexander—R. D. Little	Princeton
1901	H. A. Plummer—S. L. Russell	Yale

PAST NCAA DOUBLES CHAMPIONS—MEN (*Continued*)

Year	Player	School
1902	W. J. Clothier—E. W. Leonard	Harvard
1903	B. Colston—E. Clapp	Yale
1904	K. H. Behr—G. Bodman	Yale
1905	E. B. Dewhurst—H. B. Register	Pennsylvania
1906	F. B. Sells—Spaulding	Yale
1907	N. W. Niles—A. S. Dabney	Harvard
1908	H. M. Tilden—A. Thayer	Pennsylvania
1909	W. F. Johnson—A. Thayer	Pennsylvania
1910	D. Mathey—B. N. Dell	Princeton
1911	D. Mathey—C. T. Butler	Princeton
1912	G. M. Church—W. H. Mace	Princeton
1913	W. M. Washburn—J. J. Armstrong	Harvard
1914	R. N. Williams II—Richard Harte	Harvard
1915	R. N. Williams II—Richard Harte	Harvard
1916	G. C. Caner—Richard Harte	Harvard
1917	No Tournament Held	
1918	No Tournament Held	
1919	C. S. Carland—K. N. Hawkes	Yale
1920	A. Wilder—L. Wiley	Yale
1921	J. B. Fenno, Jr.—E. W. Feibleman	Harvard
1922	James Davies—Philip Neer	Stanford
1923	L. N. White—Louis Thalheimer	Texas
1924	L. N. White—Louis Thalheimer	Texas
1925	Gervais Hills—Gerald Straford	California
1926	E. G. Chandler—Tom Stow	California
1927	John Van Ryn—Kenneth Appel	Princeton
1928	Ralph McElvenny—Allan Herrington	Stanford
1929	Benjamin Gorchakoff—Arthur Kussman	Occidental
1930	Dolph Muehleisen—Robert Muench	California
1931	Bruce Barnes—Karl Kamrath	Texas
1932	Keith Gledhill—Joseph Coughlin	Stanford
1933	Joseph Coughlin—Sam Lee	Stanford
1934	Gene Mako—Phillip Caslin	Southern Cal
1935	Paul Newton—Richard Bennett	California
1936	Bennett Dey—William Seward	Stanford
1937	Richard Bennett—Paul Newton	California

PAST NCAA DOUBLES CHAMPIONS—MEN (*Continued*)

Year	Player	School
1938	Joseph Hunt—Lewis Wetherell	Southern Cal
1939	Douglas Imhoff—Robert Peacock	California
1940	Lawrence Dee—James Wade	Stanford
1941	Charles Olewine—Charles Mattman	Southern Cal
1942	Lawrence Dee—Frederick Schroeder	Stanford
1943	John Hickman—Walter Driver	Texas
1944	John Hickman—Felix Kelley	Texas
1945	Francisco Segura—Thomas Burke	Miami (Fla.)
1946	Robert Falkenburg—Thomas Falkenburg	Southern Cal
1947	Sam Match—Bob Curtis	Rice
1948	Fred Kovaleski—Bernard (Tut) Bartzen	William & Mary
1949	James Brink—Fred Fisher	Washington
1950	Herbert Flam—Gene Garrett	UCLA
1951	Earl Cochell—Hugh Stewart	Southern Cal
1952	Clifton Mayne—Hugh Ditzler	California
1953	Robert Perry—Larry Heubner	UCLA
1954	Robert Perry—Ronald Livingston	UCLA
1955	Francisco Contreras—Joaquin Reyes	Southern Cal
1956	Alex Olmedo—Francisco Contreras	Southern Cal
1957	Crawford Henry—Ronald Holmberg	Tulane
1958	Alex Olmedo—Ed Atkinson	Southern Cal
1959	Crawford Henry—Ronald Holmberg	Tulane
1960	Larry Nagler—Allen Fox	UCLA
1961	Rafael Osuna—Ramsey Earnhart	Southern Cal
1962	Rafael Osuna—Ramsey Earnhart	Southern Cal
1963	Rafael Osuna—Dennis Ralston	Southern Cal
1964	Dennis Ralston—Bill Bond	Southern Cal
1965	Ian Crookenden—Arthur Ashe	UCLA
1966	Ian Crookenden—Charles Pasarell	UCLA
1967	Stan Smith—Bob Lutz	Southern Cal
1968	Stan Smith—Bob Lutz	Southern Cal
1969	Joaquin Loyo-Mayo—Marcello Lara	Southern Cal
1970	Pat Cramer—Luis Garcia	Miami (Fla.)
1971	Haroon Rahim—Jeff Borowiak	UCLA
1972	Alex Mayer—Roscoe Tanner	Stanford
1973	Alex Mayer—Jim Delaney	Stanford

PAST NCAA DOUBLES CHAMPIONS—MEN (*Continued*)

Year	Player	School
1974	John Whitlinger—Jim Delaney	Stanford
1975	Butch Walts—Bruce Manson	Southern Cal
1976	Peter Fleming—Ferdi Taygan	UCLA
1977	Bruce Manson—Chris Lewis	Southern Cal
1978	John Austin—Bruce Nichols	UCLA
1979	Erick Iskersky—Ben McKown	Trinity (Texas)
1980	Mel Purcell—Rodney Harmon	Tennessee
1981	David Pate—Karl Richter	Texas Christian
1982	Peter Doohan—Pat Serret	Arkansas
1983	Allen Miller—Ola Malmqvist	Georgia
1984	Kelly Jones—Jerome Jones	Pepperdine
1985	Kelly Jones—Carlos DiLaura	Pepperdine
1986	Rick Leach—Tim Pawsat	Southern Cal
1987	Rick Leach—Scott Melville	Southern Cal
1988	Brian Garrow—Patrick Galbraith	UCLA

PAST NCAA TEAM CHAMPIONS— WOMEN

Year	Champion
1982	Stanford
1983	USC
1984	Stanford
1985	USC
1986	Stanford
1987	Stanford
1988	Stanford

PAST NCAA SINGLES CHAMPIONS—WOMEN

Year	Player	School
1982	Alycia Moulton	Stanford
1983	Beth Herr	USC
1984	Lisa Spain	Georgia
1985	Linda Gates	Stanford

PAST NCAA SINGLES CHAMPIONS—WOMEN (*Continued*)

Year	Player	School
1986	Patty Fendick	Stanford
1987	Patty Fendick	Stanford
1988	Patty Fendick	Stanford

PAST NCAA DOUBLES CHAMPIONS—WOMEN

Year	Players	School
1982	Ludloff-Lewis	UCLA
1983	Rush-Allen	Trinity
1984	Burgin-Gates	Stanford
1985	Gates-Eldridge	Stanford
1986	Gregory-Reis	Miami
1987	Adams-Donnelly	Northwestern
1988	Cooper-Sampras	UCLA

INDEX